CLIFFS

American College Testing

PREPARATION GUIDE

by

Jerry Bobrow, Ph.D.
William A. Covino, Ph.D.
David A. Kay, M.S.
Harold Nathan, Ph.D.

Consultants
Merritt L. Weisinger, J.D.
Peter Z Orton, M. Ed.
Dale W. Johnson, M.A.

INCORPORATED
LINCOLN, NEBRASKA   68501

ACKNOWLEDGMENTS

My loving thanks to my wife, Susan, and my children, Jennifer Lynn, 11, Adam Michael, 8, and Jonathan Matthew, 4, for their patience and support. My sincere thanks to Michele Spence of Cliffs Notes for final editing and careful attention to the production process.

Jerry Bobrow

CONTENTS

PART III: PRACTICE-REVIEW-ANALYZE-PRACTICE
Two Full-Length Practice Tests

APPENDIXES

PREFACE

Your ACT Assessment Program: ACT Tests, Interest Inventory, and Student Profile are important to your future! They can help you (1) assess your interests and skills, (2) plan your career, (3) get a scholarship, and (4) get into a college of your choice. Because of this, your study time must be used effectively. You need the most comprehensive test preparation guide that you can realistically complete in a reasonable time. It must be concise, direct, easy to use, and thorough, giving you all the assistance you need to do your best on the ACT Tests.

In keeping with the fine tradition of Cliffs Notes, this guide was developed by leading experts in the field of test preparation as part of a series to specifically meet these standards. The testing strategies, techniques, and materials have been researched, tested, and evaluated and are presently used at test preparation programs at many leading colleges and universities. This guide emphasizes the BOBROW TEST PREPARATION SERVICES approach, which focuses on the six major areas:

1. Ability Tested
2. Basic Skills Necessary
3. Understanding Directions
4. Analysis of Directions
5. Suggested Approaches with Samples
6. Practice-Review-Analyze-Practice

Two complete simulation ACT Batteries are included with answers and in-depth explanations. Each test battery is followed by analysis charts to help you analyze your results and evaluate your strengths and weaknesses. A brief review of English grammar, math formulas, and science terminology is included in a special appendix.

This guide was written to give you the edge in doing your best by maximizing your effort in a reasonable amount of time. It is meant to augment, not substitute for, formal or informal learning throughout junior high and high school. If you follow the Study Guide Checklist in this book and study regularly, you will get the best preparation possible.

STUDY GUIDE CHECKLIST

_____ 1. Read the ACT Information Bulletin.

_____ 2. Become familiar with the Test Format, page 3.

_____ 3. Familiarize yourself with the answers to Questions Commonly Asked about the ACT, page 5.

_____ 4. Learn the techniques of Two Successful Overall Approaches, page 7.

_____ 5. Carefully read Part II, Analysis of Exam Areas, beginning on page 9.

_____ 6. Strictly observing time allotments, take Practice Test Battery No. 1, section by section, beginning on page 55.

_____ 7. Check your answers, page 127.

_____ 8. Analyze your Practice Test Battery No. 1 results, page 130.

_____ 9. Fill out the Tally Sheet for Problems Missed to pinpoint your mistakes, page 130.

_____ 10. While referring to each item of Practice Test Battery No. 1, study ALL the Answers and Explanations that begin on page 133.

_____ 11. Review as necessary basic skills and techniques discussed in Part II of this book.

_____ 12. Selectively review grammar and usage information, math formulas, and science terminology given in the Appendixes of this book.

_____ 13. Strictly observing time allotments, take Practice Test Battery No. 2, section by section, beginning on page 175.

_____ 14. Check your answers, page 246.

_____ 15. Analyze your Practice Test Battery No. 2 results, page 249.

_____ 16. Fill out the Tally Sheet for Problems Missed to pinpoint your mistakes, page 249.

____ 17. While referring to each item of Practice Test Battery No. 2, study ALL the Answers and Explanations that begin on page 253.

____ 18. Again, review as needed Part II, Analysis of Exam Areas.

____ 19. Once more, selectively review essential information contained in the Appendixes.

____ 20. CAREFULLY READ "FINAL PREPARATION" on page 337.

Part I: Introduction

FORMAT OF THE ACT

English Test	45 Minutes	75 Questions
Mathematics Test	60 Minutes	60 Questions
Reading Test	35 Minutes	40 Questions
Science Reasoning Test	35 Minutes	40 Questions

Total Testing Time
175 Minutes
or 2 hours, 55 minutes   Approximately 215 Questions

GENERAL DESCRIPTION

The ACT Assessment Program helps you make important decisions about your future. It does so in many ways. First, the ACT Interest Inventory and the ACT Student Profile section collect information about your past experiences, your interests, and your goals. You will fill out these sections when you register for the ACT Assessment.

The ACT Assessment is the second phase of the program; it is a battery of tests which you take at an ACT test center on a designated national test date. The tests cover four subject areas: English, mathematics, reading, and science reasoning.

These four tests will generate twelve scaled scores—four test scores, a composite score, and seven subscores:

English Score

Subscores:
   Usage/Mechanics
   Rhetorical Skills

Mathematics Score

Subscores:
   Pre-Algebra/Elementary Algebra
   Intermediate Algebra/Coordinate Geometry
   Plane Geometry/Trigonometry

Reading Score

Subscores:
   Social Studies/Sciences
   Arts/Literature

Science Reasoning Score

Composite Score

QUESTIONS COMMONLY ASKED
ABOUT THE ACT

Q: WHO ADMINISTERS THE ACT?

A: The ACT is administered by the American College Testing Program. For further information about the ACT Assessment Program, write to ACTP, P.O. Box 168, Iowa City, Iowa, 52240 or call (319) 337-1000.

Q: WHAT IS THE STRUCTURE OF THE ACT ASSESSMENT?

A: The ACT Assessment consists of four tests. The English Test contains 75 questions and lasts 45 minutes. The Mathematics Test contains 60 questions and lasts 60 minutes. The Reading Test contains 40 questions and lasts 35 minutes. The Science Reasoning Test contains 40 questions and lasts 35 minutes. All four tests consist exclusively of multiple-choice questions.

Q: HOW IS THE ACT ASSESSMENT SCORED?

A: Each of the tests is scored from 1 to 36, with a mean score of 18. The subscores within sections are scored from 1 to 18, with a mean score of 9. The composite score is from 1 to 36.

Q: HOW DO COLLEGES USE THE INFORMATION ON MY SPR?

A: Most colleges use the information on your Student Profile Report in two ways: (1) as part of the admission process, to assess your ability to do college-level work and (2) to help you plan your program of study.

Q: MAY I TAKE THE ACT ASSESSMENT MORE THAN ONCE?

A: Yes, you may, but you should try to take it only once and do your best. If you do need to take the test a second time, check the registration/information bulletin for registration procedures.

Q: WHAT MATERIALS MAY I BRING TO THE ACT?

A: You may bring your test center admission form, fully completed; three sharpened Number 2 pencils; a good eraser; positive identification; and a watch. NO books, notes, slide rules, or calculators are permitted. Scratch paper for your figuring will be provided in the test booklet itself.

Q: MAY I CANCEL MY SCORE?
A: Yes. You may do so by notifying your test supervisor before you leave the examination.

Q: SHOULD I GUESS?
A: Yes. There is no penalty for guessing, so it is to your advantage to answer every question.

Q: HOW SHOULD I PREPARE FOR THE ACT ASSESSMENT?
A: Understanding and practicing test-taking strategies will help a great deal. Subject matter review is particularly useful for the Mathematics Test and the English Test. Both subject matter and strategies are reviewed in this book.

Q: HOW AND WHEN SHOULD I REGISTER?
A: The registration period opens about ten weeks before the test date and closes about four weeks before the test date. To register within this period, obtain an ACT registration/information booklet from your high school counselor and follow the registration instructions it includes. Within three weeks after your registration folder has been received by ACTP, you will receive a test center admission form.

Q: HOW OFTEN IS THE TEST GIVEN?
A: The test is given five times a year, in October, December, February, April, and June. The test is regularly administered on a Saturday morning.

TAKING THE ACT
TWO SUCCESSFUL OVERALL APPROACHES

I. The "Plus-Minus" System

Many who take the ACT don't get their best possible score because they spend too much time on difficult questions, leaving insufficient time to answer the easy questions. Don't let this happen to you. Since every question within each section is worth the same amount, use the following system.

1. Answer easy questions immediately.

2. When you come to a question that seems "impossible" to answer, mark a large minus sign ("−") next to it on your test booklet.

3. Then mark a "guess" answer on your answer sheet and move on to the next question.

4. When you come to a question that seems solvable but appears too time consuming, mark a large plus sign ("+") next to that question in your test booklet and register a guess answer on your answer sheet. Then move on to the next question.

Since your time allotment is usually less than one minute per question, a "time-consuming" question is a question that you estimate will take you more than a minute or two to answer. But don't waste time deciding whether a question is a "+" or "−". Act quickly, as the intent of this strategy is, in fact, to save you valuable time.

After working all the easy questions, your booklet should look something like this:

$$1.$$
$$+2.$$
$$3.$$
$$-4.$$
$$+5.$$
etc.

5. After working all the problems you can do immediately in that section (the easy ones), go back and work your "+" problems. Change your "guess" on your answer sheet, if necessary, for those problems you are able to work.

6. If you finish working your "+" problems and still have time left, you can either

(A) attempt those "−" questions—the ones that you considered "impossible." Sometimes a problem later in that section will "trigger" your memory and you'll be able to go back and answer one of the earlier "impossible" problems.

or

(B) don't bother with those "impossible" questions. Rather, spend your time reviewing your work to be sure you didn't make any careless mistakes on the questions you thought were easy to answer.

REMEMBER: You do not have to erase the pluses and minuses you made on your *question booklet.* And be sure to fill in all your answer spaces—if necessary, with a guess. As there is no penalty for wrong answers, it makes no sense to leave an answer space blank. And, of course, remember that you may work only in one section of the test at a time.

II. The Elimination Strategy

Take advantage of being allowed to mark in your testing booklet. As you eliminate an answer choice from consideration, make sure to *mark it out in your question booklet* as follows:

(A)

?(B)

(C)

(D)

?(E)

Notice that some choices are marked with question marks, signifying that they may be possible answers. This technique will help you avoid reconsidering those choices you have already eliminated. It will also help you narrow down your possible answers.

Again, these marks you make on your testing booklet do not need to be erased.

Part II: Analysis of Exam Areas

This section is designed to introduce you to each ACT area by carefully reviewing the—

1. Ability Tested
2. Basic Skills Necessary
3. Directions
4. Analysis of Directions
5. Suggested Approaches with Samples

This section emphasizes important test-taking techniques and strategies and how to apply them to a variety of problem types.

INTRODUCTION TO TEST 1: ENGLISH

The English Test is 45 minutes long and contains 75 multiple-choice questions.

Ability Tested

This section tests your ability to recognize and correct errors in standard written English. It tests your knowledge of grammar, punctuation, sentence structure, and rhetoric. It is *not* a test of spelling, vocabulary, or recall of grammar rules.

The test covers five or six prose passages of differing styles and content, upon which the multiple-choice questions are based.

Basic Skills Necessary

The basic skills necessary to perform well on the English Test include the six elements of effective writing:

USAGE/MECHANICS

- **punctuation,** with an emphasis on punctuation that influences meaning, such as that which avoids ambiguity or identifies an appositive
- **basic grammar and usage,** such as agreement, case, verb form, and idiomatic usage
- **sentence structure,** including correct subordination, parallelism, and placement of modifiers

RHETORICAL SKILLS

- **strategy,** including questions about the audience, purpose, and effectiveness of prose
- **organization,** including questions about the order, unity, and coherence of a passage
- **style,** including questions about diction, imagery, freedom from ambiguity, and economy in writing

Directions

In the left-hand column, you will find passages in a "spread-out" format with various words and phrases underlined and numbered.

11

In the right-hand column, you will find a set of responses corresponding to each underlined portion. If the underlined portion is correct standard written English, is most appropriate to the style and feeling of the passage, or best makes the intended statement, mark the letter indicating "NO CHANGE." If the underlined portion is not the best choice given, choose the one that is. For these questions, consider only the underlined portions; assume that the rest of the passage is correct as written. You will also see questions concerning parts of the passage or the whole passage. Choose the response you feel is best for these questions.

For some passages, you may also be given a box of additional directions similar to the following:

> The following paragraphs are given a number in parentheses above each one. The paragraphs may be in the most logical order, or they may not. Item ___ asks you to choose the paragraph sequence that is the most logical.

Analysis of Directions

1. Make sure you understand the passage as a whole; a correct choice must be appropriate to the meaning of the passage, the author's purpose, the audience, etc. Read through the entire passage quickly and make sure you understand it before dealing with the underlined portions.

2. You are looking for errors in standard written English, the kind of English used in most textbooks. Do not evaluate a sentence in terms of the spoken English we all use.

3. When deciding whether an underlined portion is correct or not, *assume that all parts which are not underlined are correct.*

4. Several alternatives to an underlined portion may be partially correct. You are to pick the one which *fits the meaning of the sentence and is grammatically and structurally sound.*

5. You may also be given some general questions about the rhetoric (organization, style, purpose) of the passage.

Suggested Approach with Samples

Some of the types of errors you will encounter are

- punctuation errors
- grammar errors
- sentence structure errors
- logic and organization errors
- idiom errors

A short discussion of each of these types of errors using simple problems will give you a basic understanding of the structure of the English Test. Remember, there are many other types of errors.

Punctuation errors. Suspect a punctuation error when a period, comma, semicolon, colon, or dash is part of the underlined portion.

At sunrise we assembled the climbing, gear that we had hidden the night before.

1. A. NO CHANGE
   B. the climbing gear that we had hidden
   C. the climbing; gear that we had hidden
   D. the climbing— gear that we had hidden

The comma following *climbing* makes the sentence unintelligible; one cannot assemble a climbing, but one can assemble climbing gear. So removing the comma altogether (B) restores meaning to the sentence.

Grammar errors. A grammar error requires that the *form* of a word be changed. Common grammar errors involve incorrect pronouns or disagreement between subject and verb.

Pronoun error:

The computer <u>corrected oneself</u> and

                1

continued to run the program.

1. A. NO CHANGE
   B. corrects itself
   C. corrected itself
   D. corrects one-
      self

Oneself may correctly refer to a person, but not to a thing. Since a computer is a thing, the correct pronoun is *itself,* so (C) is the best choice because it supplies *itself* without unnecessarily changing *corrected.*

Subject-verb agreement error:

The carton of roses and carnations <u>were</u>

                2

beautifully displayed in the window.

2. F. NO CHANGE
   G. was
   H. weren't
   J. OMIT the un-
      derlined por-
      tion.

The subject is singular—*carton,* so the verb must be singular, *was* instead of *were.* Choice (G) is correct.

Sentence structure errors. A sentence structure error occurs when the parts of a sentence are not arranged in a logical order or when an essential part or parts have been omitted. Common sentence structure errors are faulty parallelism and dangling modifiers.

Faulty parallelism:

He drank, smoked, and <u>watching TV</u> too

                  1

much.

1. A. NO CHANGE
   B. to watch TV
   C. watched TV
   D. will watch TV

Watching TV is not parallel to (does not have the same form as) the other terms with which it is listed; a correctly parallel phrase is *drank, smoked, and watched TV,* in which each element is a verb in the past tense.

Dangling modifier:

A piano is for sale by a woman with
―――――――――――――――――――――――
                                    2
walnut legs.
――――――――
    2

2. F. NO CHANGE
    G. piano with
        walnut legs is
        for sale by a
        woman.
    H. piano is for
        sale with wal-
        nut legs by a
        woman.
    J. with walnut
        legs a piano is
        for sale.

The sentence seems to say that the woman has walnut legs! This confusion is corrected by placing *walnut legs* after the word which it is meant to describe—*piano*—as in (G).

Logic and organization errors. These errors occur when sentences are not arranged in logical order or when paragraphing is not done properly.

Incorrect paragraphing:

The requirements for graduation are a 2.5

minimum grade-point average and two

semesters of science.

In addition to the above, a written
―――――――――――――――――――――――
                1
thesis is also required.

1. A. NO CHANGE
    B. (Begin new
        paragraph)
        Also a written
    C. (Begin new
        paragraph)
        However, a
        written
    D. (Do NOT be-
        gin new para-
        graph) A writ-
        ten

No new paragraph is needed. The final sentence continues the main idea expressed in the initial sentence. (D) is correct.

Idiom errors. Idioms are the usual way in which phrases or expressions are put together in a language. Most problems in idiom come from the improper use of prepositions (*on, of, to, by, than, from,* etc.).

His problems began <u>prior of</u> his first day
                              1
at work.

1. A. NO CHANGE
   B. prior to
   C. prior than
   D. on an occasion
      previous to

Prior to (B) is the correct idiomatic usage, not *prior of.*

Sample Passage

The following is a shorter passage than will appear on the exam but which gives examples of the kinds of questions that the English Test will ask. Most of the questions offer alternative versions or "NO CHANGE" to underlined portions of the text. Remember, you must assume that only the underlined section can be changed and that the rest of the sentence which is not underlined is correct.

The ancestor of our modern microscopes

<u>are nearly</u> four hundred years old. The
        1

1. A. NO CHANGE
   B. are near
   C. is near
   D. is nearly

early microscopes <u>were worked and</u>
                              2
<u>operated by</u> lenses that, by forcing light
        2
to bend, could focus and enlarge the

2. F. NO CHANGE
   G. were worked
      and were
   H. worked and
      operated by
   J. worked by

image of whatever object

reflecting the light. By improving
<u>3</u>   <u>4</u>

3. A. NO CHANGE
    B. was reflecting
    C. reflected
    D. will reflect

<u>lensmaking</u>, microscopes could be made
   4
to enlarge an object as much as one

thousand times its original size. The

word "telescope" derives from Greek

words meaning "to view" and "far off";

"microscope" comes from words

meaning "to view" and

"small." ⑤

4. F. NO CHANGE
    G. By having im-
       proved lens-
       making,
    H. Lensmaking
       having im-
       proved,
    J. With the im-
       provement of
       lensmaking,

5. A. NO CHANGE
    B. OMIT the pre-
       ceding sen-
       tence.
    C. OMIT the first
       half of the pre-
       ceding sen-
       tence only.
    D. OMIT the last
       half of the pre-
       ceding sen-
       tence only.

<u>But for a time microscopes could not be</u>
              6
improved beyond that point. When the

objects to be studied were smaller than

the light waves that were used to see

them, the objects could

6. F. NO CHANGE
    G. But for a time:
    H. But, for a time,
    J. But, for a
       time;

not be seen. ⁊7⁊ The first attempt to

7. What might be added to the paragraph at this point?
   A. a quotation from a famous scientist
   B. a comparison of microscopes and telescopes
   C. examples of objects too small to be seen by these instruments
   D. the names of the scientists who worked on microscopes

solve this problem, in the 1920s,
                 _____
                      8

8. F. NO CHANGE
   G. Delete the commas around ", in the 1920s,"
   H. MOVE "In the 1920s" to the beginning of the sentence.
   J. MOVE "in the 1920s" to after "attempt to."

will use shorter light waves, such as
____
  9

9. A. NO CHANGE
   B. will have used
   C. used
   D. did use

ultraviolet. And the improvement was
<u>   </u>
           10
negligible. Waves any shorter than these

could not be focused properly. The

problem was unlocked and set free by
<u>_____</u>
                11
using the much shorter electron waves,

which can be focused by magnetic
<u>_____</u>
  12

fields. | 13 |

10. F. NO CHANGE
     G. Therefore,
     H. But,
     J. Thus,

11. A. NO CHANGE
     B. problem was unlocked and opened
     C. difficulty was unlocked
     D. problem was solved

12. F. NO CHANGE
     G. and these
     H. and the waves
     J. who

13. The probable audience for this passage is
     A. elementary school children
     B. general readers with some science
     C. advanced students of the history of science
     D. advanced students of mathematics

Answers

1. (D) The subject of the sentence is the singular noun *ancestor.* The adverb *nearly* is the correct modifier of the adjectives *four hundred.*

2. (J) Though all four choices are grammatical, three of them are wordy. Since *worked and operated* mean the same, one of the verbs is all we need. The active verb *worked* is briefer than the passive *were worked.*

3. (C) So far, this sentence has used the past tense in *worked* and *could focus.* There is no reason to change to another tense here.

4. (J) Choices (F) and (G) are gerund phrases. A gerund (a verbal noun, for example, *improving*), like a participle, will dangle if it is not placed close to a noun or pronoun, the performer of the action it describes. In this sentence, there is no word like *scientists.* To correct the sentence, remove the dangling gerund, as in choice (J).

5. (B) The telescope half of this sentence has no relation to the rest of this paragraph. The explanation of the roots of the word *microscope,* though more related than the telescope, is still not appropriate here, and the paragraph is improved if the entire sentence is omitted.

6. (H) The correct punctuation here is commas setting off the phase *for a time.*

7. (C) At this point, specific references to what still could not be seen (for example, viruses, atomic particles) would make clear the need for continued improvements.

8. (H) The best place for the prepositional phrase is at the beginning of the sentence.

9. (C) The past tense is the basic verb tense in this paragraph.

10. (H) The sense of the sentence suggests the necessary conjunction is *But.*

11. (D) As it stands, the phrase is verbose and the metaphors are confused. Choice (D) is the conventional phrasing with no mixed metaphor or wordiness.

12. (F) The *which* has a specific antecedent (*waves*) and says in one word what takes two or three in choices (G) and (H).

13. (B) The level of the passage is evidently above elementary school children but below what we would expect of advanced scientific students.

In the passage and questions above, you have examples of the grammar/usage questions in numbers 1, 3, or 9. Question 6 is a punctuation question, and questions 4 and 8 are questions about sentence structure. Questions 5, 7, 11, and 12 are the sort of question that the rhetorical skills portion of the test will use.

CONTENT AREA BREAKDOWN
(Approximate Percentages)

Content/Skills	Number of Items	Percentages
Usage/Mechanics	40	53%
Punctuation	10	13%
Grammar and Usage	12	16%
Sentence Structure	18	24%
Rhetorical Skills	35	47%
Strategy	12	16%
Organization	11	15%
Style	12	16%
Total	75	

In addition to the total English score, two subscores will be reported in the following areas:

Usage/Mechanics (40 items)
Rhetorical Skills (35 items)

The total English Test will be scored from 1 to 36 with a mean score being 18. The subscores will range from 1 to 18, with a mean of 9.

INTRODUCTION TO TEST 2: MATHEMATICS

The Mathematics Test is 60 minutes in length and contains 60 questions.

Abililty Tested

The Mathematics Test evaluates your ability to solve mathematical problems by using reasoning, problem-solving insight, logic, and the application of basic and advanced skills learned in high school.

Basic Skills Necessary

The basic skills necessary to do well on this test include high school arithmetic, elementary and intermediate algebra, coordinate geometry, plane geometry, and trigonometry, along with some logical insight into problem-solving situations. The three skill levels covered include: using the basic skills, applying math skills to different situations, and analyzing when and why operations will and will not yield a solution.

Directions

In the Mathematics Test, each of the problems includes five choices (A, B, C, D, E or F, G, H, J, K). You are to solve each problem and choose the correct answer.

Analysis of Directions

You are looking for the *one* correct answer; therefore, although other answers may be close, there is never more than one right answer.

Approximating can be a valuable tool, *except* its value is greatly diminished when one of the choices is "None of these." In this case, you must get an exact answer and cannot merely select the closest one.

All scratchwork is to be done in the test booklet; get used to doing this while practicing, because no scratch paper is allowed into the testing area.

Suggested Approach with Samples

1. Take advantage of being allowed to mark on the test booklet by always underlining or circling what you are looking for. This will make you sure that you are answering the right question. *Sample:*

If $x + 6 = 9$, then $3x + 1 =$

(A) 3   (B) 9   (C) 10   (D) 34   (E) 46

You should first circle or underline $3x + 1$, because this is what you are solving for. Solving for x leaves $x = 3$ and then substituting into $3x + 1$ gives $3(3) + 1$, or 10. The most common mistake is to solve for x, which is 3, and mistakenly choose (A) as your answer. But remember, you are solving for $3x + 1$, not just x. You should also notice that most of the other choices would all be possible answers if you made common or simple mistakes. The correct answer is (C). *Make sure that you are answering the right question.*

2. Substituting numbers for variables can often be an aid to understanding a problem. Remember to substitute simple numbers, since *you* have to do the work. *Sample:*

If $x > 1$, which of the following decreases as x decreases?

$$\text{I. } x + x^2$$

$$\text{II. } 2x^2 - x$$

$$\text{III. } \frac{1}{x + 1}$$

(F) I only   (J) I and II only
(G) II only   (K) II and III
(H) III only

This problem is most easily solved by taking each situation and substituting simple numbers. However, in the first situation, I, $x + x^2$, you should recognize that this expression will decrease as x decreases. Trying $x = 2$, gives $2 + (2)^2$, which equals 6. Now trying $x = 3$, gives $3 + (3)^2 = 12$. Notice that choices (G), (H), and (K) are already eliminated because they do not contain I. You should also realize that now you only need to try the values in II; since III is not paired with I as a possible choice, III cannot be one of the answers.

Trying $x = 2$ in the expression $2x^2 - x$, gives $2(2)^2 - 2$, or $2(4) - 2$, which leaves 6. Now trying $x = 3$ gives $2(3)^2 - 3$, or $2(9) - 3 = 18 - 3 = 15$. This expression also decreases as x decreases. Therefore the correct answer is choice (J). Once again notice that III was not even attempted, because it was not one of the possible choices.

3. Sometimes you will immediately recognize the proper formula or method to solve a problem. If this is not the situation, try a reasonable approach and then work from the answers. *Sample:*

> Barney can mow the lawn in 5 hours, and Fred can mow the lawn in 4 hours. How long will it take them to mow the lawn together?
>
> (A) 1 hour   (D) $4\frac{1}{2}$ hours
> (B) $2\frac{2}{9}$ hours   (E) 5 hours
> (C) 4 hours

Suppose that you are unfamiliar with the type of equation for this problem. Try the "reasonable" method. Since Fred can mow the lawn in 4 hours by himself, he will take less than 4 hours if Barney helps him. Therefore, choices (C), (D), and (E) are ridiculous. Taking this method a little further, suppose that Barney could also mow the lawn in 4 hours. Then together it would take Barney and Fred 2 hours. But since Barney is a little slower than this, the total time should be a little more than 2 hours. The correct answer is (B), $2\frac{2}{9}$ hours.

Using the equation for this problem would give the following calculations:

$$\frac{1}{5} + \frac{1}{4} = \frac{1}{x}$$

In 1 hour, Barney could do $\frac{1}{5}$ of the job, and in 1 hour, Fred could do $\frac{1}{4}$ of the job; unknown x is that part of the job they could do together in one hour. Now, solving, you calculate as follows:

$$\frac{4}{20} + \frac{5}{20} = \frac{1}{x}$$

$$\frac{9}{20} = \frac{1}{x}$$

Cross multiplying gives $\qquad 9x = 20$

Therefore $\qquad\qquad x = \frac{20}{9}$, or $2\frac{2}{9}$.

4. "Pulling" information out of the word problem structure can often give you a better look at what you are working with, and therefore, you gain additional insight into the problem. *Sample:*

> If a mixture is $\frac{3}{7}$ alcohol by volume and $\frac{4}{7}$ water by volume, what is the ratio of the volume of alcohol to the volume of water in this mixture?
>
> (F) $\frac{3}{7}$ (G) $\frac{4}{7}$ (H) $\frac{3}{4}$ (J) $\frac{4}{3}$ (K) $\frac{7}{4}$

The first bit of information that should be pulled out should be what you are looking for: "ratio of the volume of alcohol to the volume of water." Rewrite it as $A{:}W$ and then into its working form: A/W. Next, you should pull out the volumes of each; $A = \frac{3}{7}$ and $W = \frac{4}{7}$. Now the answer can be easily figured by inspection or substitution: using $(\frac{3}{7})/(\frac{4}{7})$, invert the bottom fraction and multiply to get $\frac{3}{7} \times \frac{7}{4} = \frac{3}{4}$. The ratio of the volume of alcohol to the volume of water is 3 to 4. The correct answer is choice (H). When pulling out information, actually write out the numbers and/or letters to the side of the problem, putting them into some helpful form and eliminating some of the wording.

5. Sketching diagrams or simple pictures can also be very helpful in problem solving, because the diagram may tip off either a simple solution or a method for solving the problem. *Sample:*

> What is the maximum number of pieces of birthday cake of size 4″ by 4″ that can be cut from a cake 20″ by 20″?
>
> (A) 5   (B) 10   (C) 16   (D) 20   (E) 25

Sketching the cake and marking in as follows makes this a fairly simple problem.

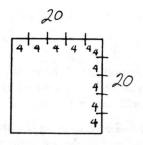

Notice that five pieces of cake will fit along each side, therefore 5 × 5 = 25. The correct answer is (E). Finding the total area of the cake and dividing it by the area of one of the 4 × 4 pieces would have also given you the correct answer, but beware of this method, because it may not work if the pieces do not fit evenly into the original area.

6. Marking in diagrams as you read them can save you valuable time. Marking can also give you insight into how to solve a problem because you will have the complete picture clearly in front of you. *Sample:*

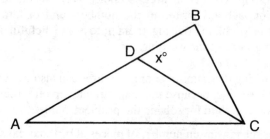

In the triangle, *CD* is an angle bisector, angle *ACD* is 30° and angle *ABC* is a right angle. Find the measurement of angle *x* in degrees.

(F) 30°   (G) 45°   (H) 60°   (J) 75°   (K) 80°

You should have read the problem and marked as follows:

In the triangle above, *CD* is an angle bisector (STOP AND MARK IN THE DRAWING), angle *ACD* is 30° (STOP AND MARK IN THE DRAWING), and angle *ABC* is a right angle (STOP AND MARK IN THE DRAWING). Find the measurement of angle *x* in degrees (STOP AND MARK IN OR CIRCLE WHAT YOU ARE LOOKING FOR IN THE DRAWING).

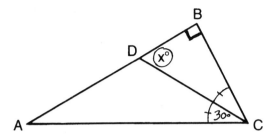

Now with the drawing marked in, it is evident that since angle *ACD* is 30°, then angle *BCD* is also 30° because they are formed by an angle bisector (divides an angle into two equal parts). Since angle *ABC* is 90° (right angle) and *BCD* is 30°, then angle x is 60°, because there are 180° in a triangle; $180 - (90 + 30) = 60$. The correct answer is (H). ALWAYS MARK IN DIAGRAMS AS YOU READ THEIR DESCRIPTIONS AND INFORMATION ABOUT THEM. THIS INCLUDES WHAT YOU ARE LOOKING FOR.

7. If it appears that extensive calculations are going to be necessary to solve a problem, check to see how far apart the choices are, and then approximate. The reason for checking the answers first is to give you a guide for how freely you can approximate. *Sample:*

The value for $(.889 \times 55)/9.97$ to the nearest tenth is

(A) .5   (B) 4.63   (C) 4.9   (D) 7.7   (E) 49.1

Before starting any computations, take a glance at the answers to see how far apart they are. Notice that the only close answers are choices (B) and (C), except choice (B) is not possible, since it is to the nearest hundredth, not tenth. Now, making some quick approximations, $.889 = 1$ and $9.97 = 10$, leaves the problem in this form

$$\frac{1 \times 55}{10} = \frac{55}{10} = 5.5$$

The closest answer is (C); therefore, it is the correct answer. Notice that choices (A) and (E) were ridiculous.

8. In some instances, it will be easier to work from the answers. Do not disregard this method, because it will at least eliminate some of the choices and could give you the correct answer. *Sample:*

Find the counting number that is less than 15 and when divided by 3 has a remainder of 1 and divided by 4 has a remainder of 2.

(F) 5   (G) 8   (H) 10   (J) 12   (K) 13

By working from the answers, you eliminate wasting time on other numbers from 1 to 14. Choices (G) and (J) can be immediately eliminated because they are divisible by 4, leaving no remainder. Choices (F) and (K) can also be eliminated because they leave a remainder of 1 when divided by 4. Therefore, the correct answer is (H); 10 leaves a remainder of 1 when divided by 3 and a remainder of 2 when divided by 4.

CONTENT AREA BREAKDOWN
(*Approximate Percentages*)

Contents/Skills	Number of Items	Percentages
Pre-Algebra and Elementary Algebra	24	40%
Intermediate Algebra and Coordinate Geometry	18	30%
Plane Geometry	14	23%
Trigonometry	4	7%
Total	60	

In addition to the total mathematics score, three subscores will be reported in the following areas:

Pre-Algebra/Elementary Algebra (24 items)
Intermediate Algebra/Coordinate Geometry (18 items)
Plane Geometry/Trigonometry (18 items)

The total Mathematics Test will be scored from 1 to 36, with a mean score being 18. The subscores will range from 1 to 18, with a mean of 9.

Additional Study Aids

For additional review and practice in math, you will find that *Cliffs Math Review for Standardized Tests* will provide you with the help you need. Unlike other general math reviews, this book focuses on *standardized test math* and gives you a practical, personalized test-preparation program. *Cliffs Math Review for Standardized Tests* is available at your local bookstore, or you may order it from Cliffs Notes, Inc., by sending in the coupon you'll find at the back of this book.

INTRODUCTION TO TEST 3: READING

The Reading Test is 35 minutes long and contains four reading passages, each followed by 10 multiple-choice questions for a total of 40 questions.

Ability Tested

The Reading Test evaluates your ability to understand, interpret, and analyze prose drawn from four types of reading passages:

- **Prose Fiction:** excerpts from short stories or novels.

- **Humanities:** architecture, art, dance, music, philosophy, theater.

- **Social Studies:** anthropology, economics, history, political science, psychology, sociology.

- **Natural Sciences:** biology, chemistry, physical science, physics.

The questions test your reading and reasoning abilities, not your prior knowledge of a subject or knowledge of vocabulary or rules of logic.

Basic Skills Necessary

The basic skills necessary to do well on this section include reading skills at the level of a high school senior or college freshman, the ability to understand what is explicitly stated in a passage, the ability to understand what is implied and what can be inferred, the ability to draw conclusions, comparisons, and generalizations. Students who have read widely and know how to read and mark a passage actively and efficiently tend to do well on the Reading Test.

Directions

Each of the four passages in this test is followed by questions. Read the passage and choose the best answer to each question. Return to the passage as often as necessary to answer the questions.

Analysis of Directions

1. Answer all the questions for one passage before moving on to the next one. If you don't know the answer, take an educated guess or skip it.

2. Use only the information given or implied in a passage. Do not consider outside information, even if it seems more accurate than the given information.

Suggested Approach with Short Sample Passage

Two strategies that will improve your reading comprehension are *prereading the questions* and *marking the passage*. Readers who use these strategies tend to score much higher on reading tests than readers who don't.

Prereading the questions. Before reading the passage, read some questions (but don't spend time reading all the multiple-choice answers) and circle the most important word or phrase. *Sample:*

1. The author's argument in favor of freedom of speech may be summarized in which of the following ways?
   (A) If every speaker is not free, no speaker is.
   (B) Speech keeps us free from the animal kingdom.
   (C) As we think, so we speak.
   (D) The Bill of Rights ensures free speech.

The most *important* part is usually the most concrete and specific one. In this case, you might circle *freedom of speech*. The question parts that you circle will be those you'll tend to remember when you read the passage. In this case, you would be likely to notice and pay close attention to *freedom of speech* when it occurs in the passage. Thus, prereading allows you to focus on the parts of the passage that contain the answers.

Marking the passage. After prereading the questions, read and mark the passage. *Always mark those spots that contain information relevant to the questions you've read. In addition, you should mark other important ideas and details.* More specific advice on marking, in reference to subareas of reading skills, follows. In general though, *remember not to overmark;* never make more than a few marks per paragraph in order to make those parts that you mark stand out.

Passage

*By the time a child starts school, he has mastered the major part of the rules of his grammar. He has managed to accomplish this remarkable feat in such a short time by experimenting with and generalizing the rules all by himself. Each child, in effect, rediscovers language in the first few years of his life.

*When it comes to vocabulary growth, it is a different story. Unlike grammar, the chief means through which vocabulary is learned is memorization. *And some people have a hard time learning and remembering words.

(The * indicates portions of the passage which refer directly to a question you've skimmed. Also marked are main points and key terms.)

1. A child has mastered many rules of grammar by about the age of
   (A) 3   (B) 5   (C) 8   (D) 10

The first sentence of the passage contains several words from this question, so it is likely to contain the correct answer. *By the time a child starts school* tells us that the answer is 5. Before choosing (B), you should look at all the answers and cross out those which seem incorrect.

2. Although vocabulary growth involves memorization and grammar learning doesn't, we may conclude that both vocabulary and grammar make use of
   (F) memorization   (H) words
   (G) study skills   (J) children

The question asks you to simply use your common sense. Choice (F) is incorrect; it contradicts both the passage and the question itself. Choice (J) makes no sense. Choice (G) is a possibility, but (H) is better because grammar learning in young children does not necessarily involve study skills but does involve words.

3. The last sentence in the passage implies that
    (A) some people have no trouble learning and remembering
        new words
    (B) some people have a hard time remembering new words
    (C) grammar does not involve remembering words
    (D) old words are not often remembered

Implies tells us that the answer is something suggested but not explicitly stated in the passage. Choice (B) is explicitly stated in the passage, so it may be eliminated. But (B) implies the opposite: if *some* people have a hard time, it must be true that *some* people don't. Choice (A) is therefore the correct choice. Choices (C) and (D) are altogether apart from the meaning of the last sentence.

Another Short Passage

St. Augustine was a contemporary of Jerome. After an early life of pleasure, he became interested in a philosophical religion called Manichaeism, a derivative of a Persian religion, in which the forces of good constantly struggle with those of evil. Augustine was eventually converted to Christianity by St. Ambrose of Milan. His *Confessions* was an autobiography that served as an inspiration to countless thousands who believed that virtue would ultimately win.

1. St. Augustine's conversion to Christianity was probably influenced by
    (A) his confessional leanings
    (B) his contemporaries
    (C) the inadequacy of a Persian religion to address Western
        moral problems
    (D) his earlier interest in the dilemma of retaining virtue

Having skimmed this question, you should have marked the portion of the passage which mentions Augustine's conversion and paid attention to the events (influences) leading to it. Choice (A) requires speculating beyond the facts in the paragraph; there is also no evidence in the passage to support choice (C). Choice (B) is too vague and general to be the best answer. (D) points toward Augustine's earlier interest in Manichaeism, and the last sentence suggests that Augustine's interest in retaining virtue continued through his Christian doctrine. Well supported as it is, (D) is the best answer.

2. From the information in the passage, we must conclude that Augustine was a
   (F) fair-weather optimist   (H) hardworking optimist
   (G) cockeyed optimist   (J) failed optimist

Skimming *this* question is not very helpful; it does not point specifically to any information in the passage. Questions of this sort usually assess your overall understanding of the meaning, style, tone, or point of view of the passage. In this case, you should recognize that Augustine is a serious person; therefore, more lighthearted terms like *fair-weather* (F) and *cockeyed* (G) are probably inappropriate. Choice (J) contradicts Augustine's success as an *inspiration to countless thousands*. (H) corresponds with his ongoing, hopeful struggle to retain virtue in the world; it is the best answer.

3. Judging from the reaction of thousands to Augustine's *Confessions*, we may conclude that much of his world at that time was in a state of
   (A) opulence   (C) heresy
   (B) misery   (D) reformation

Having skimmed this question, you should have marked the last sentence of the passage as the place to look for the answer. That Augustine's readers were inspired implies that they *required inspiration*, that they were in some sort of uninspiring, or *negative* situation. Choice (A) must therefore be eliminated because it is a positive term. Choice (D) is not necessarily a negative term and so is probably not the best answer. (C), although a negative term, does not describe a state of being which thirsts for inspiration. Choice (B) does and is therefore the best choice.

Longer Sample Passage

A social studies passage similar to this might appear in the Reading Test. Notice that this sample contains only five, not the normal ten, questions. Read the passage carefully and answer the five questions that follow.

American federalism has been described as a neat mechanical theory. The national government was said to be sovereign in certain areas of governmental concern, such as the regulation of interstate commerce. State governments were said to be sovereign in certain other areas, such as regulation of intrastate commerce and exercise of the police power. One writer has described this as the "layer cake" concept of American federalism. In the top layer are neatly compacted all the powers of the national government; in the bottom layer are found the separate and distinct functions and powers of state governments.

How nice it would be if the American federal system could be so easily and conveniently analyzed. But Professor Martin Grodzins of the University of Chicago has gone on to describe federalism in practice as more like a marble cake, with an intermingling of functions, than like a layer cake, with functions separate and distinct. This intermingling can be seen best, perhaps, by examining the example of railroad traffic. If it crosses a state line, it constitutes interstate commerce, coming under control of the national government. Rail shipments originating and ending within a single state constitute intrastate commerce, thus—the theory tells us—falling under regulation of state government. However, both the interstate and intrastate shipments may have moved over the same rails. In this simple example, one might easily read the urgent necessity for close cooperation between state and national governments. This need has not gone unrecognized by administrators of governmental programs at the state, local, and national levels.

Nonetheless, national and state interests often conflict in the political arena. Pressures may be brought to bear on state legislators which differ from those felt by members of the national Congress. Disagreement over the proper division of powers between states and the national government often lies beneath a conflict of interests. But no "best" formula has been discovered for drawing a dividing line between state powers and national powers.

The men who wrote the United States Constitution did the best they could in the face of circumstances which confronted them at the time. The state-national power dispute has raged persistently ever since. What are "states' rights"? It is obvious that, throughout United States history, "states' rights" has arisen repeatedly as the anguished wail of any interest which felt is was being treated unsympathetically at a given moment by the national government. The source of the cry would seem to depend on whose ox is being gored.

Questions

1. The best title for this passage would be
   (A) Like a Layer Cake: The Federal and the State Governments
   (B) Federal Versus State Power: An Unresolved Question
   (C) Federal Sovereignty in United States Politics
   (D) The Decline of States' Rights

2. According to Martin Grodzins, federalism is more like a marble cake than a layer cake because
   (F) the federal powers are on the top
   (G) the federal and state powers are distinct, like cake and frosting
   (H) the state and federal functions cannot be easily separated
   (J) taken together, the state and federal make up the whole cake

3. From the discussion of rail shipments in the second paragraph, we can conclude that a barge carrying freight on the Great Lakes from Chicago to Buffalo would be under the control of the

   I. government of Illinois
   II. government of New York
   III. federal government

   (A) I only
   (B) II only
   (C) III only
   (D) I and II only

4. From the distinction the passage makes between "interstate" and "intrastate," we can infer that the prefixes "inter" and "intra" mean
   (F) "between" and "within"
   (G) "inside of" and "outside of"
   (H) "to" and "from"
   (J) "around" and "through"

5. Which of the following best describes the relation of the second paragraph of the passage to the first?
   (A) It gives a specific example in support of the generalization in the first paragraph.
   (B) It questions the comparison of the first paragraph and offers a different one.
   (C) It deals with an entirely different subject.
   (D) It demonstrates the appropriateness of the comparison used in the first paragraph.

Answers

The five questions are samples of the five kinds of questions most likely to appear on the Reading Test.

Question 1. The first question is about the passage as a whole. Usually at least one question will ask for a good title, or what the central subject is, or what the author's main point is. Here the correct answer is (B). The passage is about the powers of the federal government and the states and concludes that no easy solution for determining their limits has been found. The comparison to a layer cake (choice A) is found to be inadequate, and choices (C) and (D) do not really address the central concerns of the passage.

Question 2. The second question asks for specific material from the passage. This sort of question, usually asking for an explicit supporting detail, is by far the most common type in the exam and may appear five or six times in a set of questions. Here the correct answer is (H). The passage compares the state and federal powers to a *marble cake, with an intermingling of functions.*

Questions 3 and 4. The third and fourth questions here illustrate two more question types, ones that call for an inference or an application from facts given in the passage. In answering question 3, we would note that by going from Chicago to Buffalo, the barge enters two states and infer that, like a railroad that crosses into two different states, the barge would be subject to federal rather than state law. The right answer, then, is (C).

In answering the fourth question, we would see that the *interstate* traffic is *between* two or more states, but *intrastate* traffic is *within* a single state. The correct choice is (F).

Question 5. Finally, an occasional question will ask you to describe or explain the development, logic, or purpose of part or parts of the passage. Here, for example, you are asked to relate the first and second paragraphs. The first paragraph compares the federal-state relationship to a layer cake. But the second paragraph questions this analogy, suggests a different one, and gives an example to support the new comparison. Of the four answers, (B) is clearly the best choice.

General Procedure for Answering Reading Questions

1. *Skim the questions,* circling the word or phrase that stands out in each question. *Don't* read the answer choices.

2. *Read and mark the passage,* paying special attention to information relevant to the questions you've skimmed.

3. *Answer the questions.* Base your answers *only on the material given in the passage.* Assume that the information in each passage is accurate. The questions test your understanding of the passage alone; they do *not* test the historical background of the passage, the biography of the author, or previous familiarity with the work from which the passage is taken.

READING CONTEXT BREAKDOWN
(*Approximate Percentages*)

Reading Context	Number of Items	Percentages
Prose Fiction	10	25%
Humanities	10	25%
Social Studies	10	25%
Natural Sciences	10	25%
Total	40	

In addition to the total reading score, two subscores will be reported in the following areas:

Arts/Literature (Prose Fiction, Humanities: 20 items)
Social Studies/Sciences (Social Studies, Natural Sciences: 20 items)

The total Reading Test will be scored from 1 to 36, with a mean score being 18. The subscores will range from 1 to 18, with a mean of 9.

INTRODUCTION TO TEST 4: SCIENCE REASONING

The Science Reasoning Test is 35 minutes long and contains 40 multiple-choice questions.

Ability Tested

In this test you are given several sets of scientific information, including reading passages, diagrams, and tables. Each set of information is followed by several multiple-choice questions. Your success depends on your ability to quickly understand the information presented to you. There are three different formats for the scientific information.

DATA REPRESENTATION FORMAT: The information is presented in tables, graphs, or figures which summarize the results of research.

RESEARCH SUMMARIES FORMAT: You are given a detailed description of one experiment or a series of related experiments.

CONFLICTING VIEWPOINTS FORMAT: Two or more scientists present different theories about one scientific question.

Basic Skills Necessary

The test may include information from biology, chemistry, physics, astronomy, or geology. However, you are not expected to have studied all those fields. You will be tested on your general reasoning skills applied to the scientific information given to you.

The questions will require you to understand the basic facts and concepts of the information. You will be expected to critically analyze data and scientific arguments, to perceive relationships, to draw conclusions, and to make generalizations. A few questions call for simple mathematical calculations using the data.

The test emphasizes general reasoning skills rather than your prior knowledge of science, ability to read, or skill at mathematical calculations.

Directions

Each passage in this test is followed by several questions. After you read each passage, select the correct choice for each of the questions that follow the passage. Refer back to the passage as often as necessary to answer the questions.

Analysis of Directions

Each set of scientific information is called a *passage*. A passage could be several descriptive paragraphs, a data table, a diagram of an experiment, or any combination of such information. Each passage does contain the factual information needed to answer the set of questions following the passage. You should refer back to the passage for each question rather than attempt to answer using your background knowledge or your memory of the passage.

Suggested Approach with Samples

There is considerable time pressure on this test; you will have only about 5 minutes to read each passage and answer the set of questions. Take about 2 or 3 minutes to study each passage, leaving about 20 to 30 seconds for each of the following questions. You may wish to quickly skim the questions before studying the passage. Following are sample passages illustrating the three formats on the test. The question about each passage is then discussed and solved to show you how to approach such material.

Passage I

The chart shows the total weight of air pollutants for the entire nation during a recent year. The data are cross-tabulated according to both type of pollutant and source of the material. The quantities in the chart represent millions of tons per year.

Pollutant	Cars and Trucks	Electric Plants	Industrial Plants	Waste Disposal
Carbon monoxide	67	1	2	2
Sulfur oxides	1	14	9	1
Hydrocarbons	12	1	5	1
Nitrogen oxides	7	3	2	1
Particles	1	4	6	1
Total	88	23	24	6

1. The environmental problem referred to as "acid rain" is caused by sulfur oxide pollution. Which source is the major contributor to the acid rain problem?
   (A) cars and trucks   (C) industrial plants
   (B) electric plants   (D) waste disposal

This passage is an example of the Data Representation format. You are given a table summarizing research on air pollution and asked to answer an interpretive question. You should begin by examining the table carefully to comprehend how it organizes the information. In this case, the rows show the different pollutants and the columns display the various sources of the pollution. The question asks about the acid rain problem, which it attributes to sulfur oxides. Now look at the chart and find the row for sulfur oxides. In that second row, the largest quantity is 14, so electric plants are the main contributors to the acid rain problem. The correct answer is choice (B). For the Data Representation format, the most valuable point to remember is to begin by examining the table or figure to see how it organizes the information.

Passage II

To investigate whether evaporation could cause a liquid to rise within a tube, a researcher placed an open glass tube in a large beaker filled with mercury. Water was then poured slowly into the tube until it was filled. Notice in the figure that the weight of the water displaced the mercury in the tube slightly below its level in the beaker.

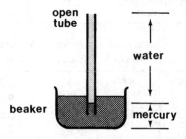

The researcher then fastened a permeable plastic membrane across the top of the tube and turned on a heat lamp to begin evaporating water through the permeable membrane. The mercury slowly rose several inches within the glass tube.

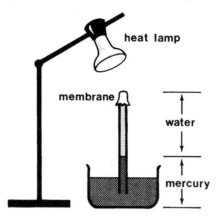

2. The rate at which the mercury rises in the tube could be accelerated by
   (F) inserting a smaller bulb in the lamp
   (G) substituting alcohol for the water
   (H) using a glass tube of smaller diameter
   (J) using a larger beaker and more mercury

This passage is an example of the Research Summaries format. You are given a detailed description of an experiment. The most important point is for you to clearly grasp the purpose of the experiment. The first sentence of the passage usually states the purpose, so return and reread that sentence. The purpose of the experiment is to "investigate whether evaporation could cause a liquid to rise within a tube." An understanding of the reason the experiment was conducted is essential to most of the questions in the Research Summaries format. Question 2, above, asks how we could get the mercury to rise faster. Since you know that evaporation causes the rise, to increase the rate of rising you must increase the rate of evaporation. The correct answer is choice (G) because alcohol evaporates much faster than water. Notice how an understanding of the purpose of the experiment aided in answering the question.

Passage III

What caused the extinction of dinosaurs? Two differing views are presented below.

Scientist 1

Throughout the long Mesozoic era, hundreds of dinosaur species dominated over smaller animals. Some dinosaurs were meat eaters and others ate only plants. Some lived in deserts, some in swamps. There were even dinosaurs swimming through the oceans and soaring through the skies. This extraordinarily successful group of reptiles all disappeared at the end of the Cretaceous period, 65 million years ago. Only a worldwide catastrophe could have simultaneously killed all dinosaurs in their diverse environmental niches. The most probable cause of the mass extinction is a close encounter with a comet, which could have abruptly altered earth's temperatures. Dinosaurs, like all reptiles, were cold-blooded animals and could not adapt to a great temperature change.

Scientist 2

It is almost certain that no single event killed all dinosaurs. Their record during the Mesozoic era is one of species continually evolving to new species; each old species is then said to have become extinct. The extinctions are not at all simultaneous. The early, egg-eating pelycosaurs disappeared in the Permian period. The largest dinosaur of all—*Brachiosaurus*—became extinct in the Jurassic. The ensuing record during the Cretaceous period is even richer and more complicated, with duck-billed hadrosaurs, predatory tyrannosaurs, and flying pterosaurs appearing and disappearing at various times. By the end of the Cretaceous, the last dinosaur species had vanished. The slow disappearance of the dinosaurs occurred as mammals evolved into more habitats. The last dinosaur and the last dinosaur egg were probably eaten by mammals.

3. A key point that would help settle the dispute about dinosaur extinction would be to know
   - (A) if cold-blooded animals could adapt to new temperatures
   - (B) when the various dinosaur species disappeared
   - (C) whether a comet could cause a change of climate
   - (D) which environmental niches were occupied by dinosaurs

This passage is an example of the Conflicting Viewpoints format, in which scientists present different theories on one issue. You should begin by rereading the opening sentence of the passage to make sure you know the scientific issue in dispute; in our example, it is the cause of dinosaur extinction. Then try to perceive the main point or points of disagreement in the theories presented, since many of the following questions cover those points of disagreement. Try not to let the details of evidence keep you from recognizing the main points of disagreement. In our sample passage, you should have noticed that Scientist 1 says that all dinosaurs were simultaneously killed, while Scientist 2 states that the different species became extinct at different times—the main point of disagreement between the two theories. In sample question 3, we could choose between the two theories if we definitely knew when the various dinosaur species disappeared, so the correct answer is choice (B). Understanding the main point or points of disagreement between the rival theories is your best help on the Conflicting Viewpoints format.

FORMAT BREAKDOWN
(Approximate Percentages)

Passage Type	Number of Items	Percentages
Data Representation	15	38%
Research Summaries	18	45%
Conflicting Viewpoints	7	17%
Total	40	

Part III: Practice-Review-Analyze-Practice
Two Full-Length Practice Tests

This section contains two full-length practice simulation ACT exams. The practice tests are followed by answers and complete explanations and analysis techniques. The format, levels of difficulty, question structure, and number of questions are similar to those on the actual ACT. The actual ACT is copyrighted and may not be duplicated and these questions are not taken directly from the actual tests.

When taking these exams, try to simulate the test conditions by following the time allotments carefully. Remember the total test is 2 hours and 55 minutes, divided as follows:

Test 1:	English	45 minutes
Test 2:	Mathematics	60 minutes
Test 3:	Reading	35 minutes
Test 4:	Science Reasoning	35 minutes

Part II: Regression Analysis—Predicting the
Two Full-Length Practice Tests

PRACTICE TEST BATTERY NO. 1

START WITH NUMBER 1 FOR EACH
NEW SECTION OF THE TEST

TEST 1

1 Ⓐ Ⓑ Ⓒ Ⓓ	26 Ⓕ Ⓖ Ⓗ Ⓙ	51 Ⓐ Ⓑ Ⓒ Ⓓ
2 Ⓕ Ⓖ Ⓗ Ⓙ	27 Ⓐ Ⓑ Ⓒ Ⓓ	52 Ⓕ Ⓖ Ⓗ Ⓙ
3 Ⓐ Ⓑ Ⓒ Ⓓ	28 Ⓕ Ⓖ Ⓗ Ⓙ	53 Ⓐ Ⓑ Ⓒ Ⓓ
4 Ⓕ Ⓖ Ⓗ Ⓙ	29 Ⓐ Ⓑ Ⓒ Ⓓ	54 Ⓕ Ⓖ Ⓗ Ⓙ
5 Ⓐ Ⓑ Ⓒ Ⓓ	30 Ⓕ Ⓖ Ⓗ Ⓙ	55 Ⓐ Ⓑ Ⓒ Ⓓ
6 Ⓕ Ⓖ Ⓗ Ⓙ	31 Ⓐ Ⓑ Ⓒ Ⓓ	56 Ⓕ Ⓖ Ⓗ Ⓙ
7 Ⓐ Ⓑ Ⓒ Ⓓ	32 Ⓕ Ⓖ Ⓗ Ⓙ	57 Ⓐ Ⓑ Ⓒ Ⓓ
8 Ⓕ Ⓖ Ⓗ Ⓙ	33 Ⓐ Ⓑ Ⓒ Ⓓ	58 Ⓕ Ⓖ Ⓗ Ⓙ
9 Ⓐ Ⓑ Ⓒ Ⓓ	34 Ⓕ Ⓖ Ⓗ Ⓙ	59 Ⓐ Ⓑ Ⓒ Ⓓ
10 Ⓕ Ⓖ Ⓗ Ⓙ	35 Ⓐ Ⓑ Ⓒ Ⓓ	60 Ⓕ Ⓖ Ⓗ Ⓙ
11 Ⓐ Ⓑ Ⓒ Ⓓ	36 Ⓕ Ⓖ Ⓗ Ⓙ	61 Ⓐ Ⓑ Ⓒ Ⓓ
12 Ⓕ Ⓖ Ⓗ Ⓙ	37 Ⓐ Ⓑ Ⓒ Ⓓ	62 Ⓕ Ⓖ Ⓗ Ⓙ
13 Ⓐ Ⓑ Ⓒ Ⓓ	38 Ⓕ Ⓖ Ⓗ Ⓙ	63 Ⓐ Ⓑ Ⓒ Ⓓ
14 Ⓕ Ⓖ Ⓗ Ⓙ	39 Ⓐ Ⓑ Ⓒ Ⓓ	64 Ⓕ Ⓖ Ⓗ Ⓙ
15 Ⓐ Ⓑ Ⓒ Ⓓ	40 Ⓕ Ⓖ Ⓗ Ⓙ	65 Ⓐ Ⓑ Ⓒ Ⓓ
16 Ⓕ Ⓖ Ⓗ Ⓙ	41 Ⓐ Ⓑ Ⓒ Ⓓ	66 Ⓕ Ⓖ Ⓗ Ⓙ
17 Ⓐ Ⓑ Ⓒ Ⓓ	42 Ⓕ Ⓖ Ⓗ Ⓙ	67 Ⓐ Ⓑ Ⓒ Ⓓ
18 Ⓕ Ⓖ Ⓗ Ⓙ	43 Ⓐ Ⓑ Ⓒ Ⓓ	68 Ⓕ Ⓖ Ⓗ Ⓙ
19 Ⓐ Ⓑ Ⓒ Ⓓ	44 Ⓕ Ⓖ Ⓗ Ⓙ	69 Ⓐ Ⓑ Ⓒ Ⓓ
20 Ⓕ Ⓖ Ⓗ Ⓙ	45 Ⓐ Ⓑ Ⓒ Ⓓ	70 Ⓕ Ⓖ Ⓗ Ⓙ
21 Ⓐ Ⓑ Ⓒ Ⓓ	46 Ⓕ Ⓖ Ⓗ Ⓙ	71 Ⓐ Ⓑ Ⓒ Ⓓ
22 Ⓕ Ⓖ Ⓗ Ⓙ	47 Ⓐ Ⓑ Ⓒ Ⓓ	72 Ⓕ Ⓖ Ⓗ Ⓙ
23 Ⓐ Ⓑ Ⓒ Ⓓ	48 Ⓕ Ⓖ Ⓗ Ⓙ	73 Ⓐ Ⓑ Ⓒ Ⓓ
24 Ⓕ Ⓖ Ⓗ Ⓙ	49 Ⓐ Ⓑ Ⓒ Ⓓ	74 Ⓕ Ⓖ Ⓗ Ⓙ
25 Ⓐ Ⓑ Ⓒ Ⓓ	50 Ⓕ Ⓖ Ⓗ Ⓙ	75 Ⓐ Ⓑ Ⓒ Ⓓ

CUT HERE

51

ANSWER SHEET FOR PRACTICE TEST BATTERY NO. 1
(Remove This Sheet and Use It to Mark Your Answers)

START WITH NUMBER 1 FOR EACH
NEW SECTION OF THE TEST

TEST 2

1 Ⓐ Ⓑ Ⓒ Ⓓ Ⓔ	26 Ⓕ Ⓖ Ⓗ Ⓙ Ⓚ	51 Ⓐ Ⓑ Ⓒ Ⓓ Ⓔ
2 Ⓕ Ⓖ Ⓗ Ⓙ Ⓚ	27 Ⓐ Ⓑ Ⓒ Ⓓ Ⓔ	52 Ⓕ Ⓖ Ⓗ Ⓙ Ⓚ
3 Ⓐ Ⓑ Ⓒ Ⓓ Ⓔ	28 Ⓕ Ⓖ Ⓗ Ⓙ Ⓚ	53 Ⓐ Ⓑ Ⓒ Ⓓ Ⓔ
4 Ⓕ Ⓖ Ⓗ Ⓙ Ⓚ	29 Ⓐ Ⓑ Ⓒ Ⓓ Ⓔ	54 Ⓕ Ⓖ Ⓗ Ⓙ Ⓚ
5 Ⓐ Ⓑ Ⓒ Ⓓ Ⓔ	30 Ⓕ Ⓖ Ⓗ Ⓙ Ⓚ	55 Ⓐ Ⓑ Ⓒ Ⓓ Ⓔ
6 Ⓕ Ⓖ Ⓗ Ⓙ Ⓚ	31 Ⓐ Ⓑ Ⓒ Ⓓ Ⓔ	56 Ⓕ Ⓖ Ⓗ Ⓙ Ⓚ
7 Ⓐ Ⓑ Ⓒ Ⓓ Ⓔ	32 Ⓕ Ⓖ Ⓗ Ⓙ Ⓚ	57 Ⓐ Ⓑ Ⓒ Ⓓ Ⓔ
8 Ⓕ Ⓖ Ⓗ Ⓙ Ⓚ	33 Ⓐ Ⓑ Ⓒ Ⓓ Ⓔ	58 Ⓕ Ⓖ Ⓗ Ⓙ Ⓚ
9 Ⓐ Ⓑ Ⓒ Ⓓ Ⓔ	34 Ⓕ Ⓖ Ⓗ Ⓙ Ⓚ	59 Ⓐ Ⓑ Ⓒ Ⓓ Ⓔ
10 Ⓕ Ⓖ Ⓗ Ⓙ Ⓚ	35 Ⓐ Ⓑ Ⓒ Ⓓ Ⓔ	60 Ⓕ Ⓖ Ⓗ Ⓙ Ⓚ
11 Ⓐ Ⓑ Ⓒ Ⓓ Ⓔ	36 Ⓕ Ⓖ Ⓗ Ⓙ Ⓚ	
12 Ⓕ Ⓖ Ⓗ Ⓙ Ⓚ	37 Ⓐ Ⓑ Ⓒ Ⓓ Ⓔ	
13 Ⓐ Ⓑ Ⓒ Ⓓ Ⓔ	38 Ⓕ Ⓖ Ⓗ Ⓙ Ⓚ	
14 Ⓕ Ⓖ Ⓗ Ⓙ Ⓚ	39 Ⓐ Ⓑ Ⓒ Ⓓ Ⓔ	
15 Ⓐ Ⓑ Ⓒ Ⓓ Ⓔ	40 Ⓕ Ⓖ Ⓗ Ⓙ Ⓚ	
16 Ⓕ Ⓖ Ⓗ Ⓙ Ⓚ	41 Ⓐ Ⓑ Ⓒ Ⓓ Ⓔ	
17 Ⓐ Ⓑ Ⓒ Ⓓ Ⓔ	42 Ⓕ Ⓖ Ⓗ Ⓙ Ⓚ	
18 Ⓕ Ⓖ Ⓗ Ⓙ Ⓚ	43 Ⓐ Ⓑ Ⓒ Ⓓ Ⓔ	
19 Ⓐ Ⓑ Ⓒ Ⓓ Ⓔ	44 Ⓕ Ⓖ Ⓗ Ⓙ Ⓚ	
20 Ⓕ Ⓖ Ⓗ Ⓙ Ⓚ	45 Ⓐ Ⓑ Ⓒ Ⓓ Ⓔ	
21 Ⓐ Ⓑ Ⓒ Ⓓ Ⓔ	46 Ⓕ Ⓖ Ⓗ Ⓙ Ⓚ	
22 Ⓕ Ⓖ Ⓗ Ⓙ Ⓚ	47 Ⓐ Ⓑ Ⓒ Ⓓ Ⓔ	
23 Ⓐ Ⓑ Ⓒ Ⓓ Ⓔ	48 Ⓕ Ⓖ Ⓗ Ⓙ Ⓚ	
24 Ⓕ Ⓖ Ⓗ Ⓙ Ⓚ	49 Ⓐ Ⓑ Ⓒ Ⓓ Ⓔ	
25 Ⓐ Ⓑ Ⓒ Ⓓ Ⓔ	50 Ⓕ Ⓖ Ⓗ Ⓙ Ⓚ	

ANSWER SHEET FOR PRACTICE TEST BATTERY NO. 1
(Remove This Sheet and Use It to Mark Your Answers)

START WITH NUMBER 1 FOR EACH
NEW SECTION OF THE TEST

TEST 3

1 Ⓐ Ⓑ Ⓒ Ⓓ
2 Ⓕ Ⓖ Ⓗ Ⓙ
3 Ⓐ Ⓑ Ⓒ Ⓓ
4 Ⓕ Ⓖ Ⓗ Ⓙ
5 Ⓐ Ⓑ Ⓒ Ⓓ

6 Ⓕ Ⓖ Ⓗ Ⓙ
7 Ⓐ Ⓑ Ⓒ Ⓓ
8 Ⓕ Ⓖ Ⓗ Ⓙ
9 Ⓐ Ⓑ Ⓒ Ⓓ
10 Ⓕ Ⓖ Ⓗ Ⓙ

11 Ⓐ Ⓑ Ⓒ Ⓓ
12 Ⓕ Ⓖ Ⓗ Ⓙ
13 Ⓐ Ⓑ Ⓒ Ⓓ
14 Ⓕ Ⓖ Ⓗ Ⓙ
15 Ⓐ Ⓑ Ⓒ Ⓓ

16 Ⓕ Ⓖ Ⓗ Ⓙ
17 Ⓐ Ⓑ Ⓒ Ⓓ
18 Ⓕ Ⓖ Ⓗ Ⓙ
19 Ⓐ Ⓑ Ⓒ Ⓓ
20 Ⓕ Ⓖ Ⓗ Ⓙ

21 Ⓐ Ⓑ Ⓒ Ⓓ
22 Ⓕ Ⓖ Ⓗ Ⓙ
23 Ⓐ Ⓑ Ⓒ Ⓓ
24 Ⓕ Ⓖ Ⓗ Ⓙ
25 Ⓐ Ⓑ Ⓒ Ⓓ

26 Ⓕ Ⓖ Ⓗ Ⓙ
27 Ⓐ Ⓑ Ⓒ Ⓓ
28 Ⓕ Ⓖ Ⓗ Ⓙ
29 Ⓐ Ⓑ Ⓒ Ⓓ
30 Ⓕ Ⓖ Ⓗ Ⓙ

31 Ⓐ Ⓑ Ⓒ Ⓓ
32 Ⓕ Ⓖ Ⓗ Ⓙ
33 Ⓐ Ⓑ Ⓒ Ⓓ
34 Ⓕ Ⓖ Ⓗ Ⓙ
35 Ⓐ Ⓑ Ⓒ Ⓓ

36 Ⓕ Ⓖ Ⓗ Ⓙ
37 Ⓐ Ⓑ Ⓒ Ⓓ
38 Ⓕ Ⓖ Ⓗ Ⓙ
39 Ⓐ Ⓑ Ⓒ Ⓓ
40 Ⓕ Ⓖ Ⓗ Ⓙ

CUT HERE

53

ANSWER SHEET FOR PRACTICE TEST BATTERY NO. 1
(Remove This Sheet and Use It to Mark Your Answers)

START WITH NUMBER 1 FOR EACH
NEW SECTION OF THE TEST

TEST 4

1 Ⓐ Ⓑ Ⓒ Ⓓ
2 Ⓕ Ⓖ Ⓗ Ⓙ
3 Ⓐ Ⓑ Ⓒ Ⓓ
4 Ⓕ Ⓖ Ⓗ Ⓙ
5 Ⓐ Ⓑ Ⓒ Ⓓ

6 Ⓕ Ⓖ Ⓗ Ⓙ
7 Ⓐ Ⓑ Ⓒ Ⓓ
8 Ⓕ Ⓖ Ⓗ Ⓙ
9 Ⓐ Ⓑ Ⓒ Ⓓ
10 Ⓕ Ⓖ Ⓗ Ⓙ

11 Ⓐ Ⓑ Ⓒ Ⓓ
12 Ⓕ Ⓖ Ⓗ Ⓙ
13 Ⓐ Ⓑ Ⓒ Ⓓ
14 Ⓕ Ⓖ Ⓗ Ⓙ
15 Ⓐ Ⓑ Ⓒ Ⓓ

16 Ⓕ Ⓖ Ⓗ Ⓙ
17 Ⓐ Ⓑ Ⓒ Ⓓ
18 Ⓕ Ⓖ Ⓗ Ⓙ
19 Ⓐ Ⓑ Ⓒ Ⓓ
20 Ⓕ Ⓖ Ⓗ Ⓙ

21 Ⓐ Ⓑ Ⓒ Ⓓ
22 Ⓕ Ⓖ Ⓗ Ⓙ
23 Ⓐ Ⓑ Ⓒ Ⓓ
24 Ⓕ Ⓖ Ⓗ Ⓙ
25 Ⓐ Ⓑ Ⓒ Ⓓ

26 Ⓕ Ⓖ Ⓗ Ⓙ
27 Ⓐ Ⓑ Ⓒ Ⓓ
28 Ⓕ Ⓖ Ⓗ Ⓙ
29 Ⓐ Ⓑ Ⓒ Ⓓ
30 Ⓕ Ⓖ Ⓗ Ⓙ

31 Ⓐ Ⓑ Ⓒ Ⓓ
32 Ⓕ Ⓖ Ⓗ Ⓙ
33 Ⓐ Ⓑ Ⓒ Ⓓ
34 Ⓕ Ⓖ Ⓗ Ⓙ
35 Ⓐ Ⓑ Ⓒ Ⓓ

36 Ⓕ Ⓖ Ⓗ Ⓙ
37 Ⓐ Ⓑ Ⓒ Ⓓ
38 Ⓕ Ⓖ Ⓗ Ⓙ
39 Ⓐ Ⓑ Ⓒ Ⓓ
40 Ⓕ Ⓖ Ⓗ Ⓙ

TEST 1: ENGLISH

Time: 45 Minutes
75 Questions

DIRECTIONS

In the left-hand column, you will find passages in a "spread out" format with various words and phrases underlined and numbered. In the right-hand column, you will find a set of responses corresponding to each underlined portion. If the underlined portion is correct standard written English, is most appropriate to the style and feeling of the passage, or best makes the intended statement, mark the letter indicating "NO CHANGE." If the underlined portion is not the best choice given, choose the one that is. For these questions, consider only the underlined portions; assume that the rest of the passage is correct as written. You will also see questions concerning parts of the passage or the whole passage. Choose the response you feel is best for these questions.

Passage I

> The following paragraphs are given a number in parentheses above each one. The paragraphs may be in the most logical order, or they may not. Item 16 asks you to choose the paragraph sequence that is the most logical.

(1)

Salad lovers, <u>gleefully</u> contemplating
                1

the high price of lettuce at the

supermarkets, are generally unaware of

1. A. NO CHANGE
   B. gleeful
   C. glumly
   D. hopefully

the several hands outstretched for a

share of the retail price.

But the growers and the farm workers
___
2
who harvest the crop, currently

confronting each other

in a strike situation that is violent in the
_____
3
Greenland Valley, are convinced that

one is short-changed in the division of
___
4
the harvest revenue. The United

Vegetable Workers Union wants an

increase in minimum wages and

that piecework rates to bring the
_____
5
earnings of the members in line

2. F. NO CHANGE
   G. For
   H. Because
   J. OMIT the un-
      derlined por-
      tion.

3. A. NO CHANGE
   B. in a situation
      that is a vio-
      lent strike
   C. in a violent
      strike situation
   D. striking vio-
      lently

4. F. NO CHANGE
   G. they are
   H. he is
   J. both are

5. A. NO CHANGE
   B. an increase in
      piecework rates
   C. piecework rates
   D. a rise of piece-
      works

<u>with truckers.</u> Farm operators are
     6

reluctant to accept additional

costs. $\boxed{7}$

6. F. NO CHANGE
    G. with that of
       truckers.
    H. with those of
       truckers.
    J. with the earn-
       ings of truck-
       ers'.

7. Suppose you were
    obligated to elimi-
    nate one of the
    four sentences in
    the first para-
    graph. Which one
    can be left out
    with the least
    damage to the
    meaning and co-
    herence of the
    paragraph?
    A. the first
       ("Salad
       lovers . . .)
    B. the second
       ("But the
       growers . . .)
    C. the third
       ("The
       United . . .)
    D. the fourth
       ("Farm opera-
       tors . . .)

(2)

In any case, the settlement in the
———————————————————
8
Greenland Valley will have an effect on

8. F. NO CHANGE
    G. (Do NOT be-
        gin new para-
        graph) The
        settlement
    H. (Do NOT be-
        gin new para-
        graph) In any
        case, the
        settlement
    J. Nevertheless,
        the settlement

the Presidents' effort to control inflation.
———————————————
9
The wage and benefit packages adopted

at Greenland Valley will have an impact

on future farm worker negotiations

throughout the country. By adopting an

increased minimum wage,

9. A. NO CHANGE
    B. that Presi-
        dents'
    C. the President's
    D. the Presidents

an inflationary pressure has already
_____
10
been instituted by the Congress.
_____
10

10. F. NO CHANGE
    G. an inflationary
       pressure has
       already been
       instituted by
       Congress.
    H. Congress has
       already ap-
       plied an infla-
       tionary pres-
       sure.
    J. an inflationary
       pressure has
       already been
       applied.

The UVW, which wants an increase to
_____
11
$6.00 per hour. Even larger increases are

sought in piecework wages, ranging from

$10.00 to $13.00 an hour for a

person both skilled in work and
_____
12
industrious when working.
_____
12

11. A. NO CHANGE
    B. UVW which
       wants
    C. UVW wants
    D. UVW wanting

12. F. NO CHANGE
    G. skilled and
       industrious
       worker.
    H. person indus-
       trious at his
       skill.
    J. person of in-
       dustry and
       skill.

(3)

Because the threat of a lettuce
_____
13
shortage has created a consumer

demand that keeps retail prices high,

producers unaffected by the strike have

doubled their prices.

13. A. NO CHANGE
    B. Although
    C. Despite the
       fact that
    D. If

The lettuce field violence, with several
_____
14
shootings and one death, has shocked
_____
14
the nation. The farm operators have
_____
14
offered only small pay

14. F. NO CHANGE
    G. The lettuce
       field violence
       of several
       shootings and
       one death has
       shocked the
       nation.
    H. The violence
       in the lettuce
       field has
       shocked the
       nation.
    J. OMIT the un-
       derlined por-
       tion.

hikes. They have however, conceded
_____
15
that a more workable agreement might

allow greater increases at the bottom of

15. A. NO CHANGE
    B. hikes. They
       have, however,
    C. hikes; they
       have however,
    D. hikes: they
       have however

the farm worker scale

with lesser gains at the top. $\boxed{16}$

16. Choose the sequence of paragraph numbers that will make the structure of the passage most logical.
    F. NO CHANGE
    G. 1, 3, 2
    H. 2, 3, 1
    J. 3, 1, 2

Passage II

Once, there was a mouse and a rat
$\overline{}$
$\qquad$ 17
who lived in a large barn in a fertile

country. The rat was happy in this home,

for there was always plenty to

eat. But the mouse was
$\overline{}$
18

17. A. NO CHANGE
    B. Once there was
    C. Once, there were
    D. There was, once

18. F. NO CHANGE
    G. eat, and
    H. eat. And
    J. eat. The

dissatisfied. "The food was good," he
$\overline{}$
$\qquad$ 19
admitted, but the winters were cold. He
$\overline{}$
19
especially

19. A. NO CHANGE
    B. The food is good, he admitted,
    C. The food was good, he admitted,
    D. "The food was good," he would admit,

disliked to see the smoke from the
                20
fireplaces in the farmhouse while he

shivered in his nest in the barn. When he

could endure the promise of warm fires

no longer, he proposed to the rat that

they move to the house. "We should

have two houses, one for winter and one

for summer, like people do," he said.
                      21

20. F. NO CHANGE
    G. disliked that
       he saw
    H. disliked seeing
    J. disliked to
       have seen

21. A. NO CHANGE
    B. as people,
    C. like people,
    D. like people
       have

But the rat was not interested.
               22

22. F. NO CHANGE
    G. But the rat was
       not interested!
    H. OMIT the un-
       derlined por-
       tion.
    J. MOVE the
       underlined
       portion to be-
       come the first
       sentence of
       the second
       paragraph.

His fur was thicker, his weight

greater, <u>and he had a better insulated</u>
<u>   23   </u>
<u>nest</u>, so he did not mind the chill. "I like
<u>23</u>
the change of seasons," he said.

"Besides," he went on, "the neighbors

here in the barn are friendly and

familiar. Who knows <u>what they will be</u>
<u>   24   </u>
<u>like in the house?</u> I'll stay right here. If
<u>   24   </u>
you don't go looking for trouble, trouble

won't come looking for

you. <u>Nothing ventured, nothing gained.</u>
<u>   25   </u>
Safety first. A bird in the hand is worth

two in the bush." Several more proverbs

followed these, and the mouse thought

that one more advantage of moving to

the farmhouse

23. A. NO CHANGE
    B. and his nest
       was better in-
       sulated,
    C. and his was a
       better insu-
       lated nest,
    D. and his nest
       better insu-
       lated,

24. F. NO CHANGE
    G. what they are
       like in the
       house
    H. what it is like
       in the house.
    J. if they will like
       you in the
       house.

25. The proverb, com-
    pared to the three
    others in this se-
    ries, is
    A. appropriate
       and briefer.
    B. identical in
       meaning.
    C. opposite in
       meaning.
    D. similar in
       meaning to
       "Safety first."

would be to escape from the tedious
_____
26

moralizing and infernal proverbs of the
_____
27

rat. [28] [29]

26. F. NO CHANGE
    G. will be to es-
       cape
    H. will be the es-
       cape
    J. is to escape

27. The word "infer-
    nal" is used here
    because it is the
    diction of the
    A. rat.
    B. mouse.
    C. barnyard.
    D. author.

28. The passage uses
    all of the following
    devices EXCEPT
    F. dialogue.
    G. comedy.
    H. contrast of
       general and
       specific
    J. indirect dis-
       course.

29. The longer work
    of which this pas-
    sage is a part is
    probably a
    A. satire.
    B. novel.
    C. fable.
    D. short story.

Passage III

(1)

The City Council, Tuesday night,

approved the 450-acre annexation of

North Belmont by a 5–1 vote over the

protestations and objections of area
<u>   </u>
30

30. F. NO CHANGE
    G. objections
    H. denouncing
    J. protestation
      and objection

residents <u>who attended the meeting.</u>
               31
<u>Protesting residents filled the Council</u>
             31
Chambers. Their verbal abuse and threat

of an injunction could not alter

31. A. NO CHANGE
    B. who attended
      the meeting
      and filled the
    C. who attended
      the meeting by
      filling the
    D. who filled the

the <u>two petitions</u> they submitted
      32
did not have the needed signatures. To

bring the issue before all the voters of

the county requires

32. F. NO CHANGE
    G. the two peti-
      tions which
    H. that of the two
      petitions
    J. the fact that
      the two peti-
      tions

either the signatures of 25% of the
_____33_____
registered voters or 10% of the
_____33_____
property owners. 34

33. A. NO CHANGE
    B. the signatures
       either of 25%
       of the regis-
       tered voters or
       10% of
    C. the signatures
       of either 25%
       of the regis-
       tered voters or
       10% of
    D. the signatures
       of either 25%
       of the voters or
       of 10% of

34. The probable au-
    dience for whom
    this paragraph was
    written is
    F. readers of
       daily or weekly
       newspapers.
    G. readers of a
       monthly news
       magazine.
    H. members of
       the City Coun-
       cil.
    J. petitioners
       from North
       Belmont.

(2)

Residents filed petitions signed by 116

alleged registered voters and 48 alleged

property owners, some signatures

appearing on both lists, <u>at the last City</u>

Council meeting.

<u>35</u>

35. The best position
in this sentence
for the underlined
phrase is
A. NO CHANGE
B. at the begin-
ning of the
sentence.
C. after the verb
"signed."
D. after the noun
"owners."

But Jack <u>Cope, city manager said in a</u>

<u>36</u>

staff report that only 66 of the registered

voters' signatures—far short

36. F. NO CHANGE
G. Cope, city
manager, said
H. Cope city man-
ager said
J. Cope, who is
city manager
said

of the required 25%—<u>was valid.</u>

<u>37</u>

And only 26 of the 48

37. A. NO CHANGE
B. were valid.
C. will be valid.
D. had been valid.

supposed property owners really
                                    38
owned land in the country. "Even if all
                   38
the protest signatures were accepted,"

38. F. NO CHANGE
    G. supposedly
       property own-
       ers really
       owned land
    H. supposed
       property own-
       ers really owns
       land
    J. supposed
       property own-
       ers really own
       land

Cope concluded, "the total will still be
                                      39
short of the number required by

law. 40

39. A. NO CHANGE
    B. would still
    C. should still
    D. OMIT the un-
       derlined por-
       tion.

40. Unlike the first
    paragraph, the
    second uses
    F. loose sen-
       tences.
    G. a rhetorical
       question.
    H. direct quota-
       tion.
    J. cause and ef-
       fect reasoning.

(3)

One of the North Belmont residents

told the Council that <u>I have delivered</u>
41
today to the city clerk the signatures of

41. A. NO CHANGE
B. I delivered
C. he delivered
D. he had delivered

21 additional voters opposed to the

<u>annexation. Enough to require an</u>
42
<u>election in the county.</u> The city clerk
42
acknowledged that she had received

42. F. NO CHANGE
G. annexation, enough to require an election in the county.
H. annexation. And enough to require an election in the county.
J. annexation. Which is enough to require an election in the county.

the signatures. <u>Anna Repton, the city</u>
43

<u>clerk, has held her office for more than</u>
43

<u>twenty years next June.</u> But Mayor
43

Schulz, citing the filing deadline of three

weeks ago, refused to allow the

signatures to be counted. A heated

exchange capped by a

43. A. NO CHANGE
    B. Anna Repton, the city clerk, will hold her office for more than twenty years next June.
    C. Anna Repton, the city clerk, will have held her office for more than twenty years next June.
    D. OMIT the underlined portion.

series of <u>savagely comic</u> insults
44

44. F. NO CHANGE
    G. savage
    H. comic
    J. savage comic

followed. ⬛45 The meeting adjourned

45. The author at this point could strengthen the passage by
    A. discussing the background of Mayor Schulz.
    B. discussing the laws governing annexation.
    C. citing the names of the North Belmont representatives.
    D. quoting one or two of the insults.

at 10:35 p.m. ⬛46

46. Which of the following words or phrases does NOT describe the closing sentence of the paragraph?
    F. conventional
    G. terse
    H. deliberately anticlimactic
    J. hortatory

Passage IV

(1)

<u>Growing up</u> in Maine in the 1930s, my
₄₇
favorite room was the kitchen. Unlike

most of the farms nearby, ours had both

electricity and gas, woodburning

fireplaces in most rooms, and

<u>the house was centrally heated by oil.</u>
₄₈
Why should I remember the kitchen as

the only warm room? [49]

47. A. NO CHANGE
    B. When growing up
    C. When I was growing up
    D. While growing up

48. F. NO CHANGE
    G. the house had central heating.
    H. the house had oil central heating.
    J. oil central heating.

49. The author varies the sentences in the paragraph here by using
    A. a first person pronoun.
    B. an interrogative verb.
    C. a passive verb.
    D. a periodic sentence.

Because, I suppose, it was even warmer
<u>50</u>
than the rest of the house. My mother

50. F. NO CHANGE
    G. Because I sup-
       pose
    H. Because, I
       suppose
    J. Because.

refused to have a "newfangled" gas stove
<u>51</u>
and did all her cooking on a huge

woodburning range.

51. The author puts
    quotation marks
    around the adjec-
    tive "newfangled"
    because
    A. the word is not
       English.
    B. the word is
       slang.
    C. the word is the
       one the
       mother used.
    D. the word is
       inappropriate
       in this context.

And what cooking! There were four
<u>52</u>
ovens in the range, and my mother kept

all of them full: breads and rolls, pies

and cakes, in the ovens on the left;

roasts, casseroles, and stews, and

52. F. NO CHANGE
    G. And what
       cooking?
    H. And what's
       cooking?
    J. OMIT the un-
       derlined por-
       tion.

her giant bean pot in the ovens on the

right. 53 54

53. The punctuation of this sentence uses a colon after "full" and a semicolon after "left." The correct punctuation would be
   A. NO CHANGE
   B. a semicolon after "full" and a colon after "left."
   C. a comma after "full" and a comma after "left."
   D. a semicolon after "full" and a comma after "left."

54. Which of the following most accurately describes the point of view of the first paragraph?
   F. a male narrator using the third person
   G. a narrator using the first person and present tense
   H. a female narrator using the first person
   J. a narrator using the first person and past tense

(2)

I live now in a small, attractive

apartment in Manhattan. My rent each

month is three or four times as much as

my father's farm earned in a year, and

my kitchen is <u>hardly bigger</u> than my
                    55

mother's four-oven range. I don't know

how to make bread (I am a lawyer,

specializing in labor law)

<u>or how to bake a bean.</u> Most of the
         56

55. A. NO CHANGE
    B. not hardly big-
       ger
    C. not hardly
       larger
    D. smaller

56. F. NO CHANGE
    G. or how beans
       are baked.
    H. nor how beans
       are baked.
    J. or know how
       to bake beans.

time I eat out or <u>fix something from a</u>
                        57
<u>package in the microwave that is quick.</u>
                        57

57. A. NO CHANGE
    B. fix something
       from a pack-
       age quickly in
       the microwave.
    C. fix something
       in the micro-
       wave from a
       package that is
       quick.
    D. fix something
       that is quick in
       the microwave
       from a pack-
       age.

My kitchen is <u>no warmer than any</u>
                        58
<u>room in</u> my apartment. A thermostat
   58
keeps all rooms

58. F. NO CHANGE
    G. not warmer
       than any room
    H. no warmer
       than any other
       room
    J. not much
       warmer than
       any room

<u>exactly the same, identical, temperature</u>
                        59
<u>of heat.</u> 60
   59

59. A. NO CHANGE
    B. at exactly the
       same, identical
       temperature of
       heat.
    C. at the same,
       identical tem-
       perature.
    D. at the same
       temperature.

60. Readers are likely to regard the passage as best described by which of the following terms?
    F. inspirational
    G. sarcastic
    H. confessional
    J. nostalgic

Passage V

> The following paragraphs are given a number in parentheses above each one. The paragraphs may be in the most logical order, or they may not. Item 75 asks you to choose the paragraph sequence that is the most logical.

(1)

A police dispatcher receiving a call

about a domestic dispute must decide

whether to send one, two, or no officers
      ―――
       61

at all. If the disturbance

61. A. NO CHANGE
    B. whether or not to send
    C. weather to send
    D. weather or not to send

appears to be a routine one a single
_____
              62
officer will be dispatched to resolve the

62. F. NO CHANGE
    G. was routine,
    H. appears to be
       routine
    J. appears to be
       routine,

dispute. And if it appears that there may
         _____
                63
be an injury or crime, two or more

officers will be sent to defuse the

tensions. In incidents of domestic

violence, women and children are more

often injured than men. ☐64

63. A. NO CHANGE
    B. If, however it
       appears
    C. However if it
       appears
    D. But if it ap-
       pears

64. The omission of
    which of the four
    sentences of the
    first paragraph
    will improve its
    coherence?
    F. the first
    G. the second
    H. the third
    J. the fourth

(2)

During a family crisis, it is often a

member of the immediate family calling
                                _____
                                  65
the Police Department. The neighbors

65. A. NO CHANGE
    B. who is calling
    C. who calls
    D. that tele-
       phones

are unlikely, <u>unless the dispute becomes</u>
                              66
<u>very noisy or threatening,</u> to interfere in
              66
someone else's domestic troubles.

Sometimes a child of fighting parents will

seek refuge with a neighbor and

<u>ask for the neighbor to</u> notify the police.
            67
In-laws are frequently responsible for

reporting <u>domestic quarrels which have</u>
                              68
<u>become violent.</u>
    68

66. F. NO CHANGE
    G. OMIT the un-
       derlined por-
       tion.
    H. MOVE the
       underlined
       portion to fol-
       low "neigh-
       bors."
    J. MOVE the
       underlined
       portion to
       follow
       "troubles."

67. A. NO CHANGE
    B. ask the neigh-
       bor to
    C. ask that the
       neighbor
       should
    D. ask of the
       neighbor to

68. F. NO CHANGE
    G. domestic quar-
       rels, which
       have become
       violent.
    H. domestic quar-
       rels that are
       violent.
    J. violent domes-
       tic quarrels.

(3)

In a crime situation, emotions

run high, and officers must
___
69

69. A. NO CHANGE
    B. run highly,
    C. ran high,
    D. have run high,

maintain a steady attitude of
_____
          70
neutrality,
_____
   70

70. F. NO CHANGE
    G. keep a steady
       attitude of
       neutrality,
    H. remain neu-
       tral,
    J. steadily main-
       tain an atti-
       tude of neu-
       trality.

which is not always easy to do.
_____
              71

71. A. NO CHANGE
    B. and this is not
       always easy to
       do.
    C. and that is not
       always easy to
       do.
    D. something not
       always easy to
       do.

If someone is hurt, they must see to it
           _____
              72
that proper medical care is obtained.

72. F. NO CHANGE
    G. is hurt,then he
    H. is hurt, he
    J. is hurt they

Skilled officers will be able to reason

with the disputants, perhaps suggesting a

separation, with either the husband or

the wife staying with friends or relatives

until the air has cleared. [74] [75]
$\overline{}$
73

73. A. NO CHANGE
    B. the rain has
       stopped.
    C. the air is
       warmer.
    D. the air is
       cooler.

74. From which of the
    following would a
    quotation prob-
    ably be a most
    effective addition
    to this passage?
    F. a social worker
       who deals with
       family prob-
       lems
    G. a victim of wife
       abuse
    H. a police officer
    J. a judge

75. Choose the sequence of paragraph numbers that will make the structure of the passage most logical.
    A. NO CHANGE
    B. 1, 3, 2
    C. 2, 1, 3
    D. 3, 2, 1

STOP. IF YOU FINISH BEFORE TIME IS CALLED, CHECK YOUR WORK ON THIS SECTION ONLY. DO NOT WORK ON ANY OTHER SECTION IN THE TEST.

TEST 2: MATHEMATICS

Time: 60 Minutes
60 Problems

DIRECTIONS

In the Mathematics Test, each of the problems includes five choices (A, B, C, D, E or F, G, H, J, K). You are to solve each problem and choose the correct answer.

1. The product of x and y is a constant. If the value of x is increased by 50%, by what percentage must the value of y be decreased?
   (A) 25%
   (B) $33\frac{1}{3}$%
   (C) 40%
   (D) 50%
   (E) $66\frac{2}{3}$%

2. One hundred students will attend a dance if tickets cost 30 cents each. For each 5 cent raise in the price of the tickets, 10 fewer students will attend. What price will deliver the maximum dollar sales?
   (F) 30   (B) 35   (H) 40   (J) 45   (K) 50

3. What is the area of a rectangle if its length is 36 and its diagonal is 39?
   (A) 1404   (B) 702   (C) 540   (D) 108   (E) 75

4. Bryan needs 5 shelves for books. The longest shelf is to be the bottom shelf, and each one above is to be 4 inches shorter than the one immediately below. If the sum of the lengths of the shelves is 155 inches, what is the length of the longest shelf?
   (F) 23 inches
   (G) 28 inches
   (H) 31 inches
   (J) 36 inches
   (K) 39 inches

5. If $3x + 2y = 14$ and $3x = 2y$, what is the value of $x + y$?
   (A) 6   (B) $5\frac{5}{6}$ (C) $5\frac{1}{6}$ (D) $4\frac{5}{6}$ (E) $3\frac{1}{2}$

6. A square and a circle have the same area. What is the circumference of the circle if the perimeter of the square is $8\sqrt{\pi}$?
   (F) 4   (G) 4π (H) $\sqrt{2}\pi$ (J) 8π (K) $8\sqrt{\pi}$

7. What is the GCF of 24, 48, 60, and 78?
   (A) 2   (B) 6   (C) 12   (D) 18   (E) 78

8. During one season, a tennis team won 21 matches and lost 30% of their matches. What was the number of matches that the team lost?
   (F) 70   (G) 30   (H) 9   (J) 7   (K) 5

9. In a package of candies, 8 candies are green, 2 are red, and 6 are white. If the first candy chosen is not a white one, what is the probability that the next one randomly chosen will be white?
   (A) $\frac{5}{16}$ (B) $\frac{3}{8}$ (C) $\frac{2}{5}$ (D) $\frac{3}{5}$ (E) $\frac{2}{3}$

10. If the angles of a triangle are: $3x, x + 10$, and $2x - 40$, what is the measure of the smallest angle?
    (F) 30   (G) 35   (H) 40   (J) 45   (K) 50

11. $(x + 3)(2x + 4) =$
    (A) $2x^2 + 10x + 12$ (D) $x^2 + 3x + 6$
    (B) $x^2 + 5x + 6$ (E) $2x^2 + 2x + 12$
    (C) $2x^2 + 6x + 12$

12. What is the value of angle w?

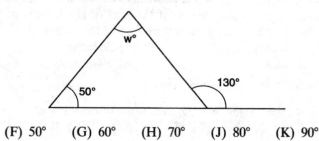

    (F) 50°   (G) 60°   (H) 70°   (J) 80°   (K) 90°

13. If A is greater than B, C is less than A, and B is greater than C, then which of the following is true?

(A) A < B < C

(D) C < A < B

(B) B < A < C

(E) C < B < A

(C) B < C < A

14. Which of the following is (are) always true about the figure?

I. ∠1 + ∠2 = ∠3
II. ∠3 > ∠2
III. 180° > ∠2 + ∠3

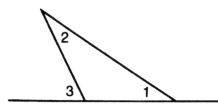

(F) I and II only

(J) I only

(G) II and II only

(K) II only

(H) I and III only

15. Simplify: $\dfrac{12x^6y^4z^2}{6x^2y^4z^8}$

(A) $\dfrac{2x^4}{z^6}$

(D) $\dfrac{2x^3}{z^4}$

(B) $2x^8y^8z^{10}$

(E) $\dfrac{2x^6}{z^4}$

(C) $6x^4z^{-6}$

16. Logan has a basketball court that is 30 feet by 50 feet in size. He needs a grass strip around it. How wide must the strip be to provide 900 square feet of grass?

(F) 3 feet

(J) 6 feet

(G) 4 feet

(K) 7 feet

(H) 5 feet

17. Two hikers leave the same point and travel at right angles to each other. At the end of 2 hours, they are 10 miles apart. If one walks 1 mile per hour faster than the other, what is the speed of the slower hiker?

    (A) 2 mph   (D) 5 mph
    (B) 3 mph   (E) 6 mph
    (C) 4 mph

18. If the three sides of a right triangle measure 3 cm, 4 cm, and 5 cm, what is the sine of the angle opposite the side with a length of 4 cm?

    (F) $\frac{3}{5}$ (J) $\frac{5}{4}$
    (G) $\frac{3}{4}$ (K) $\frac{5}{3}$
    (H) $\frac{4}{5}$

19. Which equation below has roots that are each 4 less than the roots of: $3x^2 + 2x - 4 = 0$?

    (A) $3x^2 + 14x - 12 = 0$ (D) $6x^2 + 16x + 9 = 0$
    (B) $3x^2 + 26x + 52 = 0$ (E) $3x^2 - 15x - 18 = 0$
    (C) $6x^2 + 3x - 28 = 0$

20. Which of the following could not be a solution to: $4 - 3x < -3$?

    (F) 4   (G) 3.5   (H) 3   (J) 2.5   (K) 2

21. What is the area in square units of the quadrilateral pictured below?

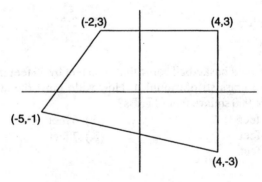

    (A) 24   (B) 27   (C) 39   (D) 46   (E) 54

22. A tank 4 inches high is to be made from a square piece of sheet metal by cutting a square out of each corner and folding up the sides. The volume of the tank is to be 900 cubic inches. What is the width of the piece of sheet metal? ($V = lwh$)
    (F) 12   (G) 15   (H) 19   (J) 21   (K) 23

23. Macey is three times as old as Mike. In 8 years, she will be twice as old as Mike. How old was Macey 3 years ago?
    (A) 5   (B) 8   (C) 21   (D) 24   (E) 27

24. What is the area of an equilateral triangle if its perimeter is 30?
    (F) 50   (J) $25\sqrt{3}$
    (G) $50\sqrt{3}$ (K) $10\sqrt{3}$
    (H) 25

25. Ellen can mow a lawn in 2 hours. Dave can mow the same lawn in $1\frac{1}{2}$ hours. About how long will it take to mow the lawn if Ellen and Dave worked together?
    (A) 210 minutes   (D) 48 minutes
    (B) 90 minutes   (E) 30 minutes
    (C) 51 minutes

26. What is the value of: $\dfrac{(x^{2y+2})(x^{6y-1})}{x^{4y-3}}$

    (F) x^{3y+4} (G) x^{4y+4} (H) x^{3y-2} (J) x^{4y-2} (K) x^{4y+1}

27. The pie graph below represents the relative sizes of a family's per-dollar budget. What is the degree measure of the central angle of the sectors labeled "Food" and "Housing"?

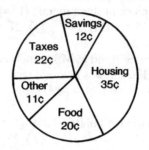

(A) 180°   (B) 188°   (C) 195°   (D) 198°   (E) 208°

28. In the figure below $AB = BC$, $CD = BD$, and angle $CAD = 70°$. Therefore, what is the measure of angle ADC?

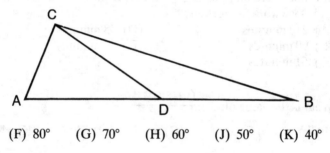

(F) 80°   (G) 70°   (H) 60°   (J) 50°   (K) 40°

29. What is the slope of a line that passes through the points $(-2, 3)$ and $(3, -2)$?
(A) −2   (B) −1   (C) 0   (D) 1   (E) 2

30. Three angles of a pentagon are 130°, 90°, and 80°. Of the remaining two angles, one is 30° more than twice the other. What is the sum of the smallest two angles?
(F) 140°   (G) 150°   (H) 160°   (J) 170°   (K) 180°

31. How much 20% solution must be added to a 60% solution to give 40 liters of a 50% solution?
    (A) 32 liters   (D) 10 liters
    (B) 30 liters   (E) 8 liters
    (C) 20 liters

32. How many times does the equation $y = x^4 - x^5$ intersect the x-axis? $y = x^4 - x^5$?
    (F) 1   (G) 2   (H) 3   (J) 4   (K) 5

33. Bryan is standing 2000 feet from objects A and C. The observed angle between the objects is 48 degrees. How far apart are objects A and C?
    (A) $4000 \sin 24°$ (D) $2000 \sin 24°$
    (B) $2000 \sin 48°$ (E) $2000 \cos 48°$
    (C) $4000 \sin 48°$

34. The current in a river is 4 mph. A boat can travel 20 mph in still water. How far up the river can the boat travel if the round trip is to take 10 hours?
    (F) 88 miles   (J) 112 miles
    (G) 96 miles   (K) 124 miles
    (H) 100 miles

35. A man walks from B to C, a distance of x miles, at 8 miles per hour and returns at 12 miles per hour. What is his average speed?
    (A) 10.2 mph   (D) 9.6 mph
    (B) 10 mph   (E) 9 mph
    (C) 9.8 mph

36. $\dfrac{x}{x-y} - \dfrac{y}{y-x} =$
    (F) $(x + y)/(x - y)$ (J) 0
    (G) 1   (K) $x - y$
    (H) $(x - y)/(x + y)$

37. Given rectangle $ABCD$ with diagonal AC, if $AB = 12$ and $BC = 9$, what is the ratio of the perimeter of rectangle $ABCD$ to the perimeter of triangle ACD?
    (A) 2:1   (B) 6:7   (C) 1:2   (D) 7:5   (E) 7:6

38. What is the sum of $4x^3 - 2x^2$, $-3x^3 + 3x^2$, and $-2x^3 - 4x^2$?
    (F) $-x^3 - 3x^2$ (J) $-3x^3 + 5x^2$
    (G) $x^3 + 3x^2$ (K) $4x^5$
    (H) $3x^3 - 5x^2$

39. If $f(x) = x^2 - 2$ and $g(x) = 2x + 2$, then $f\{g[f(\tfrac{1}{2})]\} =$
    (A) $\tfrac{1}{4}$ (B) $\tfrac{1}{2}$ (C) 1   (D) 2   (E) 4

40. What is the equation of the line that passes through the point $(1, 1)$ and is perpendicular to the line with equation $y = -\tfrac{1}{2}x + 3$?
    (F) $y = -\tfrac{1}{2}x - 2$ (J) $y = 2x - 1$
    (G) $y = -\tfrac{1}{2}x + \tfrac{3}{2}$ (K) None of these
    (H) $y = 2x + 6$

41. What is the area of the triangle in the figure below?

    (A) $8 \sin 35° \cos 35°$ (D) $4 \sin 35° + 4 \cos 35°$
    (B) $8 \tan 35°$ (E) $8 (\tan^2 35° + 1)$
    (C) $8/\tan 35°$

42. What is the equation of a line with slope $\tfrac{1}{2}$ that passes through the point $(1, 2)$?
    (F) $x - 2y + 3 = 0$ (J) $2x + y - 4 = 0$
    (G) $2x - y = 0$ (K) $4x - y - 2 = 0$
    (H) $x + 2y - 5 = 0$

43. The length of a rectangle is 6 cm greater than its width. The area of the rectangle is 18. What is the width of the rectangle?
   (A) $3(\sqrt{3} - 1)$
   (B) $3(\sqrt{3} + 1)$
   (C) $3(1 - \sqrt{3})$
   (D) $3\sqrt{3} - 1$
   (E) $3\sqrt{3} + 1$

44. Given circle O, what is the measure of angle x?

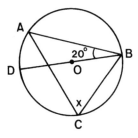

   (F) 40°
   (G) 55°
   (H) 70°
   (J) 80°
   (K) Cannot be determined

45. Dave biked 20 miles. If he had increased his average speed by 4 mph, the trip would have taken 1 hour less. What is his average speed?
   (A) $2\sqrt{21} + 2$
   (B) $2\sqrt{21} - 2$
   (C) $2\sqrt{21} - 1$
   (D) $2\sqrt{21} + 1$
   (E) $\sqrt{21} - 2$

46. The sum of two numbers is 25. The sum of their squares is 313. What is the value of the larger number?
   (F) 10   (G) 11   (H) 12   (J) 13   (K) 14

47. If a line passes through the points $(6, 4)$ and $(-2, -4)$, what is its y-intercept?
   (A) 1   (B) 0   (C) −1   (D) −2   (E) −3

48. In triangle *ABC* below, *BC* = 12, *AC* = 9, and angle *ACB* = 90°. What is the length of the height from *C* to line *AB*?

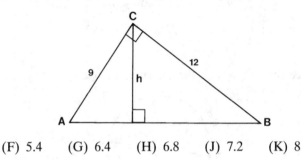

(F) 5.4   (G) 6.4   (H) 6.8   (J) 7.2   (K) 8

49. Machine A can do a job alone in 10 hours. Machine B can do the same job alone in 12 hours. Machine A is turned on at 6 a.m. Machine B is turned on at 9 a.m. Machine A breaks down at 10 a.m., and Machine B must finish the job alone. When will Machine B finish?
(A) 2:30   (D) 4:40
(B) 3:42   (E) Cannot be determined
(C) 4:12

50. The total resistance, *R*, of two resistors, *A* and *B*, connected in parallel is given by the following formula:

$$\frac{1}{R} = \frac{1}{A} + \frac{1}{B}$$

If *A* = 10 and *R* = 4, what is the value of *B*?
(F) $7\frac{1}{4}$ (G) 7   (H) $6\frac{3}{4}$ (J) $6\frac{2}{3}$ (K) 6

51. Two concentric circles have radii of 7 and 13. What is the length of a chord of the larger circle that is tangent to the smaller circle?
(A) $4\sqrt{30}$ (D) $2\sqrt{162}$
(B) $2\sqrt{30}$ (E) 22
(C) $\sqrt{30}/2$

52. In an isosceles triangle, one angle equals 120°. If one of the legs is 6 inches long, what is the length of the longest side?
    (F) $3\sqrt{3}$ (J) $3\sqrt{2}$
    (G) $6\sqrt{2}$ (K) $6\sqrt{3}$
    (H) $3\sqrt{6}$

53. Simplify: $\dfrac{2\sqrt{3} - 4}{\sqrt{3} + 2}$
    (A) $4\sqrt{3} + 7$ (D) $2(7 - 4\sqrt{3})$
    (B) $2(4\sqrt{3} - 7)$ (E) $2(4\sqrt{3} + 7)$
    (C) $2\sqrt{3} - 7$

54. Simplify: $\dfrac{78x^5y^7}{6x^2y^3}$
    (F) $\frac{1}{3}x^2y^2\sqrt{39x}$ (J) $\frac{1}{3}xy^2\sqrt{117x}$
    (G) $x^2y\sqrt{13x}$ (K) $\frac{1}{3}xy^2\sqrt{13x}$
    (H) $xy^2\sqrt{13x}$

55. $\dfrac{|8 - 3|\,|3 - 8|}{|-3 -8|\,|-8 + 3|}$
    (A) -1 (D) $5/11$
    (B) $-5/11$ (E) 1
    (C) $25/121$

56. If $x - 10 = \dfrac{-9}{x}$, what is the difference between the two roots?

    (F) 1   (G) 3   (H) 6   (J) 8   (K) 9

57. How many degrees are there in each interior angle of a regular decagon (10-sided figure)?
    (A) 15   (B) 18   (C) 120   (D) 144   (E) 172

58. If $4x^2 + 2x + A = 0$, which value of A will result in a solution for x of 2 and $-\frac{5}{2}$?
    (F) -20 (G) -10 (H) 6   (J) 12   (K) 16

59. What is the length of the diagonal of a square if the area of the square is 12 sq ft?

(A) $12\sqrt{2}$ (D) $(6\sqrt{3})/2$

(B) 6   (E) $2\sqrt{3}$

(C) $2\sqrt{6}$

60. Simplify: $\dfrac{x^2 - 7xy + 12y^2}{x^2 - 4xy + 3y^2}$

(F) $(x - 3y)/(x - y)$ (J) $3xy - 4$

(G) $(x - 6y)/(x - y)$ (K) 12

(H) $(x - 4y)/(x - y)$

STOP. IF YOU FINISH BEFORE TIME IS CALLED, CHECK YOUR WORK ON THIS SECTION ONLY. DO NOT WORK ON ANY OTHER SECTION IN THE TEST.

TEST 3: READING

Time: 35 Minutes
40 Questions

DIRECTIONS

Each of the four passages in this test is followed by questions. Read the passage and choose the best answer to each question. Return to the passage as often as necessary to answer the questions.

Passage I

Medieval thought differed radically from modern thought: whereas medieval scientists did not doubt that certain precepts of the Church or the existence of God constituted true knowledge, science today accepts as knowledge only that which can be verified scientifically. In the early Middle Ages, mystical revelation was quite common. Partly because of the relative isolation of places of learning and the loss of many classics, logical arguments were not accepted, especially in theology— the "queen of the sciences."

When many ancient classics were reintroduced into Europe (by means of translation into Latin of Arabic versions of the Greek) from Moslem Spain, new patterns of thought began to emerge: these were considerably expanded by the Crusades. When Aristotle (and the commentaries upon him by Averroës) was translated into Latin, revealed truth was no longer the accepted authority. The Bible, works of the Church fathers, and Church decrees were not rejected, but it was felt that they should be reconciled with logic and philosophy. The Scholastics were the group of clerics who undertook the task of applying logic and philosophy to theology. In his work *Sic et Non (Yes and No),* Peter Abelard of Paris stated the conflicting arguments of the various authorities in order to show their weaknesses. As a consequence, his colleagues considered him a heretic.

Not until the thirteenth century did the Latin translations of Aristotle and Averroës make their full impact. Two of the most important Scholastics of this period were Saint Albertus

Magnus and Saint Thomas Aquinas. Albertus Magnus tried to reconcile the thought of Aristotle with medieval ideals. His most famous pupil was Saint Thomas Aquinas. In his major work, the *Summa Theologica,* Thomas Aquinas held that the supreme force in the universe was God. Both God and His creations could be explained by logic. Thomas Aquinas did not reject faith or revelation; however, he said that certain things beyond the grasp of man (such as the creation of the universe and the Trinity) should be taken on faith.

By the fourteenth century, mysticism had become widespread and there was a loss of faith in logic; another system of thought, Nominalism, replaced the theories of Saint Thomas. Among the forerunners of Nominalism was Duns Scotus. Nominalists said that divine matters could be explained only by mystical faith whereas tangible objects were capable of being studied logically. This reversion to mysticism accompanied the desire to look at objects thoroughly, and this desire eventually led to the scientific approach.

1. Which of the following titles best describes the content of the passage?
   (A) The Development of Scientific Thought in the Middle Ages
   (B) Medieval vs. Modern: The Philosophy of the Middle Ages vs. Modern Thought
   (C) From Aristotle to Nominalism in the Early Middle Ages
   (D) Major Christian Thought in the Middle Ages

2. All of the following statements about Europe in the Middle Ages are true EXCEPT
   (F) in the early Middle Ages, many classical texts had not been rediscovered
   (G) many Greek works were introduced in translation
   (H) Saint Thomas Aquinas and Saint Albertus Magnus were contemporaries
   (J) at the close of the Middle Ages, mystical revelations were no longer credited

3. The language most widely used by thinkers of the European Middle Ages was probably
   - (A) Greek
   - (B) Latin
   - (C) Arabic
   - (D) Hebrew

4. According to the account in the third paragraph, Saint Thomas Aquinas would agree with all of the following EXCEPT
   - (F) logic cannot explain all things
   - (G) good works are more important than faith
   - (H) the existence of God can be proven logically
   - (J) a mystery like the Trinity must be taken on faith

5. All of the medieval writers discussed in the second and third paragraphs of the passage were
   - (A) scholars of Greek and Latin
   - (B) Crusaders
   - (C) priests
   - (D) French

6. The term *Scholasticism* is best defined as
   - (F) a system of belief that recognizes God as the Supreme Being and the Bible as divinely inspired
   - (G) Christian and medieval values
   - (H) a system of medieval schoolmen based on Aristotelian logic and early Christian writings
   - (J) the philosophical system of Albertus Magnus, Thomas Aquinas, and Duns Scotus

7. The Nominalists may be said to have contributed to the ultimate development of the scientific method because they
   - (A) accepted Christian mysticism
   - (B) revered Aristotle and Aristotelian logic
   - (C) encouraged careful study of physical objects
   - (D) avoided the attempt to explain supernatural events by natural laws

8. From the early Middle Ages to the fourteenth century, the attitude of churchmen toward logic
   (F) changed very little
   (G) went from ignorance and indifference to favor
   (H) went from increasing favor to disfavor
   (J) went from extreme disfavor to extreme favor

9. Compared to the earlier thinkers of the Middle Ages, the Nominalists had less respect for
   (A) mysticism   (C) logic
   (B) the Church fathers   (D) Church decrees

10. Which of the following best describes the attitude of the author of this passage toward the philosophers mentioned?
    (F) The most favored is Saint Thomas Aquinas.
    (G) The most disapproved of is Peter Abelard of Paris.
    (H) The most favored is Duns Scotus.
    (J) The author's personal views are not stated or implied.

Passage II

Early in the day Dorothea had returned from the school which she had set going in the village, and was taking her usual place in the sitting-room which divided the bedrooms of the sisters, bent on finishing a plan for some buildings (a kind of work which she delighted in), when Celia, who had been watching her with a hesitating desire to propose something, said—

"Dorothea dear, if you don't mind—if you are not very busy—suppose we looked at mamma's jewels to-day, and divided them? It is exactly six months to-day since uncle gave them to you, and you have not looked at them yet."

Celia's face had the shadow of a pouting expression in it, the full presence of the pout being kept back by an habitual awe of her sister.

"Well, dear, we should never wear them, you know." Dorothea spoke in a full cordial tone, half caressing, half explanatory. She had her pencil in her hand, and was making tiny side-plans on a margin.

Celia coloured, and looked very grave. "I think, dear, we are wanting in respect to mamma's memory, to put them by and take no notice of them. And," she added, after hesitating a little, "necklaces are quite usual now; and women who are stricter in some things even than you are wear ornaments. And Christians generally—surely there are women in heaven now who wore jewels." Celia was conscious of some mental strength when she really applied herself to argument.

"You would like to wear them?" exclaimed Dorothea, an air of astonished discovery animating her whole person. "Of course, then, let us have them out. Why did you not tell me before?"

The casket was soon open before them, and the various jewels spread out, making a bright parterre on the table. It was no great collection, but a few of the ornaments were really of remarkable beauty, the finest that was obvious at first being a necklace of purple amethysts set in exquisite gold work, and a pearl cross with five brilliants in it. Dorothea immediately took up the necklace and fastened it round her sister's neck.

"There, Celia! you can wear that with your Indian muslin. But this cross you must wear with your dark dresses."

Celia was trying not to smile with pleasure. "O Dodo, you must keep the cross yourself."

"No, no, dear, no," said Dorothea, putting up her hand with careless deprecation.

"Yes, indeed you must; it would suit you—in your black dress, now," said Celia, insistingly. "You *might* wear that."

"Not for the world, not for the world. A cross is the last thing I would wear as a trinket." Dorothea shuddered slightly.

"Then you will think it wicked in me to wear it," said Celia, uneasily.

"No, dear, no," said Dorothea, stroking her sister's cheek. "Souls have complexions too: what will suit one will not suit another." She was opening some ring boxes, which disclosed a fine emerald, and just then the sun passing beyond a cloud sent a bright gleam over the table.

"How very beautiful these gems are!" said Dorothea, under a new current of feeling, as sudden as the gleam. "It is strange how deeply colours seem to penetrate one, like scent. I suppose that this is the reason why gems are used as spiritual emblems in the Revelation of St. John. They look like fragments of heaven. I think that emerald is as beautiful as any of them."

"We did not notice this at first," said Celia.

"It's lovely," said Dorothea, slipping the ring on her finely-turned finger and holding it towards the window on a level with her eyes. All the while her thought was trying to justify her delight in the colours by merging them in her mystic religious joy.

11. From the passage we can infer that Celia and Dorothea are sisters
   (A) whose mother has very recently died
   (B) whose father has very recently died
   (C) who are poor and orphaned
   (D) whose mother is no longer living and whose father probably is no longer living

12. Which of the following is likely to be the most important reason for Dorothea's decision to examine the jewels?
   (F) her unwillingness to show respect to her mother's memory
   (G) her unrecognized personal vanity
   (H) her realization that Celia would like to wear them
   (J) her deeply seated Christian principles

13. Dorothea gives what at first appear to be the most beautiful and most valuable of the jewels to Celia because she
   (A) knows there are others that are even more valuable
   (B) does not understand that the jewels are valuable
   (C) wishes to remove temptations from herself
   (D) genuinely believes she herself will not wear the jewelry

14. Celia offers the jeweled cross to Dorothea because she
   (F) does not want it herself
   (G) believes it is jewelry that Dorothea might wear
   (H) does not share Dorothea's religious views
   (J) is sure that Dorothea will refuse it

15. The passage suggests that Dorothea's "strictness" is chiefly based upon her
    (A) religious principles
    (B) hypocritical wish to be well thought of
    (C) hope to marry a rich husband
    (D) insensitivity to physical beauty

16. From the presentation of Dorothea in the passage, which of the following can we suppose she would be most interested in today?
    (F) Red Cross work   (H) yachting
    (G) jewelry design   (J) conservative politics

17. Compared to Dorothea, Celia appears to be more
    (A) intellectual   (C) worldly
    (B) articulate   (D) quixotic

18. Dorothea attempts to justify her response to the beauty of the jewels by
    (F) pretending she is not interested in them
    (G) arguing that jewels are a gift of God
    (H) regarding them as religious symbols
    (J) hypocritically claiming to have religious feelings

19. Unlike the rest of the passage, the third from the last paragraph ("How very beautiful . . .") has several examples of
    (A) rhetorical question   (C) irony
    (B) simile   (D) dialogue

20. The author's attitude to Dorothea could best be described as one of
    (F) cool disinterestedness
    (G) affectionate amusement
    (H) grudging tolerance
    (J) enthusiastic approval

Passage III

Some of the developments which contributed to the growth of industrial America were a positive disadvantage to labor. Two of these we can note briefly: the mechanization of industry and the rise of the corporation. Mechanization tended, on the whole, to lower the standards of labor. The skills which workingmen had painfully acquired ceased to have their old-time value. The creative instinct of craftsmanship was largely destroyed, and workingmen were reduced to a mere part of a mechanical process.

Machinery had a tendency, too, to usurp the place of the worker in the economy of industry. It represented an enormous capital investment. The fact that furnaces had to be kept going continuously was decisive in maintaining the twelve-hour day. Machinery was in part responsible, finally, for a great deal of unemployment. It is probably true that in the end machines made more jobs than they eliminated, but it was not always the same people who got the new jobs.

Several other factors, unique to the United States, conditioned the welfare of labor. The first of these was the passing of good cheap land a generation or so after the Civil War. It would be an exaggeration to say that the West had served as a "safety valve" for labor discontent or as a refuge for very many workingmen. But it is clear that for two or three generations the open land did drain off the surplus population of the countryside, the villages, and even the cities, and the immigrants from abroad. With the rise in the cost of farming and the disappearance of good cheap land, surplus population did stay in the industrial areas. Farming was no longer a practical alternative to the factory. Labor could no longer escape the problems of an industrialized society but was forced to stand and face them.

A second factor, peculiar to the United States among industrial nations, was continuous and unrestricted immigration. In the forty years from 1870 to 1910 more than twenty million people poured into the country. This meant that every year several hundred thousand recruits joined the ranks of labor at almost any wages and under almost any conditions.

Nor was this the only competition that confronted northern labor. From the South, after the turn of the century, came tens of thousands of willing blacks ready to take their places beside the Poles, Italians, and Hungarians. For many years, the general tendency of this mass movement was to drive down wages, depress standards, and disintegrate labor unions.

A third factor—again one unique to the United States—was the existence, side by side, of a national economy and a federal political system. The problems of labor were much the same the nation over, but the power to deal with them was lodged, until very recent years, in the states alone. Competition was nationwide, but the right to regulate wages and hours was only statewide.

21. The focus of this passage is upon the
    (A) growth of labor unions in the United States
    (B) problems of labor in the United States
    (C) expansion of labor in the United States
    (D) local and federal controls of labor in the United States

22. According to the passage, one reason for the very long working day in the late nineteenth century was the
    (F) low hourly wages of the workers
    (G) greed of the corporate owners
    (H) need to keep furnaces burning continuously
    (J) state laws controlling working hours

23. Paradoxically, the development and increased use of specialized machines was
    (A) an advantage to the growth of American industry and a disadvantage to labor
    (B) an advantage to the northeast and a disadvantage to the South.
    (C) an advantage to the American worker and a disadvantage to the European
    (D) an advantage to the European immigrant and a disadvantage to the native American worker

24. The end of free lands in the West had an influence on labor in eastern cities because
   - (F) the pool of available workers became larger
   - (G) the pool of available workers became smaller
   - (H) farm labor required less training than industrial labor
   - (J) the western farmers were the potential market for food manufactured in the East

25. From information in the passage, we can infer that a sharp decline in the number of immigrants would be likely to
   - (A) bring about an increase in the wages of labor
   - (B) have little or no effect on the economy
   - (C) drive up sharply the number of unemployed workers
   - (D) have a larger influence upon coastal than on inland states

26. Like the United States, industrialized countries in Europe in the late nineteenth century would have to deal with the effects of

   - I. a large immigrant population
   - II. an increasingly mechanized industry
   - III. the recent unavailability of large areas of farmland

(F) I only	(H) I and III only
(G) II only	(J) II and III only

27. According to the passage, all of the following contributed to the growth of unemployment EXCEPT
   - (A) the development of more sophisticated machines
   - (B) the rise in the cost of farming
   - (C) the rise in the number of immigrants
   - (D) a right-to-work law

28. From information in the passage, we can infer that which of the following did NOT exist in the period from 1870 to 1910?
   - (F) a child-labor law
   - (G) a federal minimum wage
   - (H) a law limiting the powers of unions to organize
   - (J) a right-to-work law

29. According to the passage, the political system in the United States
   (A) encouraged the arrival of foreign workers
   (B) encouraged black workers to leave the South
   (C) made it difficult to deal with problems of labor
   (D) vested too much power in the states and not enough in the federal government

30. Which of the following best describes the order of topics and organization of the passage?
   (F) 1. the effects of mechanization
       2. the effects of the size of the labor force
       3. the effects of the political system
   (G) 1. the corporation
       2. the working force
       3. the national economy
   (H) 1. the effects of industrialization
       2. the effects of immigration
       3. the effects of competition
   (J) 1. mechanization
       2. farming
       3. political factors

Passage IV

One of the most interesting recent applications of radioactivity is the determination of the age of carbonaceous materials by measurement of their carbon-14 radioactivity. This technique of radiocarbon dating, which was developed by an American physical chemist, Willard F. Libby, permits the dating of samples containing carbon with an accuracy of around 200 years. At the present time the method can be applied to materials that are not over about 50,000 years old.

Carbon 14 is being made at a steady rate in the upper atmosphere. Cosmic-ray neutrons transmute nitrogen into carbon 14, which is radioactive. The radiocarbon is oxidized to carbon dioxide, which is thoroughly mixed with the nonradioactive carbon dioxide in the atmosphere, through the action of winds. The steady-state concentration of carbon 14 built up in the atmosphere by cosmic rays is about one atom of radioactive carbon to 10^{12} atoms of ordinary carbon. The carbon dioxide, radioactive and nonradioactive alike, is absorbed by plants, which fix the carbon in their tissues. Animals that eat the plants also similarly fix the carbon, containing a trace of radiocarbon, in their tissues. When a plant or animal dies, the amount of radioactivity of the carbon in its tissues is determined by the amount of radiocarbon present, which corresponds to the concentration in the atmosphere. After 5760 years (the half-life of carbon 14), however, half of the carbon 14 has undergone decomposition, and the radioactivity of the material is only half as great. After 11,520 years (or two half-lives) only one-quarter of the original radioactivity is left, and so on. Accordingly, by determining the radioactivity of a sample of carbon from wood, flesh, charcoal, skin, horn, or other plant or animal remains, the number of years that have gone by since the carbon was originally extracted from the atmosphere can be determined.

In applying the method of radiocarbon dating, a sample of material containing about 30 grams of carbon is burned to carbon dioxide, which is then reduced to elementary carbon in the form of lamp black. The beta-ray activity of the elementary carbon is then determined, with the use of Geiger counters, and compared with the beta-ray activity of recent carbon. The age of the sample may then be calculated. The method was checked by measurement of carbon from the heartwood of a giant Sequoia tree, for which the number of tree rings showed that 2928 years had passed since the heartwood was laid down. This check was satisfactory, as were also similar checks with other carbonaceous materials, such as wood in First Dynasty Egyptian tombs 4900 years old, whose dating was considered to be reliable.

31. Carbon dating may be described as

    I. a useful application of radioactivity
   II. an important technique for historians and anthropologists
  III. a technique that can be used to determine the age of plant or human remains

(A) I only
(B) II and III only
(C) I and III only
(D) I, II, and III

32. One limitation of radiocarbon dating is that it
(F) cannot be used on objects that do not contain carbon
(G) is not dependably accurate
(H) cannot be used on materials that are less than 2000 years old
(J) cannot be used on materials that are more than 30,000 years old

33. Which of the following is the best title for the passage?
(A) Carbon Dating—Its Strengths and Its Liabilities
(B) Carbon Dating—How It Works
(C) The Use of Carbon to Date Radioactive Materials
(D) Science and History

34. According to the passage, carbon dioxide

    I. is both radioactive and nonradioactive
  II. can be made from carbon 14
  III. is twelve million times more common in its nonradioactive form than in radioactive form

(F) II only
(G) I and II only
(H) I and III only
(J) I, II, and III

35. We can infer that a carnivore's bones can be dated by using carbon dating because the carnivore would have

    I. eaten plants
    II. eaten animals which had eaten plants
    III. fixed carbon in its system from breathing air

    (A) I and II only   (C) II and III only
    (B) II only   (D) I, II, and III

36. Carbon 14 is found in the tissue of plants because
    (F) of the action of cosmic-ray neutrons on plants
    (G) of photosynthesis
    (H) the plants have absorbed carbon dioxide
    (J) the carbon in the air has been caused by fires

37. From the figures given in the second paragraph of the passage, we can infer that one-eighth of the original radioactivity of carbon 14 would be left after
    (A) 5760 years   (C) 17,280 years
    (B) 11,520 years   (D) 23,040 years

38. The reliability of carbon dating has been tested by comparisons with

    I. wood from an Egyptian tomb
    II. wood dated by annual rings
    III. Geiger counters and beta-ray activity of recent carbon

    (F) I only   (H) II and III only
    (G) I and II only   (J) I, II, and III

39. Carbon dating depends upon the measurement of
    (A) beta-ray activity
    (B) cosmic-ray neutrons
    (C) steady-state concentration
    (D) carbon dioxide

40. Carbon dating could be used on all of the following ancient objects EXCEPT
    (F) a seal-bone harpoon
    (G) a linen burial garment
    (H) a turquoise ornament
    (J) an ear of corn

STOP. IF YOU FINISH BEFORE TIME IS CALLED, CHECK YOUR WORK ON THIS SECTION ONLY. DO NOT WORK ON ANY OTHER SECTION IN THE TEST.

TEST 4: SCIENCE REASONING

Time: 35 Minutes
40 Questions

DIRECTIONS

Each passage in this test is followed by several questions. After you read each passage, select the correct choice for each of the questions that follow the passage. Refer back to the passage as often as necessary to answer the questions.

Passage I

The following chart displays the results of a series of experiments which measured the viscosities of liquids at several temperatures. Viscosity is a property directly proportional to the resistance to flow. For example, molasses is more viscous than coffee.

Liquid	Molecular Weight	Viscosity (millipoises)		
		0°C	20°C	40°C
Water	16	17.92	10.05	6.56
Ethanol	46	17.73	12.01	8.34
Pentane	72	3.11	2.43	2.03
Benzene	78	9.12	6.52	5.03
Sulfuric acid	98	13.29	10.04	8.19
Heptane	100	5.24	4.09	3.41
Octane	114	7.06	5.42	4.33
Mercury	201	16.84	15.47	14.83

1. Which liquid has the highest viscosity at normal room temperature?
   (A) ethanol
   (B) mercury
   (C) sulfuric acid
   (D) water

110

2. Which of the following rules correctly states the variation of viscosity shown in the table?
   (F) higher viscosity with higher molecular weight
   (G) lower viscosity with higher temperature
   (H) lower viscosity with lower molecular weight
   (J) higher viscosity with higher temperature

3. Pentane, heptane, and octane are similar hydrocarbons with a linear molecular structure and 5, 7, or 8 carbon atoms, respectively. What is the likely viscosity at 40°C for another such hydrocarbon, hexane?
   (A) 2.72 millipoises   (C) 4.18 millipoises
   (B) 3.87 millipoises   (D) 5.25 millipoises

4. An experimenter is attempting to measure the rate at which steel ball bearings sink through water. However, at 0°C the water quickly freezes, preventing any experiment. What liquid should be substituted for the water?
   (F) benzene   (H) mercury
   (G) ethanol   (J) sulfuric acid

5. Which of the following methods could be used to measure the relative viscosity of liquids?
   (A) the amount of liquid passing through a small hole in the base of the beaker in 10 seconds
   (B) the diameter of the pool formed when 100 milliliters of liquid are carefully poured onto a table
   (C) the distance to which the liquid rises in the core of a very slender capillary tube
   (D) the intensity of light measured by a light meter when a beam shines through 5 centimeters of liquid

Passage II

To investigate the response of a primitive animal to light, a researcher selected the Great Burmese Beetle (GBB) as a subject. This large, docile insect lacks any capacity to bite or sting in self-defense. The GBB crawls rapidly enough to complete each experiment within one or two hours. It has two very prominent eyes which bulge to the sides of its head, so it was considered likely to be quite sensitive to illumination from different directions. Each of the following experiments maps the Great Burmese Beetle's movements as seen from above.

Experiment 1

The research began by studying the path of one GBB in a darkened room illuminated only by a dim red glow to permit tracking the beetle. It was found to crawl in a reasonably straight line.

Experiment 2

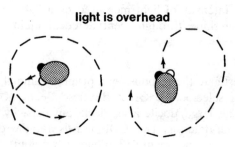

This experiment began in a darkened room. When the beetle had reached point P in the diagram, the researcher turned on one small white light on the floor to the left of the insect's path. The GBB slowly turned toward the light until it was directly facing the light, then continued straight ahead. In the map, the eyes of the GBB are shown as small open circles.

Experiment 3

The researcher then used a black enamel to paint over one eye on each of two beetles. In the diagram above, the black circles represent the painted eyes which cannot perceive light. These GBBs were placed on the floor with one bright light directly overhead. Both beetles crawled in endless circular patterns. The GBB with its right eye painted always turned to the left, while the GBB with its left eye painted invariably turned to the right. Several repetitions of this experiment yielded the same sense of turning for each GBB.

Experiment 4

Finally the two beetles with eyes covered by paint were studied in the darkened room with dim red illumination. Each GBB tended to move along a straight path.

6. At the moment when the light was turned on in Experiment 2, what was the relative illumination of the eyes of the GBB?
   (F) The left eye received more light than the right.
   (G) The right eye received more light than the left.
   (H) Both eyes were equally illuminated from floor level.
   (J) Both eyes were equally illuminated from overhead.

7. In Experiment 2, why wouldn't the GBB ever move in a circular pattern like that of Experiment 3?
   (A) The beetle had not yet been trained to crawl along a circular path.
   (B) Circular motion could occur only when the source of light is overhead.
   (C) It stops turning as soon as it is facing directly toward the light.
   (D) Neither eye of the beetle was painted to induce crawling in a circle.

8. Any change of direction of the GBB may be described as
   (F) turning away from the eye that receives the most light
   (G) turning toward the eye that receives the most light
   (H) turning away from the eye that is covered by paint
   (J) turning toward the eye that is covered by paint

9. In a lighted room, the GBB would crawl in a straight line only if
   (A) its two eyes were equally illuminated
   (B) the light bulb was in the center of the room
   (C) the light was frequently switched off
   (D) neither of its eyes were covered by paint

10. Why did the researcher need to perform Experiment 4?
    (F) to prove that dim red light cannot be perceived by the GBB
    (G) to prove that the behavior in Experiment 1 was not altered by paint
    (H) to prove that the turning in Experiment 3 was not due to the paint alone
    (J) to prove that the GBB does not learn during a series of experiments

11. In Experiment 3, how would a GBB with both eyes covered by paint behave?
    (A) It would stand still.
    (B) It would crawl in a straight line.
    (C) It would always turn in one direction.
    (D) It would turn irregularly in both directions.

Passage III

By altering the temperature or the pressure, most substances may be transformed from one state (solid, liquid, or gas) into another state. For the chemical element iodine, the following graph shows which state exists at each specific combination of temperature and pressure.

STATES OF IODINE

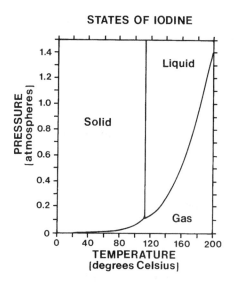

12. In which state does iodine exist at 100°C and a pressure of 0.5 atmosphere?
    (F) gas   (H) solid
    (G) liquid   (J) cannot be determined

13. What is the lowest pressure at which iodine may occur as a liquid?
    (A) 0.04 atm   (C) 0.45 atm
    (B) 0.12 atm   (D) 0.78 atm

14. At what temperature do iodine crystals melt?
    (F) 92°C   (H) 126°C
    (G) 114°C   (J) 182°C

15. The *boiling point* of any substance is defined as the temperature of the liquid/gas transition at a pressure of 1 atmosphere. What is the boiling point of iodine?
    (A) 168°C   (C) 184°C
    (B) 176°C   (D) 192°C

16. The direct transition from a solid to a gas, without an intermediate liquid state, is called *sublimation*. Which of the following statements describes the conditions under which iodine may sublime?

(F) The pressure must be less than 0.12 atm.

(G) The pressure must be more than 0.05 atm.

(H) The temperature must be less than 94°C.

(J) The temperature must be more than 110°C.

Passage IV

What was the cause of the Ice Age? Two differing viewpoints are presented below.

Scientist I

Variation in the amount of energy radiated by the sun would change the energy received by the earth. During this century, the sun's radiation has fluctuated by up to 3 percent. It is reasonable to assume a far greater variation over immensely long time spans, like the 3 million years of the Pleistocene Ice Age. If the sun's radiation were considerably higher several million years ago, the warmer atmosphere of the earth would have induced evaporation and greater humidity. The increased cloudiness must have increased the precipitation of both rain and snow. The cloud cover would also have inhibited any melting of snow during summer months. The abundant snow and its persistence throughout the year must have led to rapid expansion of the polar ice caps, yielding the great continental ice-sheets. Surprisingly, then, the Ice Age may have been initiated by the effects of a temporarily warmer sun.

Scientist 2

It has long seemed self-evident that only a cooler atmosphere could produce the great precipitation of snow needed to nourish continental glaciers. Although a warmer atmosphere might well be more humid due to evaporation from the oceans, it is not likely to precipitate as snow. The central issue seems to be whether the atmosphere was warmer or cooler at the inception of the Pleistocene glaciation. Species of mollusks which live today in cool waters at high latitudes have been found as Pleistocene fossils at numerous sites closer to the equator, indicating that Pleistocene seas were colder than the present. Seawater temperatures of both epochs may also be estimated from oxygen isotope ratios in shells of mollusks, brachiopods, and other marine creatures; these temperature determinations also show cooler oceans several million years ago. That is further supported by the distribution of temperature-sensitive ocean sediments, including limestone, chert, and red clay. All these data demonstrate that oceans were colder during the Ice Age.

17. According to the hypothesis of Scientist 1, the end of continental glaciation would be caused by
    (A) a decrease in the amount of evaporation
    (B) inadequate cloud cover during the summer
    (C) a lasting decrease in solar radiation
    (D) a warmer atmosphere melting the ice

18. The two scientists are in direct disagreement about
    (F) atmospheric humidity in the past and present
    (G) the minimum amount of variation in solar radiation
    (H) the reliability of oxygen isotope temperature determinations
    (J) temperature changes over the last 3 million years

19. The theory propounded by Scientist 1 was developed primarily to explain
    (A) the effects produced by variation in solar radiation
    (B) the increased precipitation needed for glacial expansion
    (C) the relation between humidity, precipitation, and glaciation
    (D) the temperature extremes experienced in the past

20. Although Scientist 2 opposes the theory of Scientist 1, the evidence presented by Scientist 2 is relevant to the dispute only if
    (F) cooler oceans imply a cooler atmosphere
    (G) oxygen isotope temperature determinations are accurate
    (H) several marine species have survived for millions of years
    (J) solar energy has not varied by more than 3 percent

21. Scientist 1 could best refute the temperatures calculated from oxygen isotope ratios by
    (A) pointing out that few such measurements have been made
    (B) reminding us that his theory calls for greater atmospheric humidity
    (C) showing that a factor besides temperature can affect the ratios
    (D) suggesting that chemical laws may have been different in the past

22. Coral reefs live only in water exceeding 20°C. According to Scientist 2, how should reefs have changed from the Ice Age to the present?
    (F) They have migrated toward the equator.
    (G) They have migrated toward the poles.
    (H) They have progressively decreased in size.
    (J) They have progressively increased in size.

23. The theory of Scientist 1 would be greatly strengthened by a study of data from the last 50 years showing that
    (A) more extensive cloud cover occurred during periods of high precipitation
    (B) more evaporation from the oceans occurred during periods of high air temperature
    (C) more glacial movement occurred during periods of warmer temperature
    (D) more precipitation occurred during periods of high solar radiation

Passage V

A common method of preparing a pure gas sample is to pass a mixture of two gases over a substance that reacts with one of the gases to yield a nonvolatile solid. The remaining vapor represents the gas that did not react with the substance.

GLASS TUBE WITH HEATED COPPER

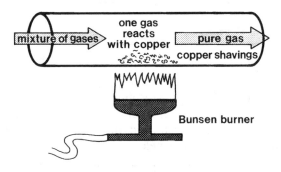

Experiment 1

Air is basically a mixture of 2 gases, oxygen and nitrogen. Many substances react with the former but not the latter, so a purified sample of nitrogen may be obtained by passing air over red-hot copper shavings to form copper oxide. The experiment was carried out and the density of the resulting nitrogen was found to be 1.256 grams per liter.

Experiment 2

A second sample of nitrogen was prepared by mixing dry air with ammonia gas and passing the mixture over heated copper.

$$4NH_3 + 3O_2 \longrightarrow 2N_2 + 6H_2O$$

ammonia   oxygen   nitrogen   water vapor

After removing the water vapor from the emerging gas, the sample should have been pure nitrogen, derived partly from the ammonia and partly from the initial air. The density of this nitrogen was measured and found to be very similar to that from the first experiment.

	Density of Nitrogen (grams/liter)
Experiment 1	1.256
Experiment 2	1.255

Experiment 3

A third sample of nitrogen was obtained without using any air by simply reacting ammonia with pure oxygen. The density of this nitrogen was also measured, and the results of the 3 density determinations are tabulated below.

	Density of Nitrogen (grams/liter)
Experiment 1	1.256
Experiment 2	1.255
Experiment 3	1.250

24. Considering the entire set of three experiments, from how many different sources was nitrogen derived?
    (F) 1   (G) 2   (H) 3   (J) 4

25. How should the differences in densities be reported?
    (A) Nitrogen obtained in early experiments is slightly denser than that in later experiments.
    (B) Nitrogen obtained in later experiments is slightly denser than that in earlier experiments.
    (C) Nitrogen obtained from air is slightly denser than that from ammonia.
    (D) Nitrogen obtained from ammonia is slightly denser than that from air.

26. Both of the first two experiments were planned by the researchers before beginning laboratory work. Why was the second
experiment considered necessary?
    (F) to check that the oxygen in the air had reacted completely
    (G) to compare nitrogen from more than one source
    (H) to contrast the properties of dry air and moist air
    (J) to ensure the copper shavings were of uniform purity

27. The third experiment was not originally planned. Why did the
researcher realize it was desirable?
    (A) to avoid contamination by material evaporated from the
        red-hot copper shavings
    (B) to check if the density difference of the first two experi-
        ments was meaningful
    (C) to determine whether any residual ammonia was mixed
        with the emerging nitrogen
    (D) to eliminate the problem of having to dehydrate the
        emerging gas

28. By volume, air contains 4 times as much nitrogen as oxygen. The
second experiment yielded ammonia-derived nitrogen equal to
two-thirds of the oxygen. In that experiment, what fraction of
the emerging nitrogen was derived from ammonia?
    (F) 1/2   (G) 1/3   (H) 1/4   (J) 1/7

29. The set of 3 experiments resulted in the discovery that air
contains about 1 percent of a previously unknown gas. What
properties of that gas were revealed by the 3 experiments?
    (A) It reacts with copper and is denser than nitrogen.
    (B) It reacts with copper and is less dense than nitrogen.
    (C) It doesn't react with copper and is denser than nitrogen.
    (D) It doesn't react with copper and is less dense than
        nitrogen.

Passage VI

Carbon is the key chemical element in the molecules necessary for life. The following diagram summarizes the recycling of carbon in our environment.

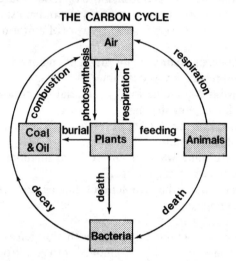

THE CARBON CYCLE

30. The carbon stored in the tissues of living animals is ultimately returned to the atmosphere by
    (F) burial or respiration
    (G) death or combustion
    (H) decay or respiration
    (J) respiration or feeding

31. Carbon dioxide is removed from the air principally by the
    (A) combustion of fossil fuels
    (B) decay of dead animals and plants
    (C) photosynthesis of green plants
    (D) respiration of animals

32. Restricting our attention to the carbon cycle, the principal ecological role of bacteria is to
    (F) prevent the animal population from becoming too large
    (G) provide nourishment for both animals and plants
    (H) release chemical elements stored in plants and animals
    (J) remove waste gases from the atmosphere

33. Photosynthesis in the green leaves of plants produces oxygen. The reverse process, which consumes oxygen, is called
    (A) combustion
    (B) metabolism
    (C) nutrition
    (D) respiration

34. A modern buildup of carbon dioxide levels threatens our climates with global warming, the highly publicized Greenhouse Effect. The diagram of the carbon cycle shows four main ways that carbon dioxide is released into the air. Only one of the four sources of carbon is the problem, because that stored carbon is being converted rapidly and completely into carbon dioxide. Which source of carbon threatens us with the Greenhouse Effect?
    (F) animals
    (G) bacteria
    (H) coal and oil
    (J) plants

Passage VII

To investigate the metabolism of phosphorous by mammals, a healthy female rat was fed a special meal containing 2 milligrams of sodium phosphate as the sole source of phosphorus. The phosphorous atoms in the sodium phosphate were radioactive P^{32}, which decays with a half-life of 17 days. Measurements of the radioactivity of organic materials permitted tracing the utilization of phosphorous by the rat. The special diet was administered only once. All subsequent meals contained common, nonradioactive phosphorous.

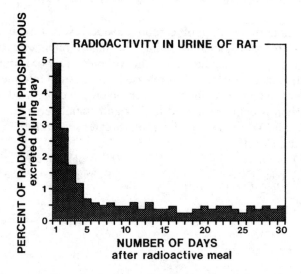

The preceding graph shows the percentage of the radioactive phosphorous excreted daily in the rat's urine. Very similar percentages were excreted each day in the feces. After one month, approximately half of the radioactive phosphorous had been excreted. The animal was then killed and the distribution of the residual phosphorous tracer was studied.

The first percentage in the chart shows the fraction of radioactive P^{32} found in the various components of the freshly killed rat, while the second percentage represents the concentration of P^{32} in each gram of dehydrated matter.

Material	Radioactive Phosphorous	
	Fresh Material (percent)	Dried Material (percent/gram)
Urine	26.3	
Feces	31.8	
Brain	0.5	14.7
Kidneys	0.2	18.2
Liver	1.7	13.9
Blood	0.4	1.8
Bones	24.8	2.8
Muscles	17.4	7.4

35. Just before the rat was killed, the total percentage of radioactive phosphorous excreted by the rat each day was about
    (A) $\frac{1}{2}$%   (B) 1%   (C) 32%   (D) 58%

36. The graph shows high amounts of radioactive phosphorous in the first few days after the special meal. Most of the P^{32} excreted during that early period was
    (F) permanently stored in the bones
    (G) temporarily stored in kidney tissue
    (H) distributed throughout the tissues of several organs
    (J) not utilized in any tissue

37. The fact that most of the phosphorous excreted by the rat was not radioactive means that
    (A) most of the phosphorous comes from the rat's tissues
    (B) the phosphorous lost its radioactivity after a few days
    (C) the rat could not utilize the radioactive phosphorous
    (D) the rat was not harmed by the radioactive phosphorous

38. The average time one phosphorous atom remains in the rat is about
    - (F) 1 week
    - (G) 17 days
    - (H) 1 month
    - (J) 2 months

39. Which one of the following reasons does NOT help to explain the dramatically different percentages in the 2 columns of the chart?
    - (A) Some of the phosphorous is lost during the drying procedure.
    - (B) No dried excreta were analyzed for radioactivity.
    - (C) Some tissues use much more phosphorous than other tissues.
    - (D) The tissue systems have very different weights.

40. Which of these statements best describes the metabolism of phosphorous by rats?
    - (F) Any phosphorous atoms in the tissues are chemically isolated until death disintegrates the tissues and releases the phosphorous.
    - (G) Only a small percentage of phosphorous atoms in the diet are utilized in the formation of tissues.
    - (H) As the tissues grow, new phosphorous atoms are required, but this process slows as time passes.
    - (J) The tissues continually take up phosphorous atoms, which will later be displaced by other phosphorous atoms.

STOP. IF YOU FINISH BEFORE TIME IS CALLED, CHECK YOUR WORK ON THIS SECTION ONLY. DO NOT WORK ON ANY OTHER SECTION IN THE TEST.

ANSWER KEY FOR PRACTICE TEST BATTERY NO. 1

Test 1: English

1. C	26. F	51. C
2. F	27. B	52. F
3. C	28. H	53. A
4. G	29. C	54. J
5. C	30. G	55. A
6. H	31. D	56. F
7. A	32. J	57. B
8. F	33. C	58. H
9. C	34. F	59. D
10. H	35. B	60. J
11. C	36. G	61. A
12. G	37. B	62. J
13. A	38. F	63. D
14. J	39. B	64. J
15. B	40. H	65. C
16. F	41. D	66. J
17. C	42. G	67. B
18. F	43. D	68. J
19. C	44. F	69. A
20. H	45. D	70. H
21. C	46. J	71. D
22. J	47. C	72. F
23. D	48. J	73. A
24. F	49. B	74. H
25. C	50. F	75. C

Test 2: Mathematics

1. B	31. D
2. H	32. G
3. C	33. A
4. K	34. G
5. B	35. D
6. G	36. F
7. B	37. E
8. H	38. F
9. C	39. A
10. F	40. J
11. A	41. A
12. J	42. F
13. E	43. A
14. F	44. H
15. A	45. B
16. H	46. J
17. B	47. D
18. H	48. J
19. B	49. C
20. K	50. J
21. C	51. A
22. K	52. K
23. C	53. B
24. J	54. H
25. C	55. D
26. G	56. J
27. D	57. D
28. F	58. F
29. B	59. C
30. G	60. H

ANSWER KEY FOR PRACTICE TEST BATTERY NO. 1

Test 3: Reading		Test 4: Science Reasoning	
1. D	21. B	1. B	21. C
2. J	22. H	2. G	22. G
3. B	23. A	3. A	23. D
4. G	24. F	4. G	24. G
5. C	25. A	5. A	25. C
6. H	26. G	6. F	26. G
7. C	27. D	7. C	27. B
8. H	28. G	8. G	28. J
9. C	29. C	9. A	29. C
10. J	30. F	10. H	30. H
11. D	31. D	11. B	31. C
12. H	32. F	12. H	32. H
13. D	33. B	13. B	33. D
14. G	34. G	14. G	34. H
15. A	35. B	15. C	35. B
16. F	36. H	16. F	36. J
17. C	37. C	17. C	37. A
18. H	38. G	18. J	38. H
19. B	39. A	19. B	39. A
20. G	40. H	20. F	40. J

SCORING YOUR ACT BATTERY

To score your test battery, total the number of correct answers for each section. Do not subtract any points for questions attempted but missed, as there is no penalty for guessing. This score is then scaled from 1 to 36 for each section and then averaged for the all-important composite score. The average score is approximately 18.

FOR YOUR OWN BENEFIT

To figure out your *percentage right* for each test, use the following formulas:

Test 1: English $\dfrac{\text{Number right}}{75} \times 100 = \underline{\hspace{1cm}} \%$

Test 2: Mathematics $\dfrac{\text{Number right}}{60} \times 100 = \underline{\hspace{1cm}} \%$

Test 3: Reading $\dfrac{\text{Number right}}{40} \times 100 = \underline{\hspace{1cm}} \%$

Test 4: Science Reasoning $\dfrac{\text{Number right}}{40} \times 100 = \underline{\hspace{1cm}} \%$

PRACTICE TEST BATTERY NO. 1: ANALYSIS SHEET

	Possible	Completed	Right	Wrong
Test 1: English	75			
Test 2: Mathematics	60			
Test 3: Reading	40			
Test 4: Science Reasoning	40			
OVERALL TOTALS	215			

WHY???????????????????????????????

ANALYSIS: TALLY SHEET FOR PROBLEMS MISSED

One of the most important parts of test preparation is analyzing WHY! you missed a problem so that you can reduce the number of mistakes. Now that you have taken the practice test and checked your answers, carefully tally your mistakes by marking them in the proper column.

REASON FOR MISTAKE

	Total Missed	Simple Mistake	Misread Problem	Lack of Knowledge
Test 1: English				
Test 2: Mathematics				
Test 3: Reading				
Test 4: Science Reasoning				
TOTAL				

Reviewing the above data should help you determine WHY you are missing certain problems. Now that you have pinpointed the type of error, take the next practice test, focusing on avoiding your most common type.

COMPLETE ANSWERS AND EXPLANATIONS FOR
PRACTICE TEST BATTERY NO. 1

TEST 1: ENGLISH

1. (C) The verbal *contemplating* requires an adverb rather than an adjective modifier. A buyer contemplating high prices is more likely to be *glum* than *gleeful*.

2. (F) The conjunction *but* makes clearer that the second sentence will contrast with the first, dealing with people who *are* aware of the fight for a share of the profits.

3. (C) Though not grammatically incorrect, the original version is wordy. Choice (D), the briefest version, is unacceptable because it distorts the meaning. The growers are not striking.

4. (G) Since *growers, farmworkers,* and *are* are all plurals, the plural *they are* should be used here.

5. (C) The sentence begins with a noun (*wages*) as object of the preposition *in.* Using a second noun (*piecework rates*) as a second object of the preposition keeps the parallelism of the sentence intact.

6. (H) The sentence is comparing the earnings of workers with the earnings (*those*) of truckers. The plural *earnings* requires a plural pronoun. Without the pronoun, the sentence compares earnings to truckers. Choice (J) repeats the noun and misuses the apostrophe.

7. (A) The introductory first sentence is the only one that does not include necessary information.

8. (F) With the move to a new topic (inflation), a new paragraph is necessary. The phrase *in any case* provides a transition.

9. (C) Since *President* is singular, the possessive is *'s.*

10. (H) The opening phrase of the sentence has no subject. Unless the subject of the verbal *adopting* follows, the phrase will dangle and seem to say that *pressure* adopted the wage increase rather than Congress. Also the more acceptable idiom is to *apply* pressure rather than *institute* it.

11. (C) As it stands, the sentence has no main verb. Omission of the *which* solves the problem.

12. (G) This is the most concise of the choices.

13. (A) The sentence as a whole makes sense with *because* as the introductory conjunction.

14. (J) This sentence has no relation to what has gone before or what follows. The paragraph is more coherent if it is omitted.

15. (B) Though either a period or a semicolon could follow *hikes,* the *however* requires two commas.

16. (F) The passage makes the most sense in the order in which it is printed here.

17. (C) With the compound subject (*mouse and rat*), a plural verb is necessary.

18. (F) Since the sentence is to contrast the attitude of the mouse with that of the rat, the conjunction *but* rather than *and* should be used.

19. (C) The phrase is not a direct quotation, so no quotation marks should be used. If it were a direct quotation, the mouse would say, "The food is good."

20. (H) Using the gerund *seeing* rather than the infinitive *to see* is more idiomatic and more concise.

21. (C) *Like* is a preposition and takes an object (*like people*), while *as* is a conjunction and may be followed by a subject and verb (*as people do*).

22. (J) The sentence fits better as the first sentence of the second paragraph, which deals with the rat. The first sentence of the second paragraph follows logically from this sentence.

23. (D) The parallelism with the second term of the series (*his weight greater*) is sustained best by choice (D).

24. (F) The sentence as written is correct. The sentence is a question and should be punctuated with a question mark at the end.

25. (C) The three other proverbs preach caution, standing pat, but *Nothing ventured, nothing gained* urges action to gain a reward.

26. (F) The *would be* is correct, a subjunctive verb.

27. (B) The word choice is that of the mouse, who has lost patience with the rat's string of proverbs.

28. (H) The passage uses dialogue, indirect discourse, and comedy.

29. (C) The passage is probably part of a fable, a moral story usually using animals as its characters.

30. (G) *Protestations* and *objections* are so close in meaning that it is unnecessary to use both. Since the next sentence uses *protesting,* the use of *objections* in the first sentence avoids the repetition.

31. (D) Though choices (A) and (B) are correct grammatically, they are much wordier than (D), which says as much, since we can assume that if they filled the Chamber, they attended the meeting.

32. (J) Here, the use of too few words causes a grammatical error. The verb *alter* requires an object like *fact,* since it is the fact, not the petitions, that cannot be altered.

33. (C) The errors in this sentence are of parallelism. The correlatives *either . . . or* should be followed by constructions that are parallel: *either 25%, or 10%.* One could also say *either the signatures of 25%* and *or the signatures of 10%,* but that construction is wordier than choice (C).

34. (F) The Council members and petitioners already know what this factual account reports. The use of *Tuesday* and the local nature of the subject suggest that a daily or weekly newspaper is more likely than a monthly news magazine to carry this story.

35. (B) As a general rule, modifiers should be near the words they modify. This phrase, modifying *filed,* fits most naturally at the beginning of the sentence.

36. (G) The phrase *city manager* is an appositive and should be set off with two commas. Choice (J) is wordier and also lacks a necessary comma.

37. (B) The subject of this verb is the plural *66.* The tense throughout the paragraph is past.

38. (F) The adjective *supposed* should be used to modify the noun *owners*. The verb should be plural and in the past tense.

39. (B) The verb here is the subjunctive *would* required by the conditional sentence.

40. (H) The second paragraph uses the direct quotation from the city manager.

41. (D) With the use of *that*, the quotation is indirect and should use the third person (*he*), not the first person (*I*), and the past perfect tense to indicate an action completed before the main verb (*told*) in the past tense.

42. (G) As it is written, the sentence beginning with *Enough* is a fragment, lacking a subject and a verb. Adding an *And* makes no difference. Choice (J) adds a verb, but there is still no subject. As a phrase that is part of a sentence that is already complete (as in G), there is no need for a subject and verb. It is simply an adjectival phrase modifying *signatures*.

43. (D) This biographical information about a minor character in the passage is unnecessary and intrusive.

44. (F) The author wishes to use the adverb *savagely* to modify the adjective *comic*. No change is warranted.

45. (D) The direct quotation of one or two of these *savagely comic insults* would, no doubt, liven up the passage.

46. (J) The author, having reached a climax, ends very quickly with words conventionally used to report a meeting's end. The effect is anticlimactic. The reader is not to find out what the insults were or what happened next. The adjective *hortatory* means *encouraging* or *exhorting* and does not at all fit this last sentence.

47. (C) As the sentence is written or in versions (B) and (D), the participial phrase dangles. By supplying a subject (*I*), choice (C) corrects the error.

48. (J) The sentence has a series of nouns as the object of the verb *had*. By using the phrase *oil central heating*, the parallelism is preserved and the meaning is expressed in the fewest words.

49. (B) The paragraph here uses a question (an interrogative verb) which the next sentence answers.

50. (F) The parenthetical *I suppose* should be set off by two commas. Though strictly speaking, the phrase is not necessary to the sense of the sentence, it affects the tone, making the speaker appear more casual and conversational.

51. (C) The word is a perfectly legitimate English adjective meaning *new* or *novel,* usually with disapproval. The author uses quotations because the word is being quoted from the mother.

52. (F) The exclamation is correct in this context. The passage loses meaning and tone if the phrase is left out.

53. (A) The punctuation is correct. The colon introduces the series and the semicolon separates the parts of a series which have internal commas.

54. (J) There is nothing in the passage to inform a reader of the gender of the speaker. As we find out later, he or she is a lawyer who does not cook. The first paragraph uses the first person and the past tense.

55. (A) Choice (D) changes the meaning. Choices (B) and (C) are double negatives.

56. (F) As it is written, the sentence is grammatically correct and the construction in the second half of the sentence is parallel to that in the first (*how to make bread*).

57. (B) The problem in this sentence is that there are two phrases modifying *something—from a package* and *that is quick.* Choice (B) does the best job of keeping the modifiers as close to the word modified as possible.

58. (H) Since the kitchen is a room, the correct phrase is *any other.*

59. (D) Since *same* and *identical* mean the same thing, only one of the two should be used. The phrase *of heat* is also unnecessary.

60. (J) Of the four choices, *nostalgic* is the best.

61. (A) The correct word here is the conjunction *whether; weather* is the noun. Since the sentence contains a *no* later, the *not* is unnecessary.

62. (J) Though not wrong, the *one* is an unneeded word. The correct punctuation sets off the introductory clause with a comma. The meaning of *appears to be,* as well as the tense, is different from the meaning and tense of *was.* The paragraph uses the present tense.

63. (D) The use of *But* or *However* is preferable here because this sentence deals with a different situation, one that is *not* routine. If the *however* is used, it should be set off by commas.

64. (J) The first three sentences of this paragraph deal with the police dispatcher, but the fourth moves to a somewhat different subject.

65. (C) The verb form here is incorrect. We need a relative pronoun that refers to a family *member* (*who,* a person, not *that,* a thing) and the present tense of the verb *call.*

66. (J) Some meaning is lost if the phrase is left out. The best place for the clause is where it will not come between the subject and main verb of the sentence, either at the beginning or at the end.

67. (B) The most concise and idiomatic phrase here is *ask . . . to.*

68. (J) Again, where there is no change of meaning, the shortest version is preferred.

69. (A) The rest of the sentence makes it clear that the verb should be in the present. To *run high* is an idiom (and a metaphor) in which *run* is a linking verb, similar in meaning to the verb *to be.* For this reason, the adjective (*high*) rather than the adverb (*highly*) is proper.

70. (H) Again, the most concise version is the best.

71. (D) Pronouns like *which, that,* and *this* should have specific antecedents. In this sentence, the antecedents of all three pronouns is the whole of the clause (*officers . . . neutrality*) but no single word in the clause. The correct version gets rid of the problem pronoun.

72. (F) Here, we must know what the *they* or *he* refers to. It is the *officers* of the first sentence, a plural, and a plural again in the third sentence. Choice (J) has the number right but omits a needed comma.

73. (A) The phrase used in the passage is correct, a common idiom which compares clear air with more controlled feelings.

74. (H) Since the passage focuses on the police, the words of a police officer who has faced these situations would be especially effective.

75. (C) Paragraph 1 talks about the police response to a call, but paragraph 2 talks about who makes the call in the first place. Paragraph 3 deals with what happens when the police arrive, that is, after the dispatch. The chronological order of the passage is 2, 1, 3, not as it is printed here.

TEST 2: MATHEMATICS

1. (B) If x is increased by 50%, we can represent it by $\frac{3}{2}x$. We must multiply this by $\frac{2}{3}y$ in order to keep the product equal to xy. Since $\frac{2}{3}$ is a $\frac{1}{3}$ reduction, answer (B) is the correct response.

2. (H) Although the answer of 40 can be determined by trial and error, there is a better way. M = (cost of ticket) (number of tickets)

   Max $= (30 + 5x)(100 - 10x)$

   $= (5)(10)(6 + x)(10 - x)$

   The roots of this symmetric curve are 10 and -6. Thus the line of symmetry is $x = 2$. Thus $(30 + 5x) = 40$.

3. (C) Since a right triangle is formed, the width of the rectangle can be found with the Pythagorean theorem. Time could be saved if you note that the triangle is a multiple of a 5, 12, 13 right triangle. The factor is 3, so the width must be 15, and $(15)(36) = 540$.

4. (K) Since the shelf lengths are 4 inches apart, first find the average shelf length by dividing 155 by 5. This gives 31. Therefore, this is the middle-length shelf. The shelf measurements are 23, 27, 31, 35, and 39. Thus, the longest shelf is 39 inches long. This problem could be approached algebraically as follows: If the longest shelf is x, the other shelves could be represented by $x - 4, x - 8, x - 12$, and $x - 16$. Add these and you get

   $$5x - 40 = 155$$
   Thus, $$5x = 195$$
   and $$x = 39$$

5. (B) Substituting, we get $3x + 3x = 14$, $6x = 14$, so $x = \frac{7}{3}$. Also $2y + 2y = 14$, $4y = 14$, so $y = \frac{1}{2}$. Therefore $x + y = \frac{7}{3} + \frac{7}{2} = \frac{14}{6} + \frac{21}{6} = \frac{35}{6} = 5\frac{5}{6}$. Thus the answer is (B).

6. (G) If the perimeter of the square is $8\sqrt{\pi}$, then each side is $2\sqrt{\pi}$ and its area is 4π. If a circle has an area of 4π, the radius is 2, the diameter is 4 and the circumference is 4π.

7. (B) The GCF cannot be larger than the smallest number. This eliminates answer (E). All four numbers are divisible by 3. This eliminates answer (A). None of the numbers is divisible by 12 or 18. This leaves the correct answer of 6.

8. (H) Since 21 is 70% of the total, the total must be 30. Thus the team lost 9 matches.

9. (C) There are a total of $8 + 2 + 6 = 16$ candies in the package. After one is chosen, 15 are left. Since there are 6 white candies out of 15 candies, the probability of getting a white one is $6/15 = 2/5$.

10. (F) Since there are 180 degrees in a triangle, $(3x) + (x + 10) + (2x - 40) = 180$. $6x - 30 = 180$, $6x = 210$, $x = 35$. Thus the three angles are 105, 45, and 30. Thus the smallest angle is 30. Answer (F).

11. (A) Remember to do all four multiplications if you use the FOIL method: First, Outer, Inner, and Last.
    An alternate method would be to line them up and multiply as follows

$$\begin{array}{r} 2x + 4 \\ x + 3 \\ \hline 6x + 12 \\ 2x^2 + 4x \quad\quad \\ \hline 2x^2 + 10x + 12 \end{array}$$

12. (J) The external angle theorem states that an exterior angle of a triangle is equal to the sum of the two remote interior angles.

    Thus, $130° = 50° + w°$

    $w = 130° - 50°$

    $= 80°$

13. (E) Remember that "<" means *less than* and ">" means *greater than*. In this problem, the middle condition is repetitious.

> "If A is greater than B" $A > B$
> "C is less than A" $C < A$
> "and B is greater than C" $B > C$

Then by making the proper connections $A > B > C$, or $C < B < A$.

14. (F) Statement I is the external angle theorem. Statement II follows from statement I. Statement III is only true some of the time.

15. (A) When dividing numbers of the same base, subtract the exponents, canceling or dividing as follows

$$\frac{\overset{2}{\cancel{12}}x^{\overset{4}{\cancel{6}}}\cancel{y}\cancel{z}}{\underset{6}{\cancel{6}}\,\cancel{x}\cancel{y}z^{8^{6}}} \text{ leaves } \frac{2x^4}{z^6}$$

16. (H) You could have made the following diagram:

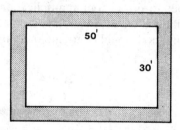

Now you could solve the problem by working from the answers. Since the answers are in order from smallest to largest, you may want to start from the middle answer and then go up or down as needed. Using the value in choice (H), 5, the diagram would look like this:

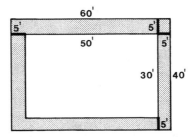

The overall area is 60′ by 40′ or 2400 sq. ft. The area of the court is 1500 sq. ft. Subtracting the area of the court from the overall area gives the area of the grass strip, which is 900 sq. ft. Therefore, the strip is 5′ wide. Solving the problem algebraically would look like this:

If the width of the strip is x, we have

$$(2x + 50)(2x + 30) - 1500 = 900$$
$$4x^2 + 160x + 1500 - 1500 = 900$$
$$x^2 + 40x - 225 = 0$$
$$(x + 45)(x - 5) = 0$$

Since distance cannot be negative, we are left with $x = 5$.

17. (B) The information would lead you to the following diagram:

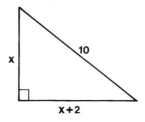

The path taken by the hikers forms a right triangle. Since the hikers hiked 2 hours and one hiker can hike 1 mph faster than the other, that hiker will be 2 miles farther than the slower one after 2 hours. Thus, the following Pythagorean relationship exists:

$$x^2 + (x + 2)^2 = 10^2$$

$$x^2 + x^2 + 4x + 4 = 100$$

$$2x^2 + 4x - 96 = 0$$

$$x^2 + 2x - 48 = 0$$

$$(x + 8)(x - 6) = 0$$

Now, solving each one independently gives

$$x + 8 = 0, \text{ so } x = -8$$

or

$$x - 6 = 0, \text{ so } x = 6$$

Since distance cannot be negative, x must be equal to 6. Thus, in 2 hours, the slower hiker walked 6 miles, which is 3 mph. Again, this problem could have been solved by working from the answers.

18. (H) The hypotenuse of the triangle is the longest side, which is 5 cm. The sine of an angle is defined as the quotient of the side opposite the angle and the hypotenuse. Thus, the sine is $\frac{4}{5}$.

19. (B) We substitute $x + 4$ in the given equation for x.

$$3(x + 4)^2 + 2(x + 4) - 4 = 0$$

$$3(x^2 + 8x + 16) + 2x + 8 - 4 = 0$$

$$3x^2 + 24x + 48 + 2x + 8 - 4 = 0$$

$$3x^2 + 26x + 52 = 0$$

20. (K) If we solve the inequality we get

$$4 - 3x < -3$$

$$-3x < -7$$

$$x > \frac{7}{3}$$

Thus, x is greater than $2\frac{1}{3}$.

21. (C) To find the area of the quadrilateral, start with the area of the large rectangle and subtract the areas of the two triangles. The height of the large rectangle is $[3 - (-3)] = 6$. The width of the large rectangle is $[4 - (-5)] = 9$. Therefore, the area of the large rectangle is 54 square units. The lower triangle has a width of $[4 - (-5)] = 9$ and a height of $[(-1) - (-3)] = 2$. Therefore, its area is $(9)(2)/2 = 9$ square units. The upper triangle has a width of $[(-2) - (-5)] = 3$ and a height of $[3 - (-1)] = 4$. Therefore, its area is $(4)(3)/2 = 6$ square units. Thus, the area of the quadrilateral is $(54 - 9) - 6 = 39$ square units.

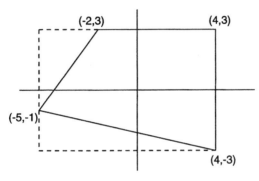

22. (K)

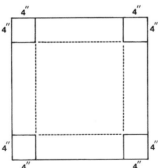

Since the square bottom of the tank can be represented by x^2, we have

$$4x^2 = 900$$

$$x^2 = 225$$

$$x = 15$$

Thus, the width of the tank is 15. Since the 4-inch sides were folded up, we must add 8 to this figure, giving 23 inches.

23. (C) Let x be Mike's age. Thus, $3x$ is Macey's age. Thus $3x + 8 = 2(x + 8)$, $3x + 8 = 2x + 16$. Thus $x = 8$. Therefore, $3x = 24$. Thus Macey *is* 24. Thus, 21, three years ago.

24. (J) The side of the triangle is 10. The area follows from the formula for the area of an equilateral triangle:

$$\left[A = \frac{x^2\sqrt{3}}{4}\right]$$

$$A = \frac{10^2\sqrt{3}}{4}$$

$$= \frac{100\sqrt{3}}{4}$$

$$= 25\sqrt{3}$$

25. (C) For this problem, change the hours to minutes, and set up the following equations.

$$\frac{x}{120} + \frac{x}{90} = 1$$

Multiply by 360. $3x + 4x = 360$, $7x = 360$, $x = 51$.

Alternate Equation: $\dfrac{1}{120} + \dfrac{1}{90} = \dfrac{1}{x}$

26. (G) When multiplying, add exponents. When dividing, subtract exponents. Thus $(2y + 2) + (6y - 1) - (4y - 3) = 4y + 4$ or finally, x^{4y+4}.

27. (D) Housing and Food together comprise 55¢ out of the family's dollar. Therefore 55¢ out of 100¢ is 55¢/100¢ or 55%. Fifty-five percent of the entire central angle of 360° is $(.55)(360°) = 198°$.

28. (F) Since $AB = BC$, angle CAD is equal to angle ACB (isosceles triangle ABC). Thus angle ACB is also 70°. This makes angle B equal to 40° (180° in a triangle). Also angle BCD equals 40° (same reason as above). Thus angle ADC equals 80° (external angle theorem).

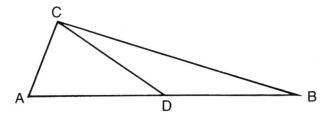

29. (B) Drawing the following x-y graph and placing the points could be helpful.

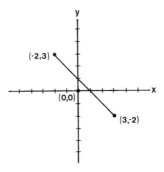

Since the line goes down to the right, the slope is negative, so the answer is either (A) or (B). From this drawing you can determine that the answer is -1, (B).

Mathematically, the formula for the slope of a line (where m = slope) given its two endpoints gives us

$$m = \frac{y_2 - y_1}{x_2 - x_1}$$

$$m = \frac{3 - (-2)}{-2 - (3)}$$

$$m = \frac{5}{-5}$$

Thus, $m = -1$

30. (G) The five angles of a pentagon add up to 540°. Thus, 240° are left over for the two unknown angles. Thus, $x + (2x + 30) = 240$, $3x = 210$, $x = 70$. Therefore, the two unknown angles are 70° and 170°. Thus the sum of the two smallest is 70° + 80° = 150°.

31. (D) To set up the following equation, let x be the number of liters of 20% solution and $(40 - x)$ be the number of 60% solution. Then $(.20)(x) + (.60)(40 - x) = (.50)(40)$. Simplifying and multiplying by 100 gives

$$20x + 2400 - 60x = 2000$$

$$-40x = -400$$

$$x = 10$$

32. (G) If we factor the equation we get $y = x^4(1 - x)$. The roots of this equation are 0 and 1, since $0 = x^4(1 - x)$ and $0 = x^4$, or $0 = 1 - x$. Thus the x-axis is intersected at the points 0 and 1, or twice.

33. (A)

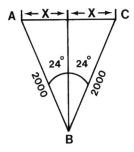

From the diagram, we see that

$$\sin 24° = \frac{x}{2000}$$

Thus, $x = 2000 \sin 24°$

Therefore, the distance between A and C is $2x$, or $4000 \sin 24°$.

34. (G) We can set up the following chart.

	D	=	R	×	T
Up	D		16		$\frac{D}{16}$
Down	D		24		$\frac{D}{24}$

Since the time is 10 hours for the whole trip,

$$\frac{D}{16} + \frac{D}{24} = 10$$

Multiplying by 48, $3D + 2D = 480, 5D = 480, D = 96$.

35. (D) Average speed is total distance/total time. The total distance is $2x$. Time going is $x/8$. Time coming back is $x/12$. Thus average speed is

$$\frac{2x}{\dfrac{x}{8} + \dfrac{x}{12}} = \frac{2x}{\dfrac{3x}{24} + \dfrac{2x}{24}}$$

$$= \frac{2x}{\dfrac{5x}{24}} = \left(\frac{2x}{1}\right)\left(\frac{24}{5x}\right) = \frac{48}{5} = 9.6$$

36. (F)   We have

$$\frac{x}{x-y} - \frac{y}{y-x} =$$

Since

$$y - x = -(x - y)$$

then

$$\frac{y}{y-x} = \frac{-y}{x-y}$$

and thus,

$$\frac{x}{x-y} - \frac{y}{y-x} = \frac{x}{x-y} + \frac{y}{x-y} = \frac{x+y}{x-y}$$

37. (E) From the Pythagorean theorem, we see that the diagonal is 15. Thus the perimeter of the rectangle is 42 and the perimeter of the triangle is 36. Thus the ratio is $\frac{42}{36} = \frac{7}{6}$, or 7:6.

38. (F) You must combine similar terms. $(4x^3) + (-3x^3) + (-2x^3) = -x^3$ and $(-2x^2) + (3x^2) + (-4x^2) = -3x^2$. Therefore, the sum is $-x^3 - 3x^2$.

39. (A) We work out from the inside.

$f(\tfrac{1}{2}) = (\tfrac{1}{2})^2 - 2 = \tfrac{1}{4} - 2 = -\tfrac{7}{4}$

Then $g[f(\tfrac{1}{2})] =$

$g(-\tfrac{7}{4}) = 2(-\tfrac{7}{4}) + 2 = -\tfrac{14}{4} + 2 = -\tfrac{14}{4} + \tfrac{8}{4} = -\tfrac{6}{4} = -\tfrac{3}{2}$

and $f\{g[f(\tfrac{1}{2})]\} = f(-\tfrac{3}{2}) = (-\tfrac{3}{2})^2 - 2 = \tfrac{9}{4} - 2 = \tfrac{9}{4} - \tfrac{8}{4} = \tfrac{1}{4}$

40. (J) Lines that are perpendicular to each other have slopes that are negative inverses of each other. Thus the equation must be of this form: $y = 2x + b$. If we substitute the given point $(1, 1)$ into this form, we can determine the value of b. $1 = (2)(1) + b$. Thus, $b = -1$, and (J) is the answer.

41. (A) The area of a triangle is $A = bh/2$. The base and height are interchangeable. Since $\sin 35° = y/4$ and $\cos 35° = x/4$, $y = 4 \sin 35°$ and $x = 4 \cos 35°$. Thus, $A = 8 \sin 35° \cos 35°$.

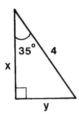

42. (F) Using the point slope form of the equation we have

$$y = \tfrac{1}{2}x + b$$

Substituting the given point into this equation allows us to find b, the y-intercept.

$$2 = \tfrac{1}{2}(1) + b$$

Thus, $b = \tfrac{3}{2}$

Therefore, $y = \tfrac{1}{2}x + \tfrac{3}{2}$

Multiplying the whole equation by 2 gives

$$2y = x + 3$$

Adding $-2y$ to each side gives

$$0 = x - 2y + 3$$

or

$$x - 2y + 3 = 0$$

43. (A) You could have made the following drawing:

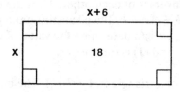

If the width of the rectangle is x, the length can be represented by $x + 6$.

Thus, $x(x + 6) = 18$

Therefore, $x^2 + 6x - 18 = 0$

Using the quadratic formula we get

$$x = \frac{-6 \pm \sqrt{36 + 72}}{2} = \frac{-6 \pm \sqrt{108}}{2} = \frac{-6 \pm 6\sqrt{3}}{2} = -3 \pm 3\sqrt{3}$$

Since x must be positive, use $+ 3\sqrt{3}$, giving

$$-3 + 3\sqrt{3} \quad \text{or} \quad 3\sqrt{3} - 3$$

Factored gives $3(\sqrt{3} - 1)$

44. (H) Single angle ABD is 20°, arc $AD = 40°$. Since arc DAB is a semicircle, arc AB must equal 140° and angle x must equal 70°.

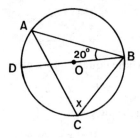

45. (B) Time equals distance divided by speed. Thus,

$$\frac{20}{x} - \frac{20}{x + 4} = 1$$

$$20(x + 4) - 20x = x^2 + 4x$$

$$20x + 80 - 20x = x^2 + 4x$$

$$x^2 + 4x - 80 = 0$$

$$x = \frac{-4 \pm \sqrt{16 + 320}}{2} = \frac{-4 \pm \sqrt{336}}{2} = \frac{-4 \pm 4\sqrt{21}}{2} = -2 \pm 2\sqrt{21}$$

Since speed must be positive, we use the $+ 2\sqrt{21}$. This gives

$$-2 + 2\sqrt{21} \quad \text{or} \quad 2\sqrt{21} - 2$$

46. (J) You could have worked this problem by plugging in from the answers. Answers (F), (G), and (H) are not reasonable because if the sum of two numbers is 25, the larger number could not be 10, 11 or 12. So plug in answer (J), 13. If 13 is the larger number, 12 is the smaller number. Now square each of them and add them together as follows:

$$12^2 + 13^2 =$$

$$144 + 169 = 313$$

Therefore, the correct answer is (J). 13 is the larger number.

Algebraically, if x represents one number, $(25 - x)$ can be used to represent the other number. Therefore

$$x^2 + (25 - x)^2 = 313$$

$$x^2 + 625 - 50x + x^2 = 313$$

$$2x^2 - 50x + 312 = 0$$

$$x^2 - 25x + 156 = 0$$

$$(x - 12)(x - 13) = 0$$

Thus, the numbers are 12 and 13.

47. **(D)** You could have made the following *x-y* graph and plotted the points.

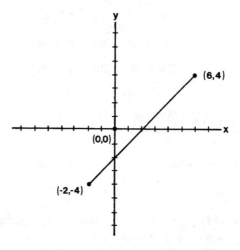

If you understand that the *y*-intercept is where the line crosses the *y*-axis, you can eliminate choices (A) and (B). From the graph, the *y*-intercept will be negative. If the graph is drawn fairly accurately, you can spot the answer of -2.

To solve for the *y*-intercept, first determine the slope of the line (m = slope of line).

$$m = \frac{y_2 - y_1}{x_2 - x_1} = \frac{4 - (-4)}{6 - (-2)} = \frac{8}{8} = 1$$

We could use the point slope formula to determine the *y*-intercept, but there is a faster way. Since the slope is 1, each unit you move to the right will result in one unit up. Therefore, if you start with the point $(-2, -4)$ and add 2 to each coordinate, you get $(0, -2)$. Thus, the *y*-intercept is -2.

48. (J)

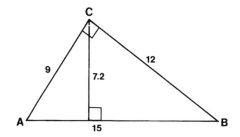

From the Pythagorean theorem, we see that side *AB* is 15. Since the height of a right triangle drawn from the right angle to the hypotenuse divides the triangle into similar triangles, we can set up the following ratio:

$$\frac{h}{9} = \frac{12}{15}$$

Thus,

$$15h = 12 \times 9$$

$$h = 7.2$$

49. (C) Machine A works for a total of 4 hours. We can substitute what we know into the following useful formula:

$$\frac{\text{A actual work}}{\text{A do job alone}} + \frac{\text{B actual work}}{\text{B do job alone}} = 1$$

In other words, the fractional part of the job that A did plus the fractional part of the job that B did must equal one complete job. Thus,

$$\frac{4}{10} + \frac{x}{12} = 1$$

Since

$$\frac{4}{10} + \frac{6}{10} = 1$$

Then

$$\frac{x}{12} = \frac{6}{10}$$

If we cross multiply, we get

$$10x = 72 \quad \text{or} \quad x = 7.2$$

Now, 7.2 hours = 7 hours, 12 minutes. Since B started at 9 a.m., B must finish at 4:12.

50. (J) Simply substitute in the formula:

$$\frac{1}{4} = \frac{1}{10} + \frac{1}{B}$$

Multiply through by the common denominator 20B to get rid of the denominators. This gives

$$5B = 2B + 20$$

$$3B = 20$$

$$B = 6\tfrac{2}{3}$$

51. (A) To get additional insight, you should draw the diagram.

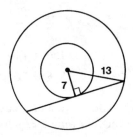

From the Pythagorean theorem, we have

$$7^2 + x^2 = 13^2$$

$$x^2 = 169 - 49$$

$$x^2 = 120$$

$$x = \sqrt{120} = 2\sqrt{30}$$

Since the length of the chord is twice the length of the leg of the right triangle,

$$2x = 4\sqrt{30}$$

52. (K) The drawing would look like this:

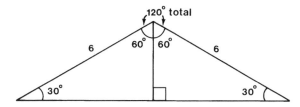

If we divide the triangle in half, we get two 30-60-90 degree right triangles. The longest side is 6. Thus, the shortest side is 3 and the third side is $3\sqrt{3}$. Thus, the length of the longest side of the large triangle is $6\sqrt{3}$.

53. (B) Perform the following:

$$\frac{2\sqrt{3} - 4}{\sqrt{3} + 2} \times \frac{\sqrt{3} - 2}{\sqrt{3} - 2} = \frac{6 - 8\sqrt{3} + 8}{3 - 4}$$

To get the numerator

$$
\begin{array}{r}
2\sqrt{3} - 4 \\
(\times) \quad \sqrt{3} - 2 \\
\hline
-4\sqrt{3} + 8 \\
6 - 4\sqrt{3} \quad\quad \\
\hline
6 - 8\sqrt{3} + 8
\end{array}
$$

To get the denominator

$$
\begin{array}{r}
\sqrt{3} + 2 \\
(\times) \quad \sqrt{3} - 2 \\
\hline
-2\sqrt{3} - 4 \\
3 + 2\sqrt{3} \quad\quad \\
\hline
3 \quad\quad\quad - 4
\end{array}
$$

Now simplifying

$$= \frac{14 - 8\sqrt{3}}{-1} = 8\sqrt{3} - 14 = 2(4\sqrt{3} - 7)$$

54. (H)

$$\sqrt{\frac{78x^5y^7}{6x^2y^3}}$$

$$\sqrt{\frac{\overset{13}{\cancel{78}}x^{\cancel{5}3}y^{\cancel{7}4}}{\cancel{6}x^{\cancel{2}}y^{\cancel{3}}}} = \sqrt{13x^3y^4} = \sqrt{13(x^2)x(y^4)} = xy^2\sqrt{13x}$$

55. (D) $\dfrac{|8-3|\,|3-8|}{|-3-8|\,|-8+3|} = \dfrac{5\times5}{11\times5} = \dfrac{25}{55} = \dfrac{5}{11}$

56. (J) Multiplying through the equation $x - 10 = \dfrac{-9}{x}$ by x gives

$$x^2 - 10x = -9$$
$$x^2 - 10x + 9 = 0$$
$$(x - 9)(x - 1) = 0$$

Thus, the roots are 9 and 1. Their difference is 8.

57. (D) The formula for the total number of degrees in an n-sided polygon is $(n - 2)180$, where n is the number of sides. Since a decagon has 10 sides, there are $(10 - 2)180 = 1440$ degrees total. Since the polygon is regular, all angles are the same size. Thus, dividing by 10, $1440/10 = 144$.

58. (F) Simply substitute either value into the equation and solve.

$$4x^2 + 2x + A = 0$$
$$4(2)^2 + (2)(2) + A = 0$$
$$16 + 4 + A = 0$$
$$A = -20$$

59. (C) To gain insight, you could have drawn the following:

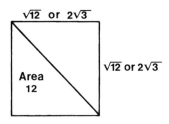

If the area of a square is 12, then each side of the square is $\sqrt{12}$ or $2\sqrt{3}$. From the relationship in the 45-45-90 degree right triangle, we know that the hypotenuse, and in this case the diagonal, is equal to the product of a side and 2. Thus,

$$d = (\sqrt{2})(2)(\sqrt{3}) = 2\sqrt{6}$$

60. (H) First factor the numerator and denominator.

$$\frac{x^2 - 7xy + 12y^2}{x^2 - 4xy + 3y^2} = \frac{(x - 3y)(x - 4y)}{(x - 3y)(x - y)} = \frac{x - 4y}{x - y}$$

TEST 3: READING

1. (D) Both (A) and (B) misrepresent the contents. The passage is not about scientific or modern thought. The passage covers more than the early Middle Ages, so the last choice, though uninspired, is at least accurate.

2. (J) The first three statements are true. The last assertion is false.

3. (B) We can make this assumption from the fact that Aristotle and Averroës were translated into Latin and all of the titles mentioned in the passage are Latin.

4. (G) The issue of faith versus works is mentioned nowhere in this passage.

5. (C) The passage identifies the Scholastics as *clerics,* that is, priests.

6. (H) The inclusion of Scotus should eliminate choice (J). Choice (F) describes most Christian belief of any era.

7. (C) Though choice (D) is true, it would not contribute so much to the development of the scientific method as would the more positive choice (C).

8. (H) According to the last paragraph, in the fourteenth century, *there was a loss of faith in logic*.

9. (C) The last paragraph explicitly states that the Nominalists had lost the *faith in logic*.

10. (J) There is nothing in this passage that reveals the author's bias for or against the schoolmen discussed. The passage is disinterested in tone.

11. (D) The mother's death had taken place at least six months earlier, when their uncle gave them the jewels. The uncle rather than a father suggests that both parents are no longer living. Their living accommodations do not suggest poverty.

12. (H) The passage is ironic when it speaks of the strength of Celia's arguments. But because Dorothea is not interested in jewels herself, it has not occurred to her that Celia might be. As soon as she realizes, she is eager to please her sister, whom she loves.

13. (D) Dorothea does not fully understand herself, but she is sincere when she first states that she will not wear jewels. Had she really been concerned about jewelry, she would not have forgotten about the jewels.

14. (G) Celia would like Dorothea to wear at least one jewel, and she hopes the cross might appeal to her sister's religious feelings.

15. (A) Celia's words suggest that Dorothea's strictness is attributable to her religious beliefs. Choices (B), (C), and (D) are very wrong answers.

16. (F) The passage presents Dorothea as indifferent to the jewels her mother has left her but interested in *good works,* such as a school in the village.

17. (C) From the passage, we can be certain that Celia is more worldly as her attitude to the jewels makes clear.

18. (H) She refers to jewels as *spiritual emblems* and *like fragments of heaven.*

19. (B) The simile, a comparison using *like* or *as,* is used several times in this paragraph. Irony and dialogue occur throughout the passage, not in this paragraph alone.

20. (G) Though the author is aware of some limitations in Dorothea, the attitude toward the character is neither hostile nor enthusiastically approving. She is presented here in a scene of light comedy.

21. (B) The difficulties of labor in the forty years from 1870 to 1910 is the subject of the passage.

22. (H) The second paragraph says that the maintenance of the furnaces was *decisive* in maintaining the twelve-hour day.

23. (A) It seems odd that industry should grow at the expense of the worker, but this was the effect of specialized machinery.

24. (F) With fewer people leaving the eastern cities for farms in the West, the eastern labor force grew larger.

25. (A) If the labor pool is small, wages are likely to rise.

26. (G) The large immigrant population and the recent unavailability of farmland are uniquely American experiences in the period.

27. (D) In fact, the move was from the South to the North.

28. (G) The last paragraph states that there was no federal authority to regulate wages, only state laws.

29. (C) The political system left most labor laws at this time to the states.

30. (F) The first two paragraphs of the passage deal with the problems caused by the mechanization of industry. Paragraphs three and four deal with the labor force (those moving west, the immigrants), while the final paragraph deals with the effects of the political situation in America.

31. (D) All three are accurate statements.

32. (F) Carbon dating can be used on plant and animal remains but not on objects that contain no carbon. It is accurate to about 200 years, according to the passage, and is unusable on objects older than 50,000 years.

33. (B) The passage does not deal with liabilities. Choice (C) is misleading, and since little is said about history, choice (D) is not appropriate.

34. (G) I and II are true. There is nothing in the passage to support III.

35. (B) A carnivore, by definition, would have eaten animals, but we can assume that some of its victims ate plants.

36. (H) According to the passage, plants absorb the carbon dioxide and fix the carbon in their tissues.

37. (C) Three half-lives, or 17,280 years, would reduce the original radioactivity to one-eighth of what it was.

38. (G) The last paragraph alludes to both I and II.

39. (A) According to the last paragraph, Geiger counters measure the beta-ray activity.

40. (H) A turquoise ornament is neither animal nor vegetable.

TEST 4: SCIENCE REASONING

1. (B) You should be aware that normal room temperature is about 68°F or 20°C. Therefore, the answer is in the middle of the three viscosity columns in the chart. Mercury has the highest viscosity, 15.47 millipoises.

2. (G) For each of the eight liquids in the chart, the viscosity decreases as you go from low temperature (0°C) toward high temperature (40°C). No simple rule relating viscosity to molecular weight is evident.

3. (A) Since the prefix *hex-* means six, hexane must have six carbon atoms. Therefore, its viscosity is likely to be midway between those of pentane (five carbons) and heptane (seven carbons). The average of those two values is 2.72 millipoises.

4. (G) In the column with viscosities at 0°C, the liquid most similar to water is ethanol. The steel bearing should sink in either at nearly the same rate.

5. (A) At the beginning of the passage, viscosity is defined as a quantity measuring the resistance to flow. The first method would accomplish that task: the higher the viscosity, the less liquid would flow through the hole in the base of the beaker. Methods (B) and (C) are related to surface tension, not viscosity.

6. (F) The light is on the floor to the left of the beetle, so its left eye received much more light than its right eye.

7. (C) All the experiments show that the beetle turns only if one eye receives more light. As soon as the beetle in Experiment 2 was facing directly toward the light, its eyes would be equally illuminated and it would stop turning.

8. (G) Experiment 2 clearly showed that the beetle would turn toward the eye that received the most light. Experiment 4 showed that paint alone would not cause the beetle to turn.

9. (A) The beetle turns if either eye receives more light, so it would crawl in a straight line only if both eyes were equally illuminated. The beetle would have to be heading directly toward any light.

10. (H) The turning in Experiment 3 could have been caused either by the light received by the open eye or irritation caused by the paint on the other eye. Experiment 4 proved that paint alone would not cause the beetle to turn.

11. (B) Since the beetle turns only if one eye receives more light, a beetle with both eyes covered with paint should crawl in a straight line even if the room contained a lone bright light off to one side of the beetle's path.

12. (H) Read the graph upward from 100°C and rightward from 0.5 atmospheres. That point falls in the solid field, so iodine would occur as crystals under such conditions.

13. (B) The lowest point in the liquid field is where it touches both the gas field and the solid field. The pressure at that *triple point* is 0.12 atmosphere. At any lower pressure, iodine can exist only as a solid or a gas.

14. (G) The vertical line between the solid field and the liquid field represents the transition from solid to liquid iodine. That vertical boundary is at a temperature of 114°C. Iodine crystals would melt to a liquid if heated to that temperature.

15. (C) Go directly to the right from a pressure of 1 atmosphere until you come to the line between the liquid and gas fields; then look downward to read the temperature. The boiling point of iodine is 184°C. Notice that the temperature of the liquid/gas transition depends on the pressure.

16. (F) Sublimation can occur only at those conditions where the solid and gas fields are in direct contact, toward the bottom of the graph. The pressure must be less than 0.12 atmosphere and the temperature must be less than 114°C.

17. (C) The fundamental idea proposed by Scientist 1 is that an increase in solar radiation causes glaciation. Therefore, an end to continental glaciation would require a lasting decrease in solar radiation, removing the condition which triggered glaciation.

18. (J) They are in direct disagreement about temperatures. Scientist 1 says that high temperatures started the Ice Age, while Scientist 2 says that low temperatures started the Ice Age.

19. (B) Both scientists agree that more snowfall is needed to start a glacial episode. The first scientist realized that a warmer atmosphere could well be more humid and have more precipitation. Choice (A) is wrong because the scientist is proposing only what effects *might* be produced by variation in the sun's energy.

20. (F) Scientist 2 makes a strong case for colder oceans during the Pleistocene epoch. However, the main issue is the temperature of the atmosphere. The implication is that if the oceans were cooler, then so would be the atmosphere.

21. (C) Unless Scientist 1 can show that some factor besides temperature affects the oxygen isotope ratios in marine shells, we will have to accept the assertion by Scientist 2 that they record temperatures accurately. Choice (A) is not the best answer because even a few measurements can be meaningful.

22. (G) According to Scientist 2, ocean waters have become progressively warmer from the Ice Age to the present. During the Ice Age, coral reefs must have been near the equator only. As the seas warmed, the reefs could migrate toward the poles.

23. (D) If data showed that periods of high solar radiation occurred during periods of high precipitation, then the theory of Scientist 1 would be greatly strengthened. As it now stands, he or she simply *asserts* that high solar radiation would lead to more precipitation.

24. (G) The nitrogen was derived from two sources, air and ammonia.

25. (C) Look at the last chart. The highest density nitrogen came from air, while the lowest density nitrogen was derived solely from ammonia. Choice (A) is not the best answer because the order of the experiments is only incidental. The source of the nitrogen is the fundamental difference between the three experiments.

26. (G) The second experiment was considered necessary because then nitrogen from two sources, air and ammonia, could be compared. Without that scientific precaution, the researcher would have missed the important discovery of the unknown gas making up about 1 percent of air.

27. (B) Look at the first chart. Although the densities of the gases are very similar, the researcher decided to perform Experiment 3 to see whether the initial difference (only 0.001 grams/liter) was meaningful. Experiment 3 then proved that the density difference was important.

28. (J) Look at the balanced chemical reaction in Experiment 2. The numbers of molecules (4, 3, 2, and 6) are proportional to the volumes of gases. Three volumes of oxygen yield *two volumes of nitrogen derived from ammonia*. However, air with three volumes of oxygen must have four times as much nitrogen, so our sample has *twelve volumes of nitrogen derived from air*. Of the total fourteen volumes of nitrogen, two were derived from ammonia. 2/14 (=1/7) of the total nitrogen came from ammonia.

29. (C) The unknown gas doesn't react with copper or it wouldn't have contaminated the "pure nitrogen" produced in the first two experiments. The densities measured in those early experiments show that the unknown gas is denser than nitrogen. The inert gas, argon, was actually discovered by this set of experiments.

30. (H) The box labeled *Air* represents carbon dioxide in the atmosphere. The carbon in animals is returned to the atmosphere either by respiration or by decay.

31. (C) The only arrow leaving the box labeled *Air* is the one for photosynthesis. In photosynthesis, green plants use carbon dioxide and water to produce sugar and oxygen.

32. (H) Without bacteria, the chemical elements in plant and animal tissues would not be recycled. Bacterial decay disintegrates the tissues and releases the elements, including carbon.

33. (D) The pair of arrows between the boxes labeled *Air* and *Plants* show that respiration is the reverse of photosynthesis. In respiration, organisms release stored energy by oxidizing sugar and producing carbon dioxide and water.

34. (H) For half a billion years, some dead organic material has been buried and gradually transformed into coal and oil. That immense quantity of stored carbon is now being used as fuel. The deposits of coal and oil will last only another century at the present rate. The vast volumes of carbon dioxide produced by burning those fuels has changed the composition of our atmosphere.

35. (B) The graph shows $\frac{1}{2}\%$ excreted in urine each day after one month of study. The passage states that a similar amount was excreted in feces. The total amount excreted must have been 1%.

36. (J) The high amounts of radioactive phosphorous excreted during the first four days must represent phosphorous that was never utilized to build any tissues of the rat.

37. (A) Throughout the study, most of the phosphorous atoms were nonradioactive. For the first few days, these nonradioactive phosphorous atoms must have been previously stored in the rat's tissues. Later in the study, the nonradioactive phosphorous came both from tissue storage and from later nonradioactive meals.

38. (H) The passage states that after one month, half the radioactive phosphorous had been excreted. The other half must still be in the live rat. Thus, the average time one phosphorous atom remains in the rat is one month.

39. (A) There is no suggestion that phosphorous is lost during drying. Look at the chart. In the first column, the high values for bones and muscles merely mean those tissues make up most of the body. The second column reveals that the kidneys, brain, and liver use much more phosphorous than equal weights of bones and muscles.

40. (J) About 90% of the radioactive phosphorous atoms were temporarily stored in the various tissues of the rat. The tissues, then, must continually take up new phosphorous atoms, which displace the old ones. This study demonstrated that phosphorous atoms are not simply locked into body tissues until the animal dies.

PRACTICE TEST BATTERY NO. 2

ANSWER SHEET FOR PRACTICE TEST BATTERY NO. 2
(Remove This Sheet and Use It to Mark Your Answers)

START WITH NUMBER 1 FOR EACH
NEW SECTION OF THE TEST

TEST 1

1 Ⓐ Ⓑ Ⓒ Ⓓ	26 Ⓕ Ⓖ Ⓗ Ⓙ	51 Ⓐ Ⓑ Ⓒ Ⓓ
2 Ⓕ Ⓖ Ⓗ Ⓙ	27 Ⓐ Ⓑ Ⓒ Ⓓ	52 Ⓕ Ⓖ Ⓗ Ⓙ
3 Ⓐ Ⓑ Ⓒ Ⓓ	28 Ⓕ Ⓖ Ⓗ Ⓙ	53 Ⓐ Ⓑ Ⓒ Ⓓ
4 Ⓕ Ⓖ Ⓗ Ⓙ	29 Ⓐ Ⓑ Ⓒ Ⓓ	54 Ⓕ Ⓖ Ⓗ Ⓙ
5 Ⓐ Ⓑ Ⓒ Ⓓ	30 Ⓕ Ⓖ Ⓗ Ⓙ	55 Ⓐ Ⓑ Ⓒ Ⓓ
6 Ⓕ Ⓖ Ⓗ Ⓙ	31 Ⓐ Ⓑ Ⓒ Ⓓ	56 Ⓕ Ⓖ Ⓗ Ⓙ
7 Ⓐ Ⓑ Ⓒ Ⓓ	32 Ⓕ Ⓖ Ⓗ Ⓙ	57 Ⓐ Ⓑ Ⓒ Ⓓ
8 Ⓕ Ⓖ Ⓗ Ⓙ	33 Ⓐ Ⓑ Ⓒ Ⓓ	58 Ⓕ Ⓖ Ⓗ Ⓙ
9 Ⓐ Ⓑ Ⓒ Ⓓ	34 Ⓕ Ⓖ Ⓗ Ⓙ	59 Ⓐ Ⓑ Ⓒ Ⓓ
10 Ⓕ Ⓖ Ⓗ Ⓙ	35 Ⓐ Ⓑ Ⓒ Ⓓ	60 Ⓕ Ⓖ Ⓗ Ⓙ
11 Ⓐ Ⓑ Ⓒ Ⓓ	36 Ⓕ Ⓖ Ⓗ Ⓙ	61 Ⓐ Ⓑ Ⓒ Ⓓ
12 Ⓕ Ⓖ Ⓗ Ⓙ	37 Ⓐ Ⓑ Ⓒ Ⓓ	62 Ⓕ Ⓖ Ⓗ Ⓙ
13 Ⓐ Ⓑ Ⓒ Ⓓ	38 Ⓕ Ⓖ Ⓗ Ⓙ	63 Ⓐ Ⓑ Ⓒ Ⓓ
14 Ⓕ Ⓖ Ⓗ Ⓙ	39 Ⓐ Ⓑ Ⓒ Ⓓ	64 Ⓕ Ⓖ Ⓗ Ⓙ
15 Ⓐ Ⓑ Ⓒ Ⓓ	40 Ⓕ Ⓖ Ⓗ Ⓙ	65 Ⓐ Ⓑ Ⓒ Ⓓ
16 Ⓕ Ⓖ Ⓗ Ⓙ	41 Ⓐ Ⓑ Ⓒ Ⓓ	66 Ⓕ Ⓖ Ⓗ Ⓙ
17 Ⓐ Ⓑ Ⓒ Ⓓ	42 Ⓕ Ⓖ Ⓗ Ⓙ	67 Ⓐ Ⓑ Ⓒ Ⓓ
18 Ⓕ Ⓖ Ⓗ Ⓙ	43 Ⓐ Ⓑ Ⓒ Ⓓ	68 Ⓕ Ⓖ Ⓗ Ⓙ
19 Ⓐ Ⓑ Ⓒ Ⓓ	44 Ⓕ Ⓖ Ⓗ Ⓙ	69 Ⓐ Ⓑ Ⓒ Ⓓ
20 Ⓕ Ⓖ Ⓗ Ⓙ	45 Ⓐ Ⓑ Ⓒ Ⓓ	70 Ⓕ Ⓖ Ⓗ Ⓙ
21 Ⓐ Ⓑ Ⓒ Ⓓ	46 Ⓕ Ⓖ Ⓗ Ⓙ	71 Ⓐ Ⓑ Ⓒ Ⓓ
22 Ⓕ Ⓖ Ⓗ Ⓙ	47 Ⓐ Ⓑ Ⓒ Ⓓ	72 Ⓕ Ⓖ Ⓗ Ⓙ
23 Ⓐ Ⓑ Ⓒ Ⓓ	48 Ⓕ Ⓖ Ⓗ Ⓙ	73 Ⓐ Ⓑ Ⓒ Ⓓ
24 Ⓕ Ⓖ Ⓗ Ⓙ	49 Ⓐ Ⓑ Ⓒ Ⓓ	74 Ⓕ Ⓖ Ⓗ Ⓙ
25 Ⓐ Ⓑ Ⓒ Ⓓ	50 Ⓕ Ⓖ Ⓗ Ⓙ	75 Ⓐ Ⓑ Ⓒ Ⓓ

171

ANSWER SHEET FOR PRACTICE TEST BATTERY NO. 2
(Remove This Sheet and Use It to Mark Your Answers)

START WITH NUMBER 1 FOR EACH
NEW SECTION OF THE TEST

TEST 2

| 1 Ⓐ Ⓑ Ⓒ Ⓓ Ⓔ |
| 2 Ⓕ Ⓖ Ⓗ Ⓙ Ⓚ |
| 3 Ⓐ Ⓑ Ⓒ Ⓓ Ⓔ |
| 4 Ⓕ Ⓖ Ⓗ Ⓙ Ⓚ |
| 5 Ⓐ Ⓑ Ⓒ Ⓓ Ⓔ |

| 6 Ⓕ Ⓖ Ⓗ Ⓙ Ⓚ |
| 7 Ⓐ Ⓑ Ⓒ Ⓓ Ⓔ |
| 8 Ⓕ Ⓖ Ⓗ Ⓙ Ⓚ |
| 9 Ⓐ Ⓑ Ⓒ Ⓓ Ⓔ |
| 10 Ⓕ Ⓖ Ⓗ Ⓙ Ⓚ |

| 11 Ⓐ Ⓑ Ⓒ Ⓓ Ⓔ |
| 12 Ⓕ Ⓖ Ⓗ Ⓙ Ⓚ |
| 13 Ⓐ Ⓑ Ⓒ Ⓓ Ⓔ |
| 14 Ⓕ Ⓖ Ⓗ Ⓙ Ⓚ |
| 15 Ⓐ Ⓑ Ⓒ Ⓓ Ⓔ |

| 16 Ⓕ Ⓖ Ⓗ Ⓙ Ⓚ |
| 17 Ⓐ Ⓑ Ⓒ Ⓓ Ⓔ |
| 18 Ⓕ Ⓖ Ⓗ Ⓙ Ⓚ |
| 19 Ⓐ Ⓑ Ⓒ Ⓓ Ⓔ |
| 20 Ⓕ Ⓖ Ⓗ Ⓙ Ⓚ |

| 21 Ⓐ Ⓑ Ⓒ Ⓓ Ⓔ |
| 22 Ⓕ Ⓖ Ⓗ Ⓙ Ⓚ |
| 23 Ⓐ Ⓑ Ⓒ Ⓓ Ⓔ |
| 24 Ⓕ Ⓖ Ⓗ Ⓙ Ⓚ |
| 25 Ⓐ Ⓑ Ⓒ Ⓓ Ⓔ |

| 26 Ⓕ Ⓖ Ⓗ Ⓙ Ⓚ |
| 27 Ⓐ Ⓑ Ⓒ Ⓓ Ⓔ |
| 28 Ⓕ Ⓖ Ⓗ Ⓙ Ⓚ |
| 29 Ⓐ Ⓑ Ⓒ Ⓓ Ⓔ |
| 30 Ⓕ Ⓖ Ⓗ Ⓙ Ⓚ |

| 31 Ⓐ Ⓑ Ⓒ Ⓓ Ⓔ |
| 32 Ⓕ Ⓖ Ⓗ Ⓙ Ⓚ |
| 33 Ⓐ Ⓑ Ⓒ Ⓓ Ⓔ |
| 34 Ⓕ Ⓖ Ⓗ Ⓙ Ⓚ |
| 35 Ⓐ Ⓑ Ⓒ Ⓓ Ⓔ |

| 36 Ⓕ Ⓖ Ⓗ Ⓙ Ⓚ |
| 37 Ⓐ Ⓑ Ⓒ Ⓓ Ⓔ |
| 38 Ⓕ Ⓖ Ⓗ Ⓙ Ⓚ |
| 39 Ⓐ Ⓑ Ⓒ Ⓓ Ⓔ |
| 40 Ⓕ Ⓖ Ⓗ Ⓙ Ⓚ |

| 41 Ⓐ Ⓑ Ⓒ Ⓓ Ⓔ |
| 42 Ⓕ Ⓖ Ⓗ Ⓙ Ⓚ |
| 43 Ⓐ Ⓑ Ⓒ Ⓓ Ⓔ |
| 44 Ⓕ Ⓖ Ⓗ Ⓙ Ⓚ |
| 45 Ⓐ Ⓑ Ⓒ Ⓓ Ⓔ |

| 46 Ⓕ Ⓖ Ⓗ Ⓙ Ⓚ |
| 47 Ⓐ Ⓑ Ⓒ Ⓓ Ⓔ |
| 48 Ⓕ Ⓖ Ⓗ Ⓙ Ⓚ |
| 49 Ⓐ Ⓑ Ⓒ Ⓓ Ⓔ |
| 50 Ⓕ Ⓖ Ⓗ Ⓙ Ⓚ |

| 51 Ⓐ Ⓑ Ⓒ Ⓓ Ⓔ |
| 52 Ⓕ Ⓖ Ⓗ Ⓙ Ⓚ |
| 53 Ⓐ Ⓑ Ⓒ Ⓓ Ⓔ |
| 54 Ⓕ Ⓖ Ⓗ Ⓙ Ⓚ |
| 55 Ⓐ Ⓑ Ⓒ Ⓓ Ⓔ |

| 56 Ⓕ Ⓖ Ⓗ Ⓙ Ⓚ |
| 57 Ⓐ Ⓑ Ⓒ Ⓓ Ⓔ |
| 58 Ⓕ Ⓖ Ⓗ Ⓙ Ⓚ |
| 59 Ⓐ Ⓑ Ⓒ Ⓓ Ⓔ |
| 60 Ⓕ Ⓖ Ⓗ Ⓙ Ⓚ |

ANSWER SHEET FOR PRACTICE TEST BATTERY NO. 2
(Remove This Sheet and Use It to Mark Your Answers)

START WITH NUMBER 1 FOR EACH
NEW SECTION OF THE TEST

TEST 3

1 Ⓐ Ⓑ Ⓒ Ⓓ	26 Ⓕ Ⓖ Ⓗ Ⓙ
2 Ⓕ Ⓖ Ⓗ Ⓙ	27 Ⓐ Ⓑ Ⓒ Ⓓ
3 Ⓐ Ⓑ Ⓒ Ⓓ	28 Ⓕ Ⓖ Ⓗ Ⓙ
4 Ⓕ Ⓖ Ⓗ Ⓙ	29 Ⓐ Ⓑ Ⓒ Ⓓ
5 Ⓐ Ⓑ Ⓒ Ⓓ	30 Ⓕ Ⓖ Ⓗ Ⓙ
6 Ⓕ Ⓖ Ⓗ Ⓙ	31 Ⓐ Ⓑ Ⓒ Ⓓ
7 Ⓐ Ⓑ Ⓒ Ⓓ	32 Ⓕ Ⓖ Ⓗ Ⓙ
8 Ⓕ Ⓖ Ⓗ Ⓙ	33 Ⓐ Ⓑ Ⓒ Ⓓ
9 Ⓐ Ⓑ Ⓒ Ⓓ	34 Ⓕ Ⓖ Ⓗ Ⓙ
10 Ⓕ Ⓖ Ⓗ Ⓙ	35 Ⓐ Ⓑ Ⓒ Ⓓ
11 Ⓐ Ⓑ Ⓒ Ⓓ	36 Ⓕ Ⓖ Ⓗ Ⓙ
12 Ⓕ Ⓖ Ⓗ Ⓙ	37 Ⓐ Ⓑ Ⓒ Ⓓ
13 Ⓐ Ⓑ Ⓒ Ⓓ	38 Ⓕ Ⓖ Ⓗ Ⓙ
14 Ⓕ Ⓖ Ⓗ Ⓙ	39 Ⓐ Ⓑ Ⓒ Ⓓ
15 Ⓐ Ⓑ Ⓒ Ⓓ	40 Ⓕ Ⓖ Ⓗ Ⓙ
16 Ⓕ Ⓖ Ⓗ Ⓙ	
17 Ⓐ Ⓑ Ⓒ Ⓓ	
18 Ⓕ Ⓖ Ⓗ Ⓙ	
19 Ⓐ Ⓑ Ⓒ Ⓓ	
20 Ⓕ Ⓖ Ⓗ Ⓙ	
21 Ⓐ Ⓑ Ⓒ Ⓓ	
22 Ⓕ Ⓖ Ⓗ Ⓙ	
23 Ⓐ Ⓑ Ⓒ Ⓓ	
24 Ⓕ Ⓖ Ⓗ Ⓙ	
25 Ⓐ Ⓑ Ⓒ Ⓓ	

CUT HERE

ANSWER SHEET FOR PRACTICE TEST BATTERY NO. 2
(Remove This Sheet and Use It to Mark Your Answers)

START WITH NUMBER 1 FOR EACH
NEW SECTION OF THE TEST

TEST 4

1 Ⓐ Ⓑ Ⓒ Ⓓ
2 Ⓕ Ⓖ Ⓗ Ⓙ
3 Ⓐ Ⓑ Ⓒ Ⓓ
4 Ⓕ Ⓖ Ⓗ Ⓙ
5 Ⓐ Ⓑ Ⓒ Ⓓ

6 Ⓕ Ⓖ Ⓗ Ⓙ
7 Ⓐ Ⓑ Ⓒ Ⓓ
8 Ⓕ Ⓖ Ⓗ Ⓙ
9 Ⓐ Ⓑ Ⓒ Ⓓ
10 Ⓕ Ⓖ Ⓗ Ⓙ

11 Ⓐ Ⓑ Ⓒ Ⓓ
12 Ⓕ Ⓖ Ⓗ Ⓙ
13 Ⓐ Ⓑ Ⓒ Ⓓ
14 Ⓕ Ⓖ Ⓗ Ⓙ
15 Ⓐ Ⓑ Ⓒ Ⓓ

16 Ⓕ Ⓖ Ⓗ Ⓙ
17 Ⓐ Ⓑ Ⓒ Ⓓ
18 Ⓕ Ⓖ Ⓗ Ⓙ
19 Ⓐ Ⓑ Ⓒ Ⓓ
20 Ⓕ Ⓖ Ⓗ Ⓙ

21 Ⓐ Ⓑ Ⓒ Ⓓ
22 Ⓕ Ⓖ Ⓗ Ⓙ
23 Ⓐ Ⓑ Ⓒ Ⓓ
24 Ⓕ Ⓖ Ⓗ Ⓙ
25 Ⓐ Ⓑ Ⓒ Ⓓ

26 Ⓕ Ⓖ Ⓗ Ⓙ
27 Ⓐ Ⓑ Ⓒ Ⓓ
28 Ⓕ Ⓖ Ⓗ Ⓙ
29 Ⓐ Ⓑ Ⓒ Ⓓ
30 Ⓕ Ⓖ Ⓗ Ⓙ

31 Ⓐ Ⓑ Ⓒ Ⓓ
32 Ⓕ Ⓖ Ⓗ Ⓙ
33 Ⓐ Ⓑ Ⓒ Ⓓ
34 Ⓕ Ⓖ Ⓗ Ⓙ
35 Ⓐ Ⓑ Ⓒ Ⓓ

36 Ⓕ Ⓖ Ⓗ Ⓙ
37 Ⓐ Ⓑ Ⓒ Ⓓ
38 Ⓕ Ⓖ Ⓗ Ⓙ
39 Ⓐ Ⓑ Ⓒ Ⓓ
40 Ⓕ Ⓖ Ⓗ Ⓙ

TEST 1: ENGLISH

Time: 45 Minutes
75 Questions

DIRECTIONS

In the left-hand column, you will find passages in a "spread-out" format with various words and phrases underlined and numbered. In the right-hand column, you will find a set of responses corresponding to each underlined portion. If the underlined portion is correct standard written English, is most appropriate to the style and feeling of the passage, or best makes the intended statement, mark the letter indicating "NO CHANGE." If the underlined portion is not the best choice given, choose the one that is. For these questions, consider only the underlined portions; assume that the rest of the passage is correct as written. You will also see questions concerning parts of the passage or the whole passage. Choose the response you feel is best for these questions.

Passage I

Notwithstanding <u>its</u> scientific

excellence in selected fields, the Soviet

Union badly needed the collaboration of

the rest of the world's scholars. During

the Cold War, a number of American

scientists <u>who chose to restrict their</u>

cooperation as a protest against

Moscow's suppression of human

1. A. NO CHANGE
   B. it's
   C. their
   D. there

2. F. NO CHANGE
   G. whose choice to restrict
   H. who choose to restrict
   J. chose to restrict

175

rights. <u>Computers are an area in which</u>
3

<u>the Russians are far behind.</u> The list of
3

American scientists who joined in this

collective expression of conscience

included thirteen Nobel laureates and

eighteen directors of major laboratories.

What most of them found

<u>in the Soviet regime that</u>
4

<u>most disturbed them</u> was a
4

<u>contempt for</u> the notion that each
5

individual has intrinsic moral worth.

"Detente and the promises of Helsinki

are empty catchwords to those dissenters

locked up in the vast Gulag

Archipelago," said Yale biologist Arthur

Martins. Physicists and chemists from

3. A. NO CHANGE
   B. Computers is an area in which the Russians are far behind.
   C. In computers, the Russians are far behind.
   D. OMIT the underlined portion.

4. F. NO CHANGE
   G. in the Soviet regime that disturbed them most
   H. most disturbing in the Soviet regime
   J. OMIT the underlined portion.

5. A. NO CHANGE
   B. contemptuous attitude toward
   C. feeling of contempt for
   D. OMIT the underlined portion.

universities all over the country agree.
_____
                    6

6. F. NO CHANGE
    G. throughout the
        country agree.
    H. throughout the
        country are in
        agreement.
    J. all over the
       country
       agreed.

The response to the Western scientists
_____
                7
from Moscow was icy silence. The
_____
              7
release of scientists like Liepa and

7. A. NO CHANGE
    B. The response
        from Moscow
        to the Western
        scientists was
        icy silence.
    C. From Moscow,
        the response
        to the Western
        scientists was
        icy silence.
    D. (Begin new
        paragraph)
        The response
        from Moscow
        to the Western
        scientists was
        icy silence.

Tchelikov, who the authorities had
_____
             8
imprisoned on vague and unproved

8. F. NO CHANGE
    G. Tchelikov who
        the
    H. Tchelikov
        whom the
    J. Techikov,
       whom the

charges, might have <u>untied the deadlock</u>
　　　　　　　　　　　　　　9
with the scientists in the West but would

have had potentially dangerous effects in

Russia. There was some restlessness

already in the <u>predominant Moslem</u>
　　　　　　　　　　10
states. Once again, the grain harvest in

the Ukraine <u>was expected to be</u>
　　　　　　　　11

<u>as small, if not than smaller than,</u>
　　　　　　　　12
<u>the previous year's. And</u>
　　　　　12

9. A. NO CHANGE
　　B. severed the deadlock
　　C. broken the deadlock
　　D. overturned the deadlock

10. F. NO CHANGE
　　G. predominant Muslim
　　H. predominantly Moslem
　　J. Muslim

11. A. NO CHANGE
　　B. will be
　　C. may be
　　D. were expected to be

12. F. NO CHANGE
　　G. as small if not smaller than the previous year's.
　　H. as small, if not smaller than the previous year's.
　　J. as small as, if not smaller than, the previous year's.

there was, as usual a dearth
                                    ‾‾‾‾
                                     13
of consumer goods in the shops of the

cities.

13. A. NO CHANGE
    B. there was as
       usual, a dearth
    C. there was usu-
       ally, a dearth
    D. there was, as
       usual a dearth

Passage II

> The following paragraphs are given a number in parentheses above each one. The paragraphs may be in the most logical order, or they may not. Item 32 asks you to choose the paragraph sequence that is the most logical.

(1)

Even as a small child, cooking had
                                ‾‾‾‾‾‾‾‾
                                    14
interested me. My mother encouraged
‾‾‾‾‾‾‾‾‾‾‾‾
      14
my curiosity, since in those days cooking

14. F. NO CHANGE
    G. cooking inter-
       ested me.
    H. cooking was of
       interest to me.
    J. I was inter-
       ested in cook-
       ing.

was thought to be a suitable interest for
           ‾‾‾‾‾‾‾‾‾‾‾‾‾‾‾‾‾‾‾‾‾‾‾‾‾‾
                      15
a little girl, and I was the only daughter

among six children. Not, of course, that

anyone ever imagined I would cook

15. A. NO CHANGE
    B. suitably inter-
       esting
    C. of interest
    D. interesting

professionally. ⟦16⟧ Anyway,

16. The preceding sentence differs from the others in this paragraph because it
   F. has no direct object.
   G. uses a metaphor.
   H. is not a complete sentence.
   J. poses a rhetorical question.

before I had graduated from high school,
                    17
I was very good by American standards. I

did most of the cooking at home,

17. A. NO CHANGE
   B. before I had been graduated from
   C. before graduating from
   D. before I graduated from

and sold my cakes, cookies and
                  18
breads to neighbors. I had learned
  18
enough French in school to be able to

make my way through the articles and

recipes I found in the illustrated

18. F. NO CHANGE
   G. cakes, cookies, and my breads
   H. cakes, cookies, and breads
   J. cakes, my cookies, and my breads

European magazines, which I bought
                    _____
                           19
at the second-hand book shops. I'm

certain that mine were the first croissants

ever put on sale in New

Hampshire, though nowadays you can
_____
        20
buy them in any store that sells Wonder

Bread. | 21 |

19. A. NO CHANGE
    B. magazines I bought
    C. magazines, which I purchased
    D. magazines which had been bought

20. F. NO CHANGE
    G. Hampshire and
    H. Hampshire, and
    J. Hampshire, because

21. In the first paragraph, the author uses all of the following devices to give a conversational tone EXCEPT
    A. contraction.
    B. incomplete sentence.
    C. specific commonplace detail.
    D. simile.

(2)

<u>While in the first two years of college,</u>
22

cooking more or less slipped my mind. I

went to a women's college, where we all

ate the appalling institutional food in

elegant dining rooms with spotless linen

on the tables. In my junior year, I was

living in a small dorm when the college

<u>workers, they were criminally underpaid,</u>
23

went out on strike. We divided up the

chores in the dorm, and I volunteered to

cook the dinners. It was

<u>really not greatly different than</u>
24

cooking for my large family.

22. F. NO CHANGE
    G. While in my freshman and sophomore years,
    H. When in the two first years of college,
    J. In my first two years of college,

23. A. NO CHANGE
    B. , they were criminal and underpaid,
    C. —they were criminally underpaid—
    D. which was criminally underpaid,

24. F. NO CHANGE
    G. no different than
    H. not really greatly different than
    J. really not greatly different from

Compared to the college <u>cooks I looked</u>
<u>like Escoffier.</u> My studies slipped badly
because I was clearly more interested in

crisp vegetables than in Russian history

and more engaged by the problems of

nutrition <u>than I was by the problems of</u>

<u>mathematics.</u>

25. A. NO CHANGE
    B. cooks I looked
       as good as Es-
       coffier.
    C. cooks, I looked
       like Escoffier.
    D. cooks—I
       looked like
       Escoffier.

26. F. NO CHANGE
    G. than I was by
       mathematics.
    H. than by the
       problems of
       mathematics.
    J. than math-
       ematics.

(3)

One of the other residents of my dorm

was a <u>rich, rather snooty girl</u> from New

York who had hardly spoken to me

before the strike. Nancy loved good

food, and for the first time

since she came to college could now

actually look forward to dinner. She

knew more about cooking than anyone I

had ever met. It turned out that her

27. A. NO CHANGE
    B. rich and con-
       ceited girl
    C. rich, conceited
       girl
    D. rich girl

family owned a posh hotel and two
                  ‾‾‾‾‾‾‾‾‾‾‾‾‾‾‾‾‾‾
                         28
restaurants in New York City, one
‾‾‾‾‾‾‾‾‾‾‾‾‾‾‾‾‾‾‾‾‾‾‾‾‾‾‾‾‾‾‾‾‾‾
                  28
Italian and a French one. We were
‾‾‾‾‾‾‾‾‾‾‾‾‾‾‾‾‾‾‾‾‾‾‾‾‾‾‾‾‾‾
                  28
soon best friends. She had a crazy idea

of running the family business

herself, in those days as likely as a

28. **F.** NO CHANGE
    G. a posh hotel and an Italian and a French restaurant in New York City.
    H. in New York City a posh hotel and two restaurants, one Italian and one that was French.
    J. a posh hotel, a French restaurant, and an Italian restaurant, all in New York City.

woman being an astronaut, a college
‾‾‾‾‾‾‾‾‾‾‾‾‾‾‾‾‾‾‾‾‾‾‾‾‾‾‾‾‾‾‾‾‾‾
                  29
president, or on the Supreme Court.
‾‾‾‾‾‾‾‾‾‾‾‾‾‾‾‾‾‾‾‾‾‾‾‾‾‾‾‾‾‾‾‾‾‾
                  29

29. **A.** NO CHANGE
    B. woman's being an astronaut, a college president, or on the Supreme Court.
    C. woman astronaut, college president, or Supreme Court justice.
    D. female astronaut, college president, or being on the Supreme Court.

And she said <u>"I was to become the best</u>
                              30

<u>chef in the city."</u> 31 32
        30

30. F. NO CHANGE
     G. said "I would
         be the best
         chef in the
         city."
     H. said, "I was to
         become the
         best chef in
         the city."
     J. said that I was
         to become the
         best chef in
         the city.

31. The passage is
     best described as
     A. didactic
     B. autobiographi-
         cal
     C. formal
     D. inspirational

32. Choose the se-
     quence of para-
     graph numbers
     that will make the
     passage's structure
     most logical.
     F. NO CHANGE
     G. 2, 1, 3
     H. 2, 3, 1
     J. 1, 3, 2

Passage III

(1)

The number of local armed robberies

in the past week <u>rose by two more</u>
                       33
Tuesday night,

33. A. NO CHANGE
    B. rose by two
    C. has risen by
       two more
    D. had risen by
       two

<u>but they reported two suspects arrested</u>
                    34
<u>this morning by city police.</u> One suspect,
                    34

34. F. NO CHANGE
    G. but two re-
       ported sus-
       pects were
       arrested this
       morning by
       city police.
    H. but city police
       reported the
       arrest of two
       suspects this
       morning.
    J. but city police
       reportedly ar-
       rested two sus-
       pects this
       morning.

John Hugo, was arrested <u>after spotting</u>
                            35
in the Eastview Mall carrying a

suspicious looking package. Security

guards at the Mall held the suspect

35. A. NO CHANGE
    B. having been
       spotted
    C. after he is
       spotted
    D. after spotting
       him

until city police had arrived and the
                  —————————————
                        36
package proved to be cash and jewels
————————
  36
taken earlier this week from an

Astromart. Hugo has a long history of

criminal activity. Later this morning, a
                   ————————————————
                          37
second suspect was arrested while
——————————————————————————
              37
attempting to break into the storage
——————————————————————————————
              37
room of an electronics store.
——————————————————————————
          37

36. F. NO CHANGE
     G. arrived, and
         the package
     H. had arrived.
         The package
     J. arrived. The
         package

37. A. NO CHANGE
     B. OMIT the un-
         derlined por-
         tion.
     C. Begin the sec-
         ond paragraph
         with this sen-
         tence.
     D. End the sec-
         ond paragraph
         with this sen-
         tence.

(2)

Michael Marshall was armed

according to the sheriff's deputy who
                38
arrested him with a handgun and a knife.
                38
He attempted to escape

38. F. NO CHANGE
     G. according to a sheriff's deputy, who arrested him with a handgun and a knife.
     H. with a handgun and a knife, according to the sheriff's deputy who arrested him.
     J. with a handgun and a knife, according to the sheriff's deputy, who arrested him.

by commandeering an automobile from a
           39
worker in the parking lot, but the deputy

blocked the only exit from the area

before Marshall could get his car started.

Described as a heavy man of unusual

39. A. NO CHANGE
     B. by commandeering of
     C. by commanding
     D. by commandment of

height, <u>police said the suspect</u> is almost

40

certainly the man they have been looking

for in connection with the Western

Savings robbery.

(3)

<u>Police spokesman were</u> especially

41

eager to discuss the arrest of Marshall

<u>who they have been pursuing</u> for more

42

than four months. If he is convicted of

the Western robbery, he can be

sentenced to as many as ten years in

prison, since two innocent bystanders

---

40. F. NO CHANGE
    G. police said
that the sus-
pect
    H. the suspect,
according to
police,
    J. the suspect,
say the police,

41. A. NO CHANGE
    B. Police spokes-
man was
    C. (Do NOT be-
gin new para-
graph) Police
spokesmen
were
    D. (Do NOT be-
gin new para-
graph) Police
spokesmen
was

42. F. NO CHANGE
    G. who they have
pursued
    H. whom they
have been pur-
suing
    J. whom has
been pursued

were injured <u>committing that crime.</u>
                        43

43. A. NO CHANGE
    B. while commit-
       ting that
       crime.
    C. when commit-
       ting that
       crime.
    D. when that
       crime was
       committed.

<u>As a repeat offender, the sentence for</u>
                     44

44. F. NO CHANGE
    G. A repeat of-
       fender,
    H. Because a re-
       peat offender,
    J. Because he is
       a repeat of-
       fender,

Hugo could be just as long. [45]

45. The passage may
    best be described
    as an example of
    A. analytic ex-
       pository prose.
    B. newswriting.
    C. editorial prose.
    D. biography.

Passage IV

(1)

In the 1980s, the Treasury

Department took a close look at

regulations limiting the interest that

banks and savings and loan associations

were permitted to pay on deposits. Small

depositors rarely got more than four

percent interest and <u>often got less.</u> At
46.

the time, Americans saved just under five

percent of their personal income.

Supply-side government economists

46. F. NO CHANGE
   G. often received a lower rate
   H. frequently received less interest.
   J. often received less than four percent interest.

argued that if the interest rates paid by

banks <u>were allowed to increase,</u>
47.

Americans would soon be saving eight to

ten percent of their personal income.

<u>At the time, treasury bills in</u>
48.
<u>denominations of $10,000 paid up to</u>
48.
<u>six percent interest.</u>
48.

47. A. NO CHANGE
   B. increased,
   C. went up,
   D. should go up,

48. F. NO CHANGE
   G. MOVE the underlined portion to follow the first sentence of the first paragraph.
   H. MOVE the underlined portion to become the first sentence of the second paragraph.
   J. OMIT the underlined portion.

(2)

With the removal of the cap on bank
49
interest rates, savers received twice as
49
much interest on bank deposits.

49. A. NO CHANGE
    B. Having re-
       moved the cap
       on bank inter-
       est rates,
    C. The cap on
       bank interest
       rates having
       been removed,
    D. OMIT the un-
       derlined por-
       tion.

And many new safe savings vehicles
50

50. F. NO CHANGE
    G. Many new safe
       savings ve-
       hicles
    H. And many are
       the new safe
       savings ve-
       hicles
    J. Many new,
       safe, savings
       vehicles

became available such as money market
51
accounts. And how much of personal
51
income did Americans save? Three and

one half percent, compared to six

percent in Europe or eight percent in

51. A. NO CHANGE
    B. available, such
       as money mar-
       ket accounts.
    C. available as
       money market
       accounts.
    D. available, one
       being the
       money market
       account.

Japan. 52 More savings and loan institutions failed in the ten years following deregulation than in the first seventy years of the twentieth century. The percentage of personal income saved by Americans continued to decline each year. Supply-side economists continued to argue

that deregulation would solve all our problems. 53

52. The third and fourth sentences of this paragraph are different from the rest of the passage because they
   F. both contain errors of grammar.
   G. are a question and an exclamation.
   H. are a question and an incomplete sentence.
   J. ask and answer a question by using a metaphor.

53. The passage is probably best described as an example of
   A. newswriting.
   B. editorial prose.
   C. investigative journalism.
   D. economic analysis.

Passage V

(1)

Some years ago a small book called
The Pilgrim's Scrip was published
                        54
anonymously. A collection of
    54

aphorisms the book was noticeable for
          55
its quaint earnestness and its perversity

of view of women who the writer
             56
appeared to rank as creatures in

service to the Serpent. The author, if

he did not always say things new,

evidently spoke from

reflection, feeling, and experience. His
                57
thoughts were sad enough, occasionally

dark, here and there comical in their

oddness, and yet with an element of

hope.

54. F. NO CHANGE
     G. is anonymously
        published.
     H. had been pub-
        lished anony-
        mously.
     J. anonymously
        was published.

55. A. NO CHANGE
     B. aphorism the
        book was
     C. aphorisms, the
        book was
     D. aphorisms
        were

56. F. NO CHANGE
     G. woman who
     H. women, whom
     J. women, who

57. A. NO CHANGE
     B. reflex, feeling
        and experi-
        ence.
     C. reflection feel-
        ing, and expe-
        rience.
     D. reflection feel-
        ing and experi-
        ences.

(2)

Curious enough, the objectionable
58
feature in this little book preserved it

from obscurity. 59 Men read it and

tossed it aside, amused or weary. By the

ladies, however,

58. F. NO CHANGE
    G. Curiously enough, the objectionable
    H. Curiously, the objectionable
    J. Curiously, the objective

59. A. Keep the new paragraph beginning with the preceding sentence.
    B. Do NOT begin a new paragraph with the preceding sentence.
    C. OMIT the preceding sentence and begin a new paragraph with "Men read. . ."
    D. End the first paragraph with the preceding sentence, and begin the second paragraph with "Men read. . ."

the book <u>was welcomed</u>. These
                60
extraordinary creatures, whose actions

it is impossible to predict and

<u>who will now and then love, or affect to</u>
                    61
<u>love, their enemies</u> better than their
        61
friends, cherished the book, and asked

for its author. He had not put his name

on the title page. In place of an author's

name was a griffin between

<u>wheatsheaves, perhaps a</u>
                62
<u>symbol</u> or a family crest. Many inquired
    62   .
of the publisher for further

enlightenment, but he kept the author's

secret and increased the mystery.

60. F. NO CHANGE
     G. had been wel-
         comed.
     H. is welcomed.
     J. was welcome.

61. A. NO CHANGE
     B. who will now
         and then love,
         or effect to
         love, their en-
         emies
     C. who will love,
         or effect to
         love their en-
         emies.
     D. who will now
         and then love
         or affect to
         love their en-
         emies

62. F. NO CHANGE
     G. wheatsheaves,
         perhaps sym-
         bolic of
     H. wheatsheaves,
         perhaps, a
         symbol, or
     J. wheatsheaves,
         perhaps

(3)

One adventurous lady went to the

Herald's College and there, after

immense labor, <u>ascertained that</u> griffin
                         63

between wheatsheaves was the crest of

Sir Austin Feverel, a man of wealth,

honor, and a somewhat lamentable

history. Sir Austin had been married,

<u>and he had been deserted by his</u>
                    64

<u>wife for another man.</u> He must surely be
          64

the author the lady concluded and

published her conclusions

to the world. ⬜65

63. A. NO CHANGE
    B. found out the discovery that
    C. made the discovery that
    D. discovered the fact that

64. F. NO CHANGE
    G. and he was deserted by his wife for another man.
    H. and his wife deserted him for another man.
    J. and for another man he had been deserted by his wife.

65. The passage is probably an excerpt taken from
    A. a newspaper editorial.
    B. a novel.
    C. a biography.
    D. a history.

Passage VI

(1)

When <u>usual, conservative</u>
 ₆₆
businesspeople call for government

controls on hospital costs, it's a sure sign

that the hospitals are losing the public

opinion battle to the regulators. And no

wonder. The cost of hospital care

<u>quadrupling</u> in the last ten years, while
 ₆₇
the consumer price index has not quite

doubled in the same period. Nationwide,

hospital costs are now rising at a rate of

16% yearly, <u>and this is three times the</u>
 ₆₈
<u>current state of inflation.</u> To impose a
 ₆₈
form of price control would be to use a

66. F. NO CHANGE
    G. usual conser-
       vative
    H. usual and con-
       servative
    J. usually conser-
       vative

67. A. NO CHANGE
    B. having quad-
       rupled
    C. has quad-
       rupled
    D. having in-
       creased four
       times

68. F. NO CHANGE
    G. which is a rate
       three times the
       current infla-
       tion rate.
    H. and this is
       three times the
       current rate of
       inflation.
    J. three times the
       current infla-
       tion rate.

method with a poor track record. ☐69

The average hospital bill today is $4000,

three times the average only four

years ago. ☐70

69. A. NO CHANGE
    B. MOVE the preceding sentence to begin the first paragraph.
    C. MOVE the preceding sentence to end the first paragraph.
    D. OMIT the preceding sentence.

70. The preceding statistic would be more significant if we were also told
    F. what the average bill two years ago was.
    G. how long a hospital stay this bill represents.
    H. how many hospitals have a higher average bill.
    J. what the average doctor's bill is.

These <u>dismal statistics</u> translate into
                 71
steadily rising insurance premiums for

companies which offer health insurance

to their workers.

71. A. NO CHANGE
    B. These statistics
    C. These figures
    D. Figures like
       these

(2)

Hospital economics are simply too

insulated from the normal competitive

pressures <u>that restrains</u> costs elsewhere
             72
in the economy. With ninety percent of

all hospital bills paid by government

health care programs on a cost incurred

basis, hospitals have no <u>insistence</u> to
                          73
control costs. A government task force

has urged insurers to negotiate directly

with hospitals to revise payment

formulas and impose <u>economizing</u>
                      74
<u>discipline</u> on hospital expenditures.
   74

72. F. NO CHANGE
    G. which restrains
    H. that restrain
    J. to restrain

73. A. NO CHANGE
    B. instinct
    C. insurance
    D. incentive

74. F. NO CHANGE
    G. economic dis-
       cipline
    H. economic dis-
       cretion
    J. economics and
       discipline

But the <u>key to blocking the skyrocket</u>
                        75
<u>of hospital cost spiral</u> without
        75
government interference remains in the

hands of hospital administrators.

75. A. NO CHANGE
    B. the key to
       stopping the
       skyrocketing
       hospital cost
       spiral
    C. unlocking the
       skyrocket of
       hospital costs
    D. stopping fast-
       rising hospital
       costs

STOP. IF YOU FINISH BEFORE TIME IS CALLED, CHECK
YOUR WORK ON THIS SECTION ONLY. DO NOT WORK
ON ANY OTHER SECTION IN THE TEST.

TEST 2: MATHEMATICS

Time: 60 Minutes
60 Problems

DIRECTIONS

In the Mathematics Test, each of the problems includes five choices (A, B, C, D, E or F, G, H, J, K). You are to solve each problem and choose the correct answer.

1. If 20% of a class averages 80% on a test, 50% of the class averages 60% on the test, and the remainder of the class averages 40% on the test, what is the overall class average?
   (A) 64   (B) 60   (C) 58   (D) 56   (E) 54

2. A full container holds $\frac{5}{8}$ gallon of liquid. If the container is $\frac{4}{5}$ full and then 25% of the liquid is lost due to evaporation, how much liquid is left in the container?
   (F) $\frac{1}{4}$ gallon   (J) $\frac{5}{8}$ gallon
   (G) $\frac{3}{8}$ gallon   (K) $\frac{3}{4}$ gallon
   (H) $\frac{1}{2}$ gallon

3. Two similar polygons have perimeters in the ratio of 3 to 4. If the smaller has an area of 36, what is the area of the larger?
   (A) $20\frac{1}{4}$ (B) 27   (C) 48   (D) 64   (E) 72

4. If $f(x) = 2x + 4$ and $g(x) = x^2 - 2$, then $f[g(3)] =$
   (F) 12   (G) 14   (H) 18   (J) 70   (K) 98

5. What is the 10th term in the following sequence: 5, 6, 8, 11, 15, . . . ?
   (A) 20   (B) 35   (C) 41   (D) 50   (E) 60

6. In 6 years, Tony will be twice as old as he was 4 years ago. How old will Tony be in 4 years?
   (F) 12 years   (J) 18 years
   (G) 14 years   (K) 20 years
   (H) 16 years

7. The chart on the right represents an inventory of the number of toys in the storeroom of Acme Toy Company. If a child were to choose one of these toys at random, what would be the probability that the chosen toy is worth under $5.00?

Number of Toys	Value Each
140	$3.98
60	$4.98
178	$5.98
122	$6.98
500 total	

(A) 3/25   (B) 7/25   (C) 2/5   (D) 1/2   (E) 3/5

8. Tom's collection of 50 coins consists of dimes and quarters totaling $7.10. How many more dimes than quarters does Tom have?

(F) 14   (G) 20   (H) 22   (J) 26   (K) 36

9. Evaluate: $3 + \cfrac{3}{3 + \cfrac{3}{3 + \cfrac{3}{3 + 3}}}$

(A) $3\frac{23}{27}$ (B) $3\frac{7}{9}$ (C) $3\frac{19}{27}$ (D) $3\frac{17}{27}$ (E) $3\frac{1}{3}$

10. If you bicycle 10 miles per hour for y hours and y miles per hour for 10 hours, how far have you bicycled?

(F) $20 + 2y$ (J) $100/y^2$
(G) $20y$ (K) $100y^2$
(H) $(y^2 + 100)/10y$

11. In the figure below, $\angle w + \angle z = 170°$.

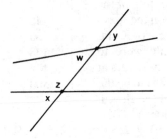

Which of the following is (are) true?

     I. $\angle x > \angle y$
     II. $\angle x$ and $\angle z$ are supplementary
     III. $\angle x < 90°$

(A) I only
(B) I and II only
(C) I and III only
(D) II and III only
(E) I, II, and III

12. An empty fuel tank is filled with brand Z gasoline. When the tank is half empty, it is filled with brand Y gasoline. When the tank is half empty again, it is filled with brand Z gasoline. When the tank is half empty again it is filled with brand Y gasoline. At this time, what percent of the gasoline in the tank is brand Z?

(F) 50%
(G) 40%
(H) $33\frac{1}{3}\%$
(J) 25%
(K) None of these

13. What is 0.7% of 30?

(A) 0.021   (B) 0.21   (C) 2.1   (D) 21   (E) 210

14. $\dfrac{(4^{2x})(4^{x})(2^{4x})}{(2^{6x})(4^{3x})(2^{2x})} =$

(F) 2^{4x} (G) 4^{2x} (H) $\dfrac{1}{4^{2x}}$ (J) $\dfrac{1}{2^{2x}}$ (K) $\dfrac{1}{4^{x}}$

15. How many 3-person committees can be formed in a club with 8 members?

(A) 8   (B) 24   (C) 48   (D) 56   (E) 336

16. In rectangle *ABCD* below, *BC* = 4, *CD* = 10, and *BE* = *x*. What is the area of the shaded region?

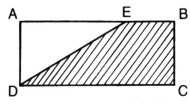

(F) 20 + 2*x*
(G) 20 + 4*x*
(H) (40 −*x*)/2

(J) 20 + *x*
(K) 40 + 2*x*

17. At a party there were 5 times as many females as males. There were 3 times as many adults as children. Which of the following could not be the number of people at the party?
    (A) 72   (B) 120   (C) 216   (D) 258   (E) 384

18. Which of the following is the largest?
    (F) Half of 30% of 280
    (G) One third of 70% of 160
    (H) Twice 50% of 30
    (J) Three times 40% of 40
    (K) 60% of 60

19. $\dfrac{12\sqrt{6} - 6\sqrt{50}}{\sqrt{72}} =$

    (A) 2
    (B) $(\sqrt{3} - \sqrt{2})/2$
    (C) $3\sqrt{2} - 6\sqrt{3}$

    (D) $2\sqrt{3} - 5$
    (E) None of these

20. If electricity costs *x* cents per kilowatt hour for the first 30 kilowatt hours and *y* cents per kilowatt hour for each additional kilowatt hour, what is the cost of *z* kilowatt hours (*z* > 30)?
    (F) 30(*x* − *y*) + *yz*
    (G) (*z* − 30)*x* + 30*y*
    (H) 30*y* − 30*x* + *yz*

    (J) 30*x* + (*y* − 30)*z*
    (K) 30(*x* + *y*) − *yz*

21. What is the point of intersection of the two lines with the following equations: $3y + 2x = 18$ and $y = 4x - 8$?
   (A) $(8, -3)$ (D) $(2, 0)$
   (B) $(4, 3)$ (E) $(-3, 8)$
   (C) $(3, 4)$

22. In the figure below, $AB \parallel CE$, $AE = 12$, $DE = 6$, and $CE = 4$. What is the length of AB?

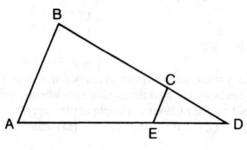

   (F) 6   (G) 8   (H) 10   (J) 12   (K) 18

23. Using 3 standard dice, what is the approximate probability of rolling a combination totaling 4?
   (A) $\frac{1}{18}$ (B) $\frac{1}{36}$ (C) $\frac{1}{64}$ (D) $\frac{1}{72}$ (E) $\frac{1}{108}$

24. Where does the graph of the equation $y + 4 = 2x^2$ cross the graph of the equation $x = -1$?
   (F) -6 (G) -2 (H) 0   (J) 2   (K) 6

25. If $6x - 3y = 30$ and $4x = 2 - y$, then what is the value of $x + y$?
   (A) -8 (B) -6 (C) -4 (D) 2   (E) 8

26. If a 32-inch chord is drawn in a circle of radius 20 inches, how far is the chord from the center of the circle?
   (F) 4 inches   (J) 10 inches
   (G) 6 inches   (K) 12 inches
   (H) 8 inches

27. If $7x = 3y$, what is the ratio of x to y?
   (A) 7/3   (B) 7/4   (C) 4/3   (D) 4/7   (E) 3/7

28. If $\dfrac{3}{y} + \dfrac{4}{2y} = \dfrac{3}{4}$, what is the value of y?

    (F) 8   (G) $6\frac{2}{3}$ (H) $4\frac{1}{2}$ (J) $2\frac{3}{4}$ (K) $1\frac{1}{3}$

29. What are the coordinates of one endpoint of a segment if the other endpoint has coordinates (x, y) and the midpoint has coordinates $(3x, -3y)$?

    (A) $(2x, -y)$ (D) $(4x, -2y)$

    (B) $(-2x, y)$ (E) $(7x, -5y)$

    (C) $(5x, -7y)$

30. Tim's weight is 12 kg more than twice Jane's weight. What is Tim's weight if they weigh 135 kg together?

    (F) 94 kg   (J) 61.5 kg

    (G) 82 kg   (K) 41 kg

    (H) 73.5 kg

31. If $i = \sqrt{-1}$, simplify $\dfrac{1}{3 + i}$

    (A) $\dfrac{3 - i}{10}$ (D) $\dfrac{i - 3}{8}$

    (B) $\dfrac{i - 3}{10}$ (E) $\dfrac{1}{3i}$

    (C) $\dfrac{3 - i}{8}$

32. Find the product of $(5x^2y)$, $(-2xy^2)$, and $(-3y^4)$.

    (F) $30x^2y^8$ (J) $-30x^2y^8$

    (G) $-30x^3y^7$ (K) $60x^3y^7$

    (H) $30x^3y^7$

33. An item that normally sells for \$40.00 has been marked down 10%. If 10% sales tax is added to the discount price, how much will the item cost including tax?

    (A) \$36.10   (D) \$40.40

    (B) \$39.60   (E) \$44.00

    (C) \$40.00

34. In the figure below, $AB \perp BC$, $BD \perp AC$, and each triangle is scalene. What is the length of AC?

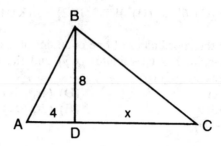

   (F) 12   (J) 32
   (G) 16   (K) Cannot be determined
   (H) 20

35. If 6 apples and 2 pears weigh the same as 3 apples and 6 pears, how many apples will it take to balance 12 pears?
   (A) 3   (B) 5   (C) 6   (D) 9   (E) 12

36. In the figure below, angle x and angle z are complementary. In terms of angle y, what is the measure of angle z?

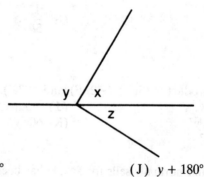

   (F) $y - 90°$ (J) $y + 180°$
   (G) $180° - y$ (K) $90° - y$
   (H) $90° + y$

37. What is the approximate value of $\sqrt{2491/103}$?
   (A) 50   (B) 25   (C) 24   (D) 5   (E) 4

38. $1 - 2 + 3 - 4 + 5 - \cdots + 99 =$
    (F) 100   (G) 50   (H) 0   (J) -50 (K) -100

39. Twenty-seven cubes are arranged as shown below and placed on a flat board. Then the exposed surfaces are painted. Not counting the bottom surfaces on the board, how many unpainted sides are there?

    (A) 41   (D) 82
    (B) 44   (E) 84
    (C) 76

40. If $12 < 2x < 18$ and $-9 < 3y < 6$, then which of the following is (are) true?

$$\text{I. } 3 < x + y < 11$$
$$\text{II. } -12 < y - x < -4$$
$$\text{III. } x > 7$$

    (F) I only   (J) I and III only
    (G) III only   (K) I and II only
    (H) II and III only

41. A student received the following scores on 5 exams: 32, 20, 40, 42, 36. Which of the following scores would the student need to receive on the sixth test so that the median score and the mean score would be the same:
    (A) 46   (B) 48   (C) 52   (D) 58   (E) 60

42. Three consecutive odd numbers add up to 15 more than twice the smallest. What is the sum of the 3 numbers?
    (F) 33   (G) 31   (H) 29   (J) 28   (K) 26

43. $\dfrac{(5^2 + 5^1)(5^3 + 5^2)}{5^2} =$

    (A) 625   (D) 150

    (B) 180   (E) 15

    (C) 156

44. The longest side of a right triangle is 6 feet in length. The second side is half the length of the third side. What is the length of the third side?

    (F) $\dfrac{6\sqrt{5}}{5}$ (J) $5\sqrt{5}$

    (G) $\dfrac{3\sqrt{5}}{5}$ (K) $12\sqrt{5}$

    (H) $\dfrac{12\sqrt{5}}{5}$

45. If parallelogram $ABCD$ below has a height of 6 inches and a base of 8 inches and angle A is equal to $60°$, what is the perimeter of the parallelogram?

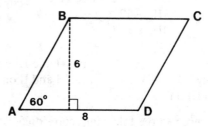

    (A) $16(1 + 3\sqrt{3})$ (D) $8(1 + \sqrt{3})$

    (B) $8(4 + \sqrt{3})$ (E) $8(2 + \sqrt{3})$

    (C) $4(4 + \sqrt{3})$

46. Line A has a slope of $\frac{3}{4}$. What is the equation of a line that passes through the point $(0, 1)$ and is perpendicular to line A?

    (F) $4x - 3y = 3$ (J) $4x - 3y = -3$

    (G) $3x - 4y = -4$ (K) $4x + 3y = 3$

    (H) $3x + 4y = 4$

47. If the supplement of angle x is 4 times its complement, what is the measure of angle x?

(A) 30°   (B) 45°   (C) 60°   (D) 120°   (E) 150°

48. Which of the following is equivalent to $\dfrac{\sqrt{5}+2}{\sqrt{3}}$?

(F) $\dfrac{\sqrt{5}+\sqrt{6}}{3}$

(J) $\dfrac{2\sqrt{15}+\sqrt{3}}{3}$

(G) $\sqrt{15}+\sqrt{6}$

(K) $\dfrac{\sqrt{15}+2\sqrt{3}}{3}$

(H) $\dfrac{\sqrt{5}+2\sqrt{3}}{3}$

49. Triangle ABC has its vertices at $(2, 8)$, $(9, 7)$, and $(4, 2)$. What is the area of triangle ABC?

(A) 20   (B) 24   (C) 24.5   (D) 28   (E) 32

50. As shown in the drawing below, a tower casts a shadow 60 feet long. If the angle of elevation of the sun is 40°, what is the height of the tower?

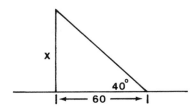

(F) 60 sin 40°   (J) 60 cot 40°
(G) 60 tan 40°   (K) 60 cot 50°
(H) 60 tan 50°

51. If a regular hexagon has a perimeter 48 inches, what is its area?

(A) $60\sqrt{2}$ (D) $96\sqrt{2}$
(B) $96\sqrt{3}$ (E) $72\sqrt{3}$
(C) $48\sqrt{3}$

52. Three lines intersect as shown below to form the indicated angles. If $b + c = 160°$ and if $a = 50°$, what is the measure of angle d?

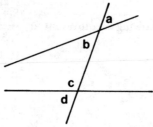

(F) 50°
(G) 60°
(H) 70°
(J) 80°
(K) Cannot be determined

53. Lou scored an average of 60 of his first four tests. What must he score on his fifth test so that the average of the five tests will be 70?

(A) 80
(B) 90
(C) 95
(D) 100
(E) 110

54. A circle and a square have the same area. What is the ratio of the perimeter of the square to the circumference of the circle?

(F) 1:1   (G) π:3   (H) 4:π (J) $\sqrt{\pi}$:2   (K) $2\sqrt{\pi}$:π

55. $\dfrac{9 - \dfrac{1}{p^2}}{3 - \dfrac{1}{p}} =$

(A) $3 - \dfrac{1}{p}$

(B) $3 + \dfrac{1}{p^2}$

(C) $\dfrac{3p - 1}{p}$

(D) $\dfrac{3p + 1}{p}$

(E) $6 - p$

56. A racetrack is made up of 2 straight sections and 2 semicircular sections as shown below. How many meters is it around the racetrack?

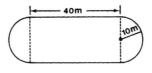

(F) $20(4 + \pi)$

(J) $40(2 + \pi)$

(G) $20(6 + \pi)$

(K) None of the above

(H) $100(8 + \pi)$

57. $\dfrac{(m^6n)^{-2}(mn^{-2})^3}{(m^{-2}n^{-2})^{-2}} =$

(A) $\dfrac{1}{m^{13}n^{12}}$

(D) $\dfrac{n^3}{n^4}$

(B) m^6n^4

(E) $\dfrac{m}{n^8}$

(C) $\dfrac{m^2}{n^8}$

58. What is the value of X in the figure below?

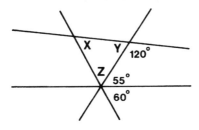

(F) $65°$ (G) $60°$ (H) $55°$ (J) $50°$ (K) $45°$

59. Using the figure below, what is the value in meters of x?

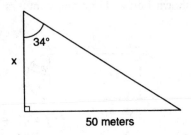

50 meters

(A) 50 sin 34°

(D) 50/tan 34°

(B) 50 cos 34°

(E) 50/cos 34°

(C) 50 tan 34°

60. One half a number is 6 greater than twice a second number. If the second number is 9 greater than the first number, then what is the value of the larger number?

(F) −20   (G) −16   (H) −7   (J) 4   (K) 10

STOP. IF YOU FINISH BEFORE TIME IS CALLED, CHECK YOUR WORK ON THIS SECTION ONLY. DO NOT WORK ON ANY OTHER SECTION IN THE TEST.

TEST 3: READING

Time: 35 Minutes
40 Questions

DIRECTIONS

Each of the four passages in this test is followed by questions. Read the passage and choose the best answer to each question. Return to the passage as often as necessary to answer the questions.

Passage I

Is it useful to compare the works of the greatest artists? Should an art student be encouraged to paint like Leonardo *and* Goya, though one is Italian and the other Spanish, and they lived in different centuries? It is, indeed, true that there *is* a relative merit, that a peach is nobler than a hawthorn berry. But in each rank of fruits, as in each rank of masters, one is endowed with one virtue, and another with another; their glory is their dissimilarity, and they who propose in the training of an artist that he should unite the coloring of Tintoretto, the finish of Durer, and the tenderness of Correggio are no wiser than a horticulturist would be who made it the object of his labor to produce a fruit which should unite in itself the lusciousness of the grape, the crispness of the nut, and the fragrance of the pine.

And from these considerations one most important practical corollary is to be deduced, namely, that the greatness or smallness of a man is, in the most conclusive sense, determined for him at his birth, as strictly as it is determined for a fruit whether it is to be a currant or an apricot. Education, favorable circumstances, resolution, and industry can do much; in a certain sense they do *everything;* that is to say, they determine whether the apricot shall fall blighted by the wind, or whether it shall reach maturity. But apricot out of currant—great man out of small—did never yet art or effort make; and, in a general way, men have their excellence nearly fixed for them when they are born; a little cramped and frostbitten on one side, a little sun-burned and fortune-spotted on the other, they reach between good and evil chances, such size and taste as generally belong to the men of their caliber.

Therefore it is, that every system of teaching is false which holds forth "great art" as in any wise to be taught to students or even to be aimed at by them. Great art is precisely that which never was, nor will be, taught. It is preeminently and finally the expression of the spirits of great men; so that the only wholesome teaching is that which simply endeavors to fix those characters of nobleness in the pupil's mind, without holding out to him, as a possible or even probable result, that he should ever paint like Titian or carve like Michael Angelo. Such teaching enforces upon him the assured duty of endeavoring to draw in a manner at least honest and intelligible and cultivates in him those general charities of heart, sincerities of thought, and graces of habit which are likely to lead him, throughout life, to prefer openness to affectation, realities to shadows, and beauty to corruption.

1. Which of the following is the best title for this passage?
   (A) The Comparison of Great Artists
   (B) The Uniqueness of Artistic Genius
   (C) How to Train an Artist
   (D) Artists are Made, Not Born

2. According to the first paragraph of the passage, the great artists are
   (F) alike
   (G) dissimilar
   (H) poor models for student artists
   (J) no wiser than horticulturists

3. The development of the first paragraph of the passage depends chiefly upon
   (A) the posing of a question and the offering of a series of answers
   (B) an extended analogy
   (C) a series of rhetorical questions
   (D) a contrast of the specific and the general

4. In the second paragraph, the author compares men to fruits to stress
   (F) the importance of inborn ability
   (G) the importance of good luck
   (H) the importance of determination and hard work
   (J) man's ability to control his destiny

5. The comparison of artists to fruits is employed in
   (A) the second paragraph only
   (B) the first and second paragraphs only
   (C) the first and third paragraphs only
   (D) all three paragraphs

6. The author of the passage would probably believe that a great dancer achieved success chiefly because of
   (F) hard work
   (G) an intense will to succeed
   (H) inborn ability
   (J) excellent coaching

7. The author would probably approve of all of the following qualities in a work of art EXCEPT
   (A) reality   (C) tenderness
   (B) finish   (D) vagueness

8. The author would probably disagree with all of the following EXCEPT
   (F) all artists are equally valuable
   (G) contemporary artists should be taught to imitate the works of the great artists of the past
   (H) greatness in art is unteachable
   (J) birth alone will determine artistic success

9. The author would be likely to condemn a work of art for all of the following reasons EXCEPT
   (A) dishonesty   (C) unreality
   (B) simplicity   (D) affectation

10. What the last paragraph suggests should be taught to prospective artists implies that the author believes
    (F) there is no significant connection between the character of the artists and the work of art
    (G) an evil artist might produce noble art
    (H) there is a relation between the character of the artist and the work of art
    (J) a virtuous artist may produce corrupt art

Passage II

I had shut the door to. Then I turned around, and there he was. I used to be scared of him all the time, he tanned me so much. I reckoned I was scared now, too; but in a minute I see I was mistaken—that is, after the first jolt, as you may say, when my breath sort of hitched, he being so unexpected; but right away after I see I warn't scared of him worth bothring about.

He was most fifty, and he looked it. His hair was long and tangled and greasy, and hung down, and you could see his eyes shining through like he was behind vines. It was all black, no gray; so was his long, mixed-up whiskers. There warn't no color in his face, where his face showed; it was white; not like another man's white, but a white to make a body sick, a white to make a body's flesh crawl—a tree-toad white, a fish-belly white. As for his cloths—just rags, that was all. He had one ankle resting on t'other knee; the boot on that foot was busted, and two of his toes stuck through, and he worked them now and then. His hat was laying on the floor—an old black slouch with the top caved in, like a lid.

I stood a-looking at him; he set there a-looking at me, with his chair tilted back a little. I set the candle down. I noticed the window was up; so he had clumb in by the shed. He kept a-looking me all over. By and by he says:

"Starchy clothes—very. You think you're a good deal of a big-bug, *don't* you?"

"Maybe I am, maybe I ain't," I says.

"Don't you give me none o' your lip," says he. "You've put on considerable many frills since I been away. I'll take you down a peg before I get done with you. You're educated, too,

they say—can read and write. You think you're better'n your
father, now, don't you, because he can't? *I'll* take it out of you.
Who told you you might meddle with such hifalut'n foolishness,
hey?—who told you you could?"

"The widow. She told me."

"The widow, hey?—and who told the widow she could put in
her shovel about a thing that ain't none of her business?"

"Nobody never told her."

"Well, I'll learn her how to meddle. And looky here—you
drop that school, you hear? I'll learn people to bring up a boy to
put on airs over his own father and let on to be better'n what *he*
is. You lemme catch you fooling around that school again, you
hear? Your mother couldn't read, and she couldn't write,
nuther, before she died. None of the family couldn't before *they*
died. *I* can't; and here you're a-swelling yourself up like this. I
ain't the man to stand it—you hear? Say, lemme hear you
read."

I took up a book and begun something about General
Washington and the wars. When I'd read about a half a minute,
he fetched the book a whack with his hand and knocked it
across the house. He says:

"It's so. You can do it. I had my doubts when you told me.
Now looky here; you stop that putting on frills. I won't have it.
I'll lay for you, my smarty; and if I catch you about that school
I'll tan you good. First you know you'll get religion, too. I never
see such a son."

11. The two characters who appear in the scene are
    (A) an uncle and his nephew
    (B) a father and his daughter
    (C) a father and his son
    (D) two former friends meeting again after a separation

12. From details in the passage, we can infer that this scene takes
place
    (F) out of doors in warm weather
    (G) indoors in winter
    (H) indoors at night
    (J) indoors during the day

13. The state of mind of the speaker in the first paragraph is best
    described as
    (A) terrified
    (B) startled, but not frightened
    (C) frightened at first, then pleased
    (D) unaffected

14. The description in the second paragraph differs from the rest of
    the passage because it several times uses
    (F) indirect discourse   (H) denotative language
    (G) simile and metaphor   (J) incorrect grammar

15. The effect of the description in the second paragraph is to make
    the man described appear
    (A) pitiable   (C) repulsive
    (B) interesting   (D) mysterious

16. When the visitor says "Starchy clothes—very. You think you're
    a good deal of a big-bug, *don't* you, " he is expressing his
    (F) surprise at how much the other has grown
    (G) admiration of the clothes the other is wearing
    (H) contempt at the other's supposed complacence
    (J) amusement at the way the other is dressed

17. In narrating the passage, the author uses which three of the
    following?
    (A) a first person narrator, dialogue, action that took place in
        the past
    (B) a third person narrator, action taking place in the present,
        monologue
    (C) a second person narrator, dialogue, action taking place in
        the present
    (D) a first person narrator, action taking place in the present,
        monologue

18. From details in the passage, we can infer that the narrator's mother
    (F) is a widow
    (G) was uneducated and is no longer alive
    (H) came from a social position above that of the father
    (J) deserted his father before her death

19. Why does the second speaker ask to hear the first speaker read?
    (A) because he is interested in war
    (B) because he wishes to find out if the other can read
    (C) because he hates reading and readers
    (D) because he cannot read himself

20. In the course of the passage, the visitor expresses his contempt for all of the following EXCEPT
    (F) school   (H) ignorance
    (G) decent clothes   (J) religion

Passage III

Scholars concede that Tutankhamen's is "the richest royal tomb of antiquity ever found." Yet, since it belonged to an obscure "boy king" who ruled only nine years (from about 1334 to 1325 B.C.), it has been assumed that mightier pharoahs must indeed have had richer tombs, although most of the evidence has long since vanished.

Tutankhamen was more than a pharaoh. He was a milestone, a symbol of restored order after an interlude of chaos. Egypt had long been dominated by the vast priesthood of the state god Amun-Re. The priests profited from the spoils of Egypt's foreign conquests, and they shared power with the pharoahs. Then, under Amenophis III, the stage was set for the dwindling of the priests' power, and under his son, who became known as Akhenaten, disaster struck. Akhenaten had the effrontery to sponsor a universal sun god called Aten. He abandoned the priestly stronghold at Thebes, sailed down the Nile to a site he called Akhenaten, and built a new religious capital.

The priests were irate, and the rest of Egypt worried. The populace hated to give up all their beloved gods, and when Akhenaten died, the reaction was inevitable. The priests recaptured their power, and the boy Tutankhamen became pharaoh. To many of his subjects, he represented a welcome return to "old times," For this reason, one modern scholar suggests that, when Tutankhamen died at about the age of 18, this tomb may have been outfitted with extra elegance.

Whatever the case, the contents of the tomb are full of clues to Egyptian history. Take the little alabaster unguent jar. Represented in the handle are two long-stemmed flowers, the lotus of Upper Egypt and the papyrus plant of Lower Egypt. After a fierce battle, these two regions were united about 3000 B.C. and subsequently the flowers were often pictured with their stems knotted together as an emblem of peaceful unity.

The early Egyptian, like most of mankind, tried to protect himself against misfortune. His gods, amulets, and magic writings were all part of his protective equipment. Tutankhamen's mirror case was shaped like an ankh, a cross with a loop at the top. Potent symbols of life, ankhs were seen everywhere. Another ubiquitous emblem was the eye, which appears on the clasp on Tutankhamen's bracelet. One of the holiest symbols of Egyptian religion, the eye at different periods was identified with the sun and moon.

The uses of tomb treasure were both magical and practical, with no sharp line between them. An example of double usefulness is Tutankhamen's ivory headrest, with two lions on its base and Shu, the god of air, holding up the curved head support. This would serve the king in a practical way in the afterworld—just as it did on earth—but, also, since the human head was regarded as the seat of life, a headrest had a magical efficacy in the attempt to defy death.

21. The central concern of the passage is
    (A) Egyptian gods
    (B) Egyptian dynastic history
    (C) Egyptian symbols
    (D) Tutankhamen's tomb

22. The first paragraph of the passage is logically related to the second and third paragraphs because
   (F) all three deal with Egyptian pharaohs
   (G) paragraphs two and three discuss the pharaohs who followed Tutankhamen
   (H) paragraphs two and three discuss Egyptian religion in the reigns before Tutankhamen
   (J) paragraphs two and three offer an explanation for the richness of Tutankhamen's tomb

23. Tutankhamen was probably born in
   (A) 1325 B.C.   (C) 1343 B.C.
   (B) 1334 B.C.   (D) 1352 B.C.

24. The words *disaster* and *effrontery* in the second paragraph represent the point of view of
   (F) the author of the passage
   (G) scholars of Egyptian history
   (H) Akhenaten
   (J) the priests

25. According to the passage, the accession of Tutankhamen was welcomed by many Egyptians because
   (A) the religious capital at Thebes was restored
   (B) polytheism was restored
   (C) the kingdoms of Upper and Lower Egypt were reunited
   (D) the priests were removed from power

26. From information in the passage, we can infer that the priests were able to reclaim their authority at the death of Akhenaten because

   I. the people wished to return to the old religion
   II. the new king was only a child
   III. the populace was enraged by the cost of Akhenaten's tomb

   (F) I and II only   (H) II and III only
   (G) I and III only   (J) I, II, and III

27. It is significant that the plants chosen to represent Upper Egypt and Lower Egypt are both plants
    (A) associated with writing
    (B) associated with water
    (C) associated with food
    (D) with beautiful flowers

28. From details of the passage, we can infer that ancient Egyptians were believers in

      I. a life after death
     II. magic
    III. the efficacy of the priesthood

    (F) I and II only   (H) II and III only
    (G) I and III only   (J) I, II, and III

29. All of the following are Egyptian gods EXCEPT
    (A) Ankh   (C) Shu
    (B) Amun-Re   (D) Aten

30. That the kings who ruled longer and were more important historically than Tutankhamen had richer and larger tombs is
    (F) disproved in this passage
    (G) unresolved by this passage
    (H) an issue this passage never raises
    (J) proven in this passage

Passage IV

Comparatively few freshwater species of fishes are limited in their distribution to a single river system, yet not many are found on both sides of a high mountain ridge, such as the Rocky Mountains in North America. That is to say, the fishes of the Mississippi Valley are generally different and distinct from those of the Pacific slope.

While it is a well-known fact that the fish life in no two river systems, even though they empty into the sea on the same side of a divide, is identical, such streams do have many species in common. The principal rivers of the Atlantic slope of the

United States, for example, contain several species common to all of them, including the bullhead catfish, the bluegill sunfish, and the largemouth bass. None of these species can endure salt water, so they cannot now migrate from one river system to another. On the other hand, the more northern streams contain species not found in the southern ones, and vice versa. The common pike, for example, is found in the Atlantic streams from Maryland northward, and the brook trout and yellow perch occur only in the streams from North Carolina southward.

How the present distribution came about must remain a matter of conjecture. It is quite probable that some of the streams, including those on opposite sides of a divide, may have been connected at one time. Again, streams may be entirely separate during normal weather, but an exceptionally heavy rainfall or the sudden melting of snow in the uplands sometimes causes floods which may form a temporary connection between them, providing a passageway for fishes. It is possible, also, that water birds may accidentally carry fish or spawn from one stream to another, or that man may be instrumental in such a transfer.

Evidently, then, freshwater fishes may become distributed far beyond the confines of the stream of their origin. The chief factor in limiting the still wider distribution of species is temperature. This forms such an efficient barrier that comparatively few species of freshwater fishes of the United States extend their range into Mexico. In Panama only one fish common to the fresh waters of the States has been found, and that is the eel, which is not strictly a freshwater form, as it enters salt water to spawn and is taken in fairly salty water at other times.

31. According to the first paragraph of the passage, in which of the following pairs of states should we expect the freshwater fishes to be most similar?
    (A) Oregon and New Jersey
    (B) New York and Delaware
    (C) California and Kentucky
    (D) Washington and Vermont

32. The freshwater fish life found in two river systems at approximately the same latitude and on the same side of a continental divide is
    (F) never just the same
    (G) likely to be very different
    (H) always just the same
    (J) often just the same

33. In which of the following lists are all three species of freshwater fish likely to be found in waters of South Carolina?
    (A) bullhead catfish, largemouth bass, pike
    (B) bluegill sunfish, pike, largemouth bass
    (C) largemouth bass, yellow perch, pike
    (D) bullhead catfish, brook trout, bluegill sunfish

34. According to the passage, exceptionally heavy rains or exceptionally large snow meltings may explain
    (F) sudden rises in freshwater fish populations
    (G) sudden declines in freshwater fish populations
    (H) why fish of the same species are found in different water systems
    (J) why fish of different species are seldom found in water systems on different sides of a high mountain ridge

35. Which of the following statements helps to explain why the freshwater system on one side of a high mountain ridge has so few species in common with the freshwater system on the other side?

    I. It is possible that the streams on both sides of the ridge were once connected.
    II. Most species of freshwater fish cannot endure salt water.
    III. Water birds that cross mountain ridges often carry fish spawn from one stream to another.

    (A) I only   (C) I and III only
    (B) II only   (D) II and III only

36. Of the following, which fish is evidently least sensitive to variations in temperature?
    (F) the pike   (H) the eel
    (G) the bluegill sunfish (J) the brook trout

37. According to the last paragraph of the passage, in which of the following pairs of states should we expect the species of freshwater fish to be most similar?
    (A) New York and Rhode Island
    (B) Michigan and Georgia
    (C) Maine and Florida
    (D) Minnesota and Mississippi

38. According to the passage, the chief deterrent to a wider distribution of the species of freshwater fish is
    (F) water pollution
    (G) the loss of habitat due to human encroachment on nature
    (H) temperature
    (J) the salinity of the oceans

39. We should expect the largest number of freshwater fish species found in the northeastern United States to be found also in
    (A) Mexico   (C) Panama
    (B) Canada   (D) Peru

40. The best title for this passage would be
    (F) Temperature, Geography, and the Distribution of Fish
    (G) North American Fish and Their Separation by Mountain Ridges
    (H) The Distribution of Freshwater Fish Species in North America
    (J) The Distribution of Freshwater Fish and Its Causes

STOP. IF YOU FINISH BEFORE TIME IS CALLED, CHECK YOUR WORK ON THIS SECTION ONLY. DO NOT WORK ON ANY OTHER SECTION IN THE TEST.

TEST 4: SCIENCE REASONING

Time: 35 Minutes
40 Questions

DIRECTIONS

Each passage in this test is followed by several questions. After you read each passage, select the correct choice for each of the questions that follow the passage. Refer back to the passage as often as necessary to answer the questions.

Passage I

The following graph shows the variation of temperature with altitude in our atmosphere. The four layers of different shades correspond to atmospheric zones, which are named in the right side of the graph.

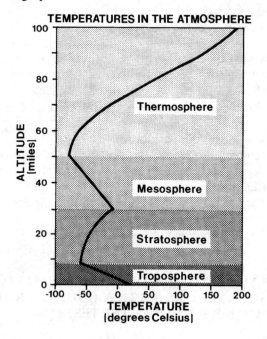

TEMPERATURES IN THE ATMOSPHERE

1. What is the temperature of the atmosphere at an altitude of 70 miles?
   (A) −80°C   (C) 27°C
   (B) −15°C   (D) 50°C

2. Which of the 4 atmospheric zones has the smallest range of temperatures?
   (F) mesosphere   (H) thermosphere
   (G) stratosphere   (J) troposphere

3. Which two atmospheric zones show decreasing temperature with increasing altitude?
   (A) mesosphere and troposphere
   (B) stratosphere and thermosphere
   (C) thermosphere and mesosphere
   (D) troposphere and stratosphere

4. Air pressure at any given altitude is caused by the weight of the air above that level. Which of the atmospheric zones has the highest air pressure?
   (F) mesosphere   (H) thermosphere
   (G) stratosphere   (J) troposphere

5. Conditions are most favorable in the stratosphere for the formation of ozone molecules from oxygen. At that altitude, oxygen absorbs ultraviolet radiation and is transformed into ozone. How does ozone formation explain the temperature pattern in the stratosphere?
   (A) The absorption of solar energy causes a rise in temperature.
   (B) Energy released by ozone formation causes a rise in temperature.
   (C) The loss of oxygen molecules causes a fall in temperature.
   (D) Ozone molecules absorb energy and cause a fall in temperature.

Passage II

To determine the types of crystals making up a coarse-grained rock, the researcher had only 2 analytical methods available.

The semiquantitative *X-ray fluorescence unit* could detect the presence of certain chemical elements, but it could not measure their abundances precisely. The chemical compositions for all crystals likely to be found in the rock are given in the following chart.

CRYSTAL VARIETIES	ATOMIC PERCENTAGES							
	Oxygen	*Silicon*	*Aluminum*	*Iron*	*Magnesium*	*Calcium*	*Sodium*	*Potassium*
Magnetite	57	0	0	43	0	0	0	0
Olivine	57	14	0	13	16	0	0	0
Hypersthene	60	20	0	9	11	0	0	0
Augite	60	20	0	4	6	10	0	0
Hornblende	57	19	5	7	5	5	2	0
Biotite	60	15	5	9	6	0	0	5
Plagioclase	61	19	12	0	0	4	4	0
Quartz	67	33	0	0	0	0	0	0
Orthoclase	61	23	8	0	0	0	0	8

The second apparatus available was a *heavy liquids kit* containing 3 bottles of organic liquids of known specific gravity, an alternate method of reporting density. The specific gravity of crystals may be estimated by seeing whether they sink or float in each liquid. The following chart states the specific gravity for each liquid and all crystal varieties suspected to be in the rock.

		SPECIFIC GRAVITY
LIQUIDS	Methylene Iodide	3.33
	Bromoform	2.89
	Acetone	0.79
CRYSTALS	Magnetite	5.18
	Olivine	3.65
	Hypersthene	3.45
	Augite	3.25
	Hornblende	3.20
	Biotite	3.00
	Plagioclase	2.69
	Quartz	2.65
	Orthoclase	2.57

Experiment 1

The coarse-grained rock was crushed enough to free the crystals from each other. Then 200 grams of the sandlike material was stirred into a beaker containing bromoform. Some of the material floated, while most of the material sank to the bottom of the beaker. The fraction that floated appeared uniform, as if it were only one variety of crystal. An X-ray fluorescence analysis of the floated material detected the presence of silicon and calcium, but not potassium. The other 5 elements were not checked.

Experiment 2

The fraction of the material that sank in Experiment 1 was then washed free of bromoform and dried. It was then stirred into another beaker containing methylene iodide; again the material separated into 2 fractions. Each fraction appeared to be homogeneous and composed of only one crystal type. The part that had floated in the methylene iodide was analyzed with the X-ray fluorescence unit and found to contain silicon and magnesium, but not sodium. The other 5 elements were not checked.

Experiment 3

The rock fraction that sank in the previous experiment was quickly analyzed for the presence of silicon. After that element was found to be present, the investigator discontinued his work.

6. The crystals that were analyzed by X-ray fluorescence in Experiment 1 must be
   (F) hornblende   (H) plagioclase
   (G) magnetite   (J) quartz

7. The three liquids in the kit are mutually miscible, so by mixing them a liquid of intermediate specific gravity may be obtained. Which pair of crystals could be separated by using a liquid produced by mixing equal volumes of bromoform and methylene iodide?
   (A) augite and hornblende
   (B) hornblende and biotite
   (C) hypersthene and augite
   (D) olivine and hypersthene

8. To specifically identify the crystals that were analyzed in Experiment 2, the researcher should try to detect any of the following elements EXCEPT
   (F) aluminum   (H) iron
   (G) calcium   (J) potassium

9. The usefulness of the X-ray fluorescence unit could be most improved if it could
   (A) analyze two samples of the same time
   (B) detect the presence of oxygen
   (C) measure the amount of each element
   (D) work with wet or dry samples

10. Why would it be fruitless for the researcher to analyze the material in Experiment 3 for the remaining elements?
    (F) The material could not contain any of those elements.
    (G) The possible crystals had already been narrowed to only one.
    (H) The two likely crystals contain the same elements.
    (J) The three possible crystals are all known to contain iron.

11. All rock-forming crystals are denser than the acetone included in the heavy liquids kit. How can that light liquid best be used in crystal separations?
    (A) Mix a small amount of it into bromoform to produce a liquid with a specific gravity of less than 2.89.
    (B) Mix a small amount of it into bromoform to produce a liquid with a specific gravity of more than 2.89.
    (C) Mix a small amount of it into methylene iodide to produce a liquid with a specific gravity of less than 3.33.
    (D) Mix a small amount of it into methylene iodide to produce a liquid with a specific gravity of more than 3.33.

Passage III

The following diagram shows the feeding relationships in one woodland community. The arrows point toward the dependent organism. For example, frogs eat insects.

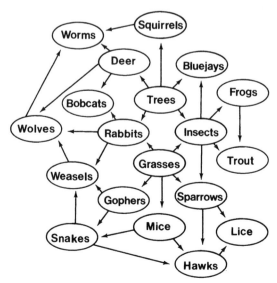

12. According to the diagram, sparrows feed on
    - (F) grasses and mice
    - (G) insects and grasses
    - (H) lice and insects
    - (J) mice and trees

13. The longest food chain in the diagram links 6 different organisms. That longest chain runs from
    - (A) grasses to deer
    - (B) trees to lice
    - (C) grasses to worms
    - (D) trees to wolves

14. Which of the following animals are natural enemies of snakes?
    - (F) gophers and mice
    - (G) hawks and weasels
    - (H) mice and hawks
    - (J) weasels and gophers

15. At the base of the network of feeding relationships are independent organisms which do not feed on other organisms. In our woodland, which organisms are at the base of the network?
    - (A) worms and lice
    - (B) frogs and snakes
    - (C) grasses and trees
    - (D) wolves and bobcats

16. A campaign by chicken farmers to eradicate weasels throughout the area could lead indirectly to
    - (F) a decrease of hawks
    - (G) a decrease of snakes
    - (H) an increase of bluejays
    - (J) an increase of bobcats

Passage IV

To investigate the ionization of air by alpha radiation, the apparatus shown below was assembled.

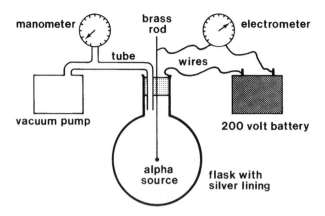

A large, round glass flask was coated with a silver lining so it would conduct electricity. Through a cork at the top, a slender brass rod supported a 10 milligram sample of polonium-210 at the center of the flask. Po^{210} is strongly radioactive, decaying by emitting alpha particles. The half-life is 138 days; in that period, half of all Po^{210} atoms decay to nonradioactive lead-206 plus high-velocity alpha particles. As the alpha particles travel through the air in the flask, some of their kinetic energy is dissipated by ionizing some of the nitrogen and oxygen molecules to electrons and positive ions. Normal air is a good electrical insulator, but ionized air allows an electrical current to flow around the circuit: battery/brass/air/silver/battery. The electrometer measures the amount of current flowing, which is directly proportional to the degree of ionization in the air.

The cork is also pierced by a tube to a pump which can lower the air pressure within the flask. The manometer permits reading the pressure at any time. Beginning at 1 atmosphere air pressure, the researcher made 9 readings of the electrical current flowing at progressively lower pressures. The prior hypothesis was that as the pressure was lowered, less of the energy of the alpha particles would be spent in ionizing air molecules. The results of the study are shown in the following graph.

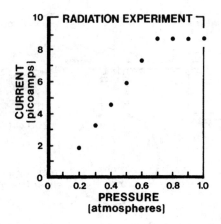

17. The prior hypothesis that amount of ionization would be proportional to air pressure is supported by readings made over the range
    (A) 0.2 to 0.7 atm   (C) 0.4 to 0.9 atm
    (B) 0.3 to 0.8 atm   (D) 0.5 to 1.0 atm

18. At the moment when the researcher records one data point to be graphed, which one of the 4 instruments could be switched off without affecting the measurement?
    (F) battery   (H) manometer
    (G) electrometer   (J) pump

19. The low currents measured at low air pressures may be explained by
    (A) the electrical resistance of a vacuum
    (B) fewer air molecules to be ionized
    (C) fewer alpha particles reaching the silver
    (D) less energetic alpha radiation

20. The researcher must complete one series of measurements within a day or two. What difference would result if the researcher tried 3 months later to check the measurements?
   (F) The measured pressure would be higher because of leakage around the cork.
   (G) The measured pressure would be lower because the pump slowly removes the air.
   (H) The measured current would be lower because the radioactive source is weaker.
   (J) The measured current would be higher because the silver lining will have tarnished.

21. The nearly constant current measured at high air pressures can be explained only if
   (A) all the alpha particles reach the silver lining without ionizing air molecules
   (B) all the energy of the alpha particles is dissipated in ionizing air molecules
   (C) all the nitrogen and oxygen molecules in the flask have been ionized
   (D) all the silver atoms have been ionized by alpha particles

22. Which of the following alterations to the apparatus would NOT significantly alter the measured current?
   (F) using aluminum to line the flask
   (G) using a larger flask
   (H) using a 150 volt battery
   (J) using radioactive cerium as the source

Passage V

Do viruses cause some human cancers? Two differing views are presented below.

Scientist 1

A seminal study in 1908 showed that healthy chickens could contract leukemia, a cancer afflicting blood, by being injected with a highly filtered extract from diseased birds. Three years later, another researcher found that a connective-tissue cancer could likewise be transferred among chickens. The latter cancer originally appeared spontaneously in one hen; highly filtered plasma injected into other chickens caused highly malignant tumors of the same kind, called *sarcomas.* Extended investigation showed that the tumor-causing agent in the filtrate was one specific virus. In 1932, a virus causing tumors in a mammal was discovered. Again, cell-free filtrates from a skin tumor in a rabbit induced malignant skin tumors, *carcinomas,* in healthy rabbits. A few years later, the first of many tumor viruses in mice was isolated. The mouse viruses are capable of causing leukemias, sarcomas, and solid tumors (*lymphomas*). Some of these cancer-inducing viruses can be transmitted from a mother mouse to her suckling offspring through the milk. By the 1950s, scientists had found tumor viruses in other mammals, including primates like the Rhesus monkey. Especially disturbing was the discovery that human adenoviruses induced cancers in laboratory mice and rats. It seems highly probable that some human cancers are caused by viral infections. The herpes viruses are prime suspects.

Scientist 2

Eighty years of searching for human viruses that induce cancerous growth have been fruitless. Not a single variety of human cancer has been shown to be due to a viral infection. Researchers have looked, and looked long, and looked well. There is not a single known human tumor virus. Cancers have been shown to be caused by genetic defects, radioactivity, light, X-rays, and numerous chemicals. Modern cancer research techniques are so advanced and sensitive that new mutagenic agents are identified each day. The widely used Ames test is capable of identifying a carcinogen that causes cancer in as few as 5 out of a billion bacterial cells. If viruses were a significant cause of human cancer, at least one tumor virus would have been found after our extensive search. In fact, even the case for viral cancer in other animals has not been positively established. Most animals infected with a virus supposed to induce malignancy in that species do not develop any tumors. Therefore, the cause of the tumors in the few cancerous animals is uncertain. Possibly the viral infection simply weakens the animals' resistance until a cancer is induced by another agent, like an ingredient of their diet. The reports of animal tumor viruses are too frequently from researchers seeking yet another grant. Surely it is time to shift our entire research budget onto known causes of cancer in humans. The search for a human tumor virus needed to be made, but by now it is known to have failed.

23. Which type of animal mentioned by Scientist 1 would be most relevant to human medicine?
    (A) chickens   (C) primates
    (B) mice   (D) rabbits

24. The strongest point that Scientist 2 raises against the belief that viral infections cause tumors in animals is that
    (F) the infections may be bacterial rather than viral
    (G) laboratory animals eat an unnatural diet
    (H) most animal researchers need results to receive grants
    (J) not all infected animals develop cancer

25. Scientist 1 also refers to a cancer of connective tissues as a
    (A) carcinoma   (C) lymphoma
    (B) leukemia   (D) sarcoma

26. All of the following points support the belief of Scientist 2 EXCEPT that
    (F) the cause of many human cancers is already known
    (G) new cancer-causing agents are discovered often
    (H) no virus has been shown to be the sole cause of any cancer
    (J) present techniques should be capable of detecting human viruses

27. In the rabbit research reported by Scientist 1, why is it important to specify that the injected liquid be cell-free?
    (A) The disease was not transmitted as cancerous cells.
    (B) Cancer might not develop in the presence of cells.
    (C) The liquid must not be contaminated with any virus.
    (D) Some cells could kill any viruses in the liquid.

28. The argument presented by Scientist 2 would be considerably weakened if Scientist 1 could prove that
    (F) human tumor viruses will be discovered soon
    (G) no animal is truly resistant to cancer
    (H) research on viruses uses only 10% of cancer research grants
    (J) some animal tumors are definitely caused by viruses.

29. The evidence presented by Scientist 1 for animal tumor viruses could be shaken if Scientist 2 showed that
    (A) adenoviruses occur in other animals as well as humans
    (B) herpes infections are not associated with any specific type of cancer
    (C) leukemia may be induced in mice by exposure to radioactivity
    (D) some particles besides the viruses passed through the filters

Passage VI

The following chart gives both the chemical symbols and atomic sizes of 6 nonmetallic elements. The last four elements are referred to as *halogens* in the questions for this passage.

Element	Symbol	Diameter of Atom (angstrom units)
Hydrogen	H	0.74
Oxygen	O	1.21
Fluorine	F	1.42
Chlorine	Cl	1.99
Bromine	Br	2.28
Iodine	I	2.67

Atoms of each of the 6 elements form chemical bonds to identical atoms and to each of the other 5 elements. A research project measured the energy required to break those chemical bonds and the results are in the next table. A higher energy corresponds to a greater force of attraction between the two atoms. Note that the chemical symbols are defined in the first table.

Bond	Energy kcal/mole
F-H	135
F-O	45
F-F	37
Cl-H	103
Cl-O	49
Cl-F	61
Cl-Cl	58
Br-H	88
Br-F	57
Br-Cl	52
Br-Br	46
I-H	71
I-Cl	50
I-Br	43
I-I	36

30. Which halogen forms the weakest bond to hydrogen?
    (F) bromine   (H) fluorine
    (G) chlorine   (J) iodine

31. The pure halogen elements occur as molecules with 2 identical atoms, like F_2. Which of those elements would have to be heated to the highest temperature to decompose the molecules into atoms?
    (A) bromine   (C) fluorine
    (B) chlorine   (D) iodine

32. Hydrogen and the halogens all react with carbon to form organic compounds with 4 such atoms bonded to a central carbon atom. Which of these organic compounds has the largest molecules?
    (F) carbon tetrachloride, CCl_4
    (G) methyl bromide, CH_3Br
    (H) methylene fluoride, CH_2F_2
    (J) methyl iodide, CH_3I

33. The bond study did not measure the energy of a bromine-oxygen bond. Estimate that energy by using the data for chlorine bonds to oxygen and fluorine.
    (A) 25 kcal/mole   (C) 65 kcal/mole
    (B) 45 kcal/mole   (D) 85 kcal/mole

34. Which of the following statements best summarizes the relative strengths of bonds between any 2 halogen atoms?
    (F) The bond is weakest between identical atoms.
    (G) The bond is stronger with hydrogen than with oxygen.
    (H) The bond is weakest if iodine is involved.
    (J) The bond is stronger between smaller atoms.

Passage VII

To investigate the possibility of gene transfer between different strains of bacteria, the following series of experiments was performed. In each case, the bacterial culture was carefully plated onto Petri dishes containing a sterilized growth medium composed of glucose and various salts. The medium did not contain any amino acids, although it is known that all organisms require amino acids for metabolism.

Experiment 1

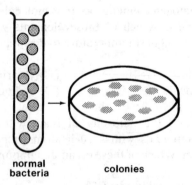

normal
bacteria   colonies

In the first experiment, a culture of normal bacteria was plated onto the growth medium which lacked any amino acids. The cluster of circular colonies which appeared were the evidence of bacterial growth. The normal bacteria were able to internally synthesize any necessary amino acids.

Experiment 2

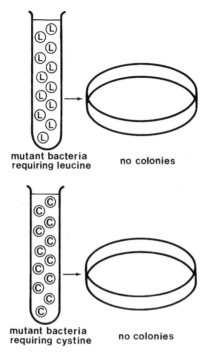

mutant bacteria
requiring leucine   no colonies

mutant bacteria
requiring cystine   no colonies

In the second experiment, the researcher used 2 mutant strains of the same bacterial species. These mutant bacteria lacked the ability to synthesize certain amino acids, leucine and cystine. One strain (L) could not synthesize leucine, but it could synthesize cystine. The other strain (C) could not synthesize cystine. As shown in the figure above, neither strain could grow on the Petri medium.

Experiment 3

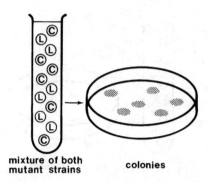

**mixture of both
mutant strains**   **colonies**

In the final experiment, the 2 mutant strains of bacteria were
mixed. That mixed culture remained in the test tube for 3 hours
to allow the bacteria an opportunity to exchange genes. When
the culture was plated onto the nutritionally deficient medium,
a number of colonies appeared.

35. The fundamental assumption of the entire set of experiments is
that the ability of bacteria to synthesize specific amino acids is
   (A) due to environmental requirements
   (B) governed by specific genes
   (C) inhibited by glucose and salts
   (D) the result of genetic mutations

36. In the set of experiments, the crucial term "synthesize" must
mean
   (F) to digest   (H) to require
   (G) to manufacture   (J) to utilize

37. The fact that the L strain of bacteria required only leucine in
order to grow on the glucose-salts medium shows that it must
have a gene to synthesize
   (A) cystine   (C) leucine
   (B) glucose   (D) all amino acids

38. If cystine had been added to both Petri dishes in Experiment 2, the result would have been
    (F) growth of the C strain only
    (G) growth of the L strain only
    (H) growth of both C and L strains
    (J) growth of neither mutant strain

39. The appearance of colonies in the third experiment can best be explained by which of these descriptions of genetic exchange?
    (A) The C strain must have received the cystine-synthesizing gene from the L strain.
    (B) The L strain must have received the leucine-synthesizing gene from the C strain.
    (C) Both the L strain received the leucine-synthesizing gene and the C strain received the cystine-synthesizing gene.
    (D) Either the C strain received the cystine-synthesizing gene or the L strain received the leucine-synthesizing gene or both.

40. If no colonies had appeared in Experiment 3, one interpretation would be that no genes were transferred between strains in the test tube. What would be another valid interpretation?
    (F) All bacteria may have starved during the 3 hours.
    (G) Both strains lacked at least one identical, vital gene.
    (H) One strain had mutated to synthesize all amino acids.
    (J) Some normal bacteria may have contaminated the culture.

STOP. IF YOU FINISH BEFORE TIME IS CALLED, CHECK YOUR WORK ON THIS SECTION ONLY. DO NOT WORK ON ANY OTHER SECTION IN THE TEST.

ANSWER KEY FOR PRACTICE TEST BATTERY NO. 2

Test 1: English

1. A	26. H	51. B
2. J	27. A	52. H
3. D	28. G	53. B
4. H	29. C	54. F
5. A	30. J	55. C
6. J	31. B	56. H
7. D	32. F	57. A
8. J	33. B	58. G
9. C	34. H	59. A
10. H	35. B	60. F
11. D	36. J	61. A
12. J	37. C	62. F
13. A	38. H	63. A
14. J	39. A	64. H
15. A	40. H	65. B
16. H	41. C	66. J
17. A	42. H	67. C
18. H	43. D	68. J
19. B	44. J	69. D
20. F	45. B	70. G
21. D	46. F	71. A
22. J	47. A	72. H
23. C	48. J	73. D
24. J	49. A	74. F
25. C	50. J	75. D

Test 2: Mathematics

1. C	31. A
2. G	32. H
3. D	33. B
4. H	34. H
5. D	35. D
6. J	36. F
7. C	37. D
8. H	38. G
9. B	39. D
10. G	40. K
11. B	41. D
12. K	42. F
13. B	43. B
14. H	44. H
15. D	45. E
16. F	46. K
17. D	47. C
18. J	48. K
19. D	49. A
20. F	50. G
21. C	51. B
22. J	52. H
23. D	53. E
24. G	54. K
25. C	55. D
26. K	56. F
27. E	57. A
28. G	58. H
29. C	59. D
30. F	60. H

ANSWER KEY FOR PRACTICE TEST BATTERY NO. 2

	Test 3: Reading			**Test 4: Science Reasoning**	
1. B	21. D		1. B	21. B
2. G	22. J		2. G	22. F
3. B	23. C		3. A	23. C
4. F	24. J		4. J	24. J
5. B	25. B		5. A	25. D
6. H	26. F		6. H	26. G
7. D	27. B		7. B	27. A
8. H	28. J		8. H	28. J
9. B	29. A		9. C	29. D
10. H	30. G		10. H	30. J
11. C	31. B		11. A	31. B
12. H	32. F		12. G	32. F
13. B	33. D		13. C	33. B
14. G	34. H		14. G	34. J
15. C	35. B		15. C	35. B
16. H	36. H		16. J	36. G
17. A	37. A		17. A	37. A
18. G	38. H		18. J	38. F
19. B	39. B		19. B	39. D
20. H	40. H		20. H	40. G

SCORING YOUR ACT BATTERY

To score your test battery, total the number of correct answers for each section. Do not subtract any points for questions attempted but missed, as there is no penalty for guessing. This score is then scaled from 1 to 36 for each section and then averaged for the all-important composite score. The average score is approximately 18.

FOR YOUR OWN BENEFIT

To figure out your *percentage right* for each test, use the following formulas:

Test 1: English $\dfrac{\text{Number right}}{75} \times 100 = \underline{\hspace{1cm}} \%$

Test 2: Mathematics $\dfrac{\text{Number right}}{60} \times 100 = \underline{\hspace{1cm}} \%$

Test 3: Reading $\dfrac{\text{Number right}}{40} \times 100 = \underline{\hspace{1cm}} \%$

Test 4: Science Reasoning $\dfrac{\text{Number right}}{40} \times 100 = \underline{\hspace{1cm}} \%$

PRACTICE TEST BATTERY NO. 2: ANALYSIS SHEET

	Possible	Completed	Right	Wrong
Test 1: English	75			
Test 2: Mathematics	60			
Test 3: Reading	40			
Test 4: Science Reasoning	40			
OVERALL TOTALS	215			

WHY??????????????????????????????

ANALYSIS: TALLY SHEET FOR PROBLEMS MISSED

One of the most important parts of test preparation is analyzing WHY! you missed a problem so that you can reduce the number of mistakes. Now that you have taken the practice test and checked your answers, carefully tally your mistakes by marking them in the proper column.

REASON FOR MISTAKE

	Total Missed	Simple Mistake	Misread Problem	Lack of Knowledge
Test 1: English				
Test 2: Mathematics				
Test 3: Reading				
Test 4: Science Reasoning				
TOTAL				

Reviewing the above data should help you determine WHY you are missing certain problems. Now that you have pinpointed the type of error, focus on avoiding your most common type.

COMPLETE ANSWERS AND EXPLANATIONS FOR
PRACTICE TEST BATTERY NO. 2

TEST 1: ENGLISH

1. (A) The singular possessive *its* is correct here. The spelling *it's* is the contraction of *it is.*

2. (J) If the *who* is preserved, the sentence has no main verb, only a verb in a relative clause. The subject of the sentence (*number*) needs a main verb to make the sentence complete.

3. (D) The paragraph is greatly improved if this sentence is left out. It might have followed the opening sentence as an example, but the paragraph moves on to its real subject, the American scientists, in the second sentence. As it stands, the third sentence is now an interruption.

4. (H) This shortest version of the phrase is the best choice. To omit the phrase altogether would completely change the meaning of the sentence.

5. (A) As in question 4, the shortest version is again the best choice, and omission changes the meaning of the sentence.

6. (J) The distinction between *all over* and *throughout* is a red herring here. Both are acceptable. The error is the verb tense. The paragraph has so far used only the past tense. There is no reason to shift to the present tense in this sentence.

7. (D) The sentence begins a new subject, the Moscow response to the American scientists, and a new paragraph should begin with this sentence. Whether the prepositional phrase *from Moscow* precedes or follows *the response* is not important.

8. (J) In the relative clause, the subject is *authorities,* the verb is *had imprisoned,* and the object of the verb is *whom,* the objective case. The comma should set off the clause because it is nonrestrictive.

9. (C) The issues here are idiom and metaphor. We untie a knot or sever it, and these metaphors can be used to mean to end an impasse. But the idiom with the word *deadlock* is *to break* or *to release.*

10. (H) The adverbial form is needed to modify the adjective *Moslem* (or *Muslim*). By omitting the adverb, choice (J) changes the meaning.

11. (D) The singular *was expected* is needed with the singular subject *harvest*. (B) and (C) are not grammatically wrong, but they change the meaning of the sentence.

12. (J) The phrase must include *as* twice. If the phrase *if not smaller than* is left out, the incompleteness of *as small the previous year's* is very easy to see.

13. (A) *Dearth* is a singular noun meaning *shortage*. The parenthetical *as usual* should be wholly set off by commas.

14. (J) The sentence begins with a phrase (*Even as a small child*) which will dangle unless the noun or pronoun that it modifies follows immediately. It is the *I*, not *cooking*, who had been a small child, so (J) is the only possible correct answer.

15. (A) The sentence is correct as it is written. The changes save words but they change the meaning. The real subject is what is suitable for a girl, not what is interesting.

16. (H) Strictly speaking, this sentence is a fragment. But in informal writing like this passage, authors will often deliberately ignore rules of grammar to give the prose naturalness. The use of *anyway* at the beginning of the next sentence also works to give the prose a relaxed tone.

17. (A) The past perfect tense, to express an action completed before the past tense (*was*) later in the sentence is correct. Choice (B) is the same tense using the passive. This is not wrong, but given a choice between active and passive, take the active. It will be at least one word shorter.

18. (H) The series should be parallel (G is not), and punctuated with commas. Choice (J) is not wrong, but it is wordier than (H).

19. (B) The best punctuation of this phrase is *that* with no comma, since the clause is restrictive. But by omitting the pronoun altogether, the problem of punctuation is solved and words are saved.

20. (F) The best word here is *though,* to indicate the difference between then and now. The *and* suggests a continuity, not a change.

21. (D) All of the first three devices are used in the paragraph. There are no similes.

22. (J) Like the opening of the first sentence of the first paragraph, this initial phrase dangles, seeming to say that *cooking* had two years of college. By using the simple prepositional phrase of (J), you eliminate the implied but unstated *I was,* which makes choices (F), (G), and (H) dangling phrases.

23. (C) The dash is the better way to set off this interruption.

24. (J) The preferred idiom is *different from* rather than *different than.* Though you should always be alert for ways to get rid of unneeded words, be sure that cutting out a word does not alter the meaning, as in choice (G).

25. (C) The introductory phrase here should be followed by a comma.

26. (H) The sentence has established a pattern by using the phrases *in crisp vegetables . . . in Russian history* and *by the problems of nutrition. . .* To maintain the parallel, use choice (H). The original version is wordy as well as not parallel. The other options are briefer but lose the balanced phrasing.

27. (A) The passage is written in a relaxed, conversational style, one that would certainly admit a word like *snooty* in place of the more formal *conceited.* Both are legitimate English words. In this context, the livelier word is the better choice. Note the use of the word *posh,* later in this paragraph, a similar choice of level of diction.

28. (G) Choice (G) is the most concise and direct way of ordering all the elements of the sentence. The other versions repeat words.

29. (C) By using the parallel nouns (*astronaut, president, Justice*), choice (C) maintains parallelism and uses fewer words.

30. (J) This is indirect discourse. If the quotation had been direct, she would have said, "You. . ."

31. (B) None of the other three choices is at all appropriate.

32. (F) The paragraphs are in a logical, chronological order.

33. (B) The paragraph uses the past tense, so the correct verb form here is *rose*. The *more* is unnecessary, as *rose* means *increased*.

34. (H) As written, the sentence is muddled and the *they* cannot be identified. In choice (G), the adjective *reported* and in (J), the adverb *reportedly* are unclear or misleading. (H) clarifies the confusion.

35. (B) The main verb of the sentence (*was arrested*) is a passive in the past tense. Since he was seen before he was arrested, the form of the verb *spot* should indicate an action earlier than that of the main verb.

36. (J) Since the clause about the package presents different information, it is clearer as an independent sentence. The basic verb tense of the paragraph is the past (*arrived*).

37. (C) The passage is clearer if this sentence begins the second paragraph. The first paragraph tells of two arrests, with details about the first. The second paragraph deals wholly with the second.

38. (H) The problem in this sentence is placing modifiers near what they modify. It is Marshall, not the deputy, who is armed with a handgun and knife, so that prepositional phrase must be close to *armed*. The *who* clause should not be set off by commas, and there should be an apostrophe in *sheriff's*.

39. (A) To *commandeer* is to *seize by force* and is the best choice of word here. The *of* is not needed.

40. (H) The participial phrase that begins this sentence dangles unless the word it modifies (*the suspect*) follows the comma. Choice (J) corrects the dangling participle but changes from the tense of the other verbs in the paragraphs.

41. (C) A case could be made on both sides of the new paragraph question. Separated, both paragraphs are short. Both do deal with Marshall. In any event, the noun *spokesman* must be changed to a plural in the absence of any article (*the* or *a*), so the verb must be the plural *were*.

42. (H) In the *who* clause, the subject is *they,* the verb is *have been pursuing,* and the object of this verb is *whom,* in the objective case.

43. (D) The phrase *committing the crime* must be closer to the word it modifies (*he*) or rephrased. It is now another dangling participle. Adding *while* or *when* does not change the error. Choice (D) gets rid of the participle.

44. (J) Another dangling modifier. By adding a subject to the phrase (*he is*), the problem is corrected.

45. (B) Though there are one or two details that could be called biographical, this is much more obviously a sample of newswriting.

46. (F) Though all of the four answers are grammatical, the original version is clear and more concise.

47. (A) Here the shorter versions do not say exactly what the original longer version says. The economists are concerned with changing the law to allow an increase in interest rates. The briefer versions leave out the issue of *allowing.*

48. (J) This sentence has no real connection with the concerns of either paragraph. The passage is improved if the sentence is omitted.

49. (A) Choices (B) and (C) are dangling participles. To omit the opening phrase is to remove essential information from the sentence, though the sentence will still make grammatical sense.

50. (J) The commas make the sentence clearer.

51. (B) The comma is helpful here. Choice (D) is wordy.

52. (H) The third sentence is a question; the fourth is an incomplete sentence which answers the question but does not use a metaphor.

53. (B) This is an editorial piece, written chiefly to criticize economists who argue for deregulation. Though the subject is economics, the passage is not really economic analysis so much as it is using a few economic facts to make a case against a political position.

54. (F) Reading through the rest of the paragraph will show that the past tense is used throughout. If possible, a subject and its verb should be kept together, so there is no reason to move the adverb between them as in choice (J).

55. (C) The opening phrase should be separated from *the book.* The past tense singular is the correct verb form.

56. (H) The clause is nonrestrictive and should be set off by a comma. In the clause, the subject is *the writer,* the verb is *appeared to rank,* and the object of this verb is *whom.* Thus the objective *whom* should be used.

57. (A) The diction of the series is correct as it stands, and the series is properly punctuated with commas.

58. (G) The adjective that fits best here is *objectionable,* which means *disagreeable* or *offensive.* The point is that the book attracted interest because of its criticism of women.

59. (A) The author has moved from the book itself (paragraph 1) to its reception. The sentence should begin the second paragraph.

60. (F) The passage is written in the past tense. Since the sentence uses the preposition *by* (*by the ladies*), the use of *welcome* would be unidiomatic. We say *welcome to, welcomed by.*

61. (A) The punctuation in the passage is correct. The phrase *or affect to love* is parenthetical and should be set off by commas. The verb *affect* means to *feign* (compare *affectation*) while the verb *effect* means to *bring about.*

62. (F) Choices (G) and (J) alter the meaning. The punctuation in the passage is correct.

63. (A) The verb *ascertain* means to *find out* and is appropriate here. There is no reason to use three or four words for what one will do.

64. (H) All things being equal, the active verb is less wordy than the passive.

65. (B) The passage is the opening of a Victorian novel, George Meredith's *The Ordeal of Richard Feverel* (1859).

66. (J) The *usual* here modifies the adjective *conservative* not the noun *businesspeople,* so the adverb *usually* should be used.

67. (C) This clause needs a main verb—one that is consistent with *has . . . doubled* in the second half of the sentence. Choices (A), (B), and (D) are all participles, not main verbs.

68. (J) The phrase *and this is* is not wrong, but it is a wordy construction. The word *state* is evidently a diction error for *rate.*

69. (D) The sentence is not closely connected to the rest of the paragraph. The passage is improved if this sentence is left out.

70. (G) If we don't know how long a stay this bill represents (one day? one month?), it is much less meaningful. None of the information of choices (F), (H), or (J) would make this statistic more significant.

71. (A) The author has chosen the adjective *dismal* to express a personal view of the situation. To omit this important adjective is to alter the effect of the paragraph.

72. (H) Choice (J) changes the meaning of the sentence. The antecedent of *that* is the plural *pressures,* so the verb must be the plural *restrain.*

73. (D) The context should make it clear that *incentive,* that is, a *motive* or *encouragement,* is the right word here.

74. (F) The meaning here of the adjective is *money-saving* (*economizing*), not the same thing as *economic* or *economics.*

75. (D) The problem here is the mixture of metaphors. We have a *key,* a *blocking,* a *skyrocket,* and a *spiral* all in the same clause. Choices (A) and (B) are only slightly better. (D) gets rid of the metaphors.

TEST 2: MATHEMATICS

1. (C) This is a weighted average.

$$\frac{(20)(80) + (50)(60) + (30)(40)}{100} = \frac{5800}{100} = 58\%$$

2. (G) If 25% is lost, 75% or $\frac{3}{4}$ remains. Thus,

$$\frac{5}{8} \times \frac{4}{5} \times \frac{3}{4} =$$

Canceling gives

$$\frac{\overset{1}{\cancel{5}}}{8} \times \frac{\overset{1}{\cancel{4}}}{\underset{1}{\cancel{5}}} \times \frac{3}{\underset{1}{\cancel{4}}} = \frac{3}{8}$$

3. (D) If the linear measure is in the ratio of 3 to 4, the areas will be in the ratio of 9 to 16.

Thus, $\dfrac{9}{16} = \dfrac{36}{x}$

Therefore, $x = \dfrac{(16)(36)}{9} = 64$

4. (H) Since $f[g(3)]$, working inside to outside gives

$$g(x) = x^2 - 2$$
$$g(3) = 3^2 - 2$$
$$g(3) = 9 - 2$$
$$g(3) = 7$$

Next, $f[g(3)] = f(7)$

And since $f(x) = 2x + 4$

then $f(7) = 2(7) + 4$

$f(7) = 14 + 4$

thus $f(7) = 18$

5. (D) To determine the next numbers in the sequence, use differences between pairs of consecutive pairs. $5 + 1 = 6$; $6 + 2 = 8$; $8 + 3 = 11$; $11 + 4 = 15$. Continuing this process, $15 + 5 = 20$, $20 + 6 = 26$; $26 + 7 = 33$; $33 + 8 = 41$; $41 + 9 = 50$. Another method of solution would be to notice that the 10th number in this sequence would be the sum of the integers 1 through 9 and the starting number of 5. The formula for finding the sum of the integers from 1 to n is $n(n + 1)/2$. Thus, if $n = 9$, the 10th number in the sequence is $5 + 45 = 50$.

6. (J) If x represents his age now,

$$x + 6 = 2(x - 4)$$
$$x + 6 = 2x - 8$$
$$x = 14$$

This is the age *now*. In 4 years, Tony will be 18.

7. (C) A subtotal of 200 toys are worth under \$5.00 ($140 + 60$). Therefore, the probability of choosing one of these toys is 200 out of a total of 500 toys all together, or $200/500 = 2/5$.

8. (H) Since the collection contains 50 coins, we can use x and $50 - x$ as the quantity of quarters and dimes. Thus,

$$25x + 10(50 - x) = 710$$
$$25x + 500 - 10x = 710$$
$$15x = 210$$
$$x = 14$$

Since the number of quarters is 14, the number of dimes is $50 - 14$ or 36. The difference is 22.

9. (B) Start solving at the bottom right with the fraction $\dfrac{3}{3+3}$

and continue as follows:

$$3 + \cfrac{3}{3 + \cfrac{3}{3 + \cfrac{3}{3 + 3}}} = 3 + \cfrac{3}{3 + \cfrac{3}{3 + \frac{3}{6}}}$$

$$= 3 + \cfrac{3}{3 + \cfrac{3}{3\frac{1}{2}}}$$

$$= 3 + \cfrac{3}{3 + \cfrac{3}{\frac{7}{2}}}$$

$$= 3 + \cfrac{3}{3 + \frac{6}{7}}$$

$$= 3 + \cfrac{3}{3\frac{6}{7}}$$

$$= 3 + \cfrac{3}{\frac{27}{7}}$$

$$= 3 + \frac{21}{27}$$

$$= 3\frac{21}{27} = 3\frac{7}{9}$$

10. (G) Distance equals rate times time. If you travel 10 miles per hour for y hours, you have traveled $10y$ miles. If you travel y miles per hour for 10 hours, you have traveled $10y$ miles. Thus, you traveled $20y$ miles all together.

11. (B) Statement II is correct, since angle x and angle z add up to a straight line. Statement I is correct, since the two lines are not parallel and meet on the left. The lower line can be rotated clockwise or the top line can be rotated counterclockwise, or a combination of the two. In each case, angle x is greater than angle y. Statement III is not necessarily true all the time.

12. (K) We can tabulate the data:

	part of tank brand Z	part of tank brand Y
after first fill up	1	0
before second fill up	$\frac{1}{2}$	0
after second fill up	$\frac{1}{2}$	$\frac{1}{2}$
before third fill up	$\frac{1}{4}$	$\frac{1}{4}$
after third fill up	$\frac{3}{4}$	$\frac{1}{4}$
before fourth fill up	$\frac{3}{8}$	$\frac{1}{8}$
after fourth fill up	$\frac{3}{8}$	$\frac{5}{8}$

Since the tank is now full, $\frac{3}{8}$ or 37.5% is brand Z.

13. (B) Change the question into an algebraic sentence and solve.

$$x = 0.7\% \text{ of } 30$$
$$= (0.007)(30)$$
$$= 0.21$$

14. (H) Change all factors to a base of 4.

$$\frac{(4^{2x})(4^x)(2^{4x})}{(2^{6x})(4^{3x})(2^{2x})} = \frac{(4^{2x})(4^x)(4^{2x})}{(4^{3x})(4^{3x})(4^x)} = \frac{4^{5x}}{4^{7x}} = \frac{1}{4^{2x}}$$

15. (D) The formula for combinations is: For n things taken r at a time

$$\binom{n}{r} = \frac{n!}{r!(n-r)!}$$

Therefore $\binom{8}{3} = \frac{8!}{3!5!} = \frac{8 \times 7 \times 6 \times 5 \times 4 \times 3 \times 2 \times 1}{3 \times 2 \times 1 \times 5 \times 4 \times 3 \times 2 \times 1} = 56$

16. (F) The shaded region is a trapezoid. $\left[\text{Area} = \left(\frac{b_1 + b_2}{2} \right) h \right]$

Thus its area is $\dfrac{(x + 10)}{(2)} (4) = (x + 10)(2)$

$$= 2x + 20, \text{ or } 20 + 2x.$$

17. (D) From the first sentence, we see that the total number of persons at the party must be divisible by 6 (5:1). From the second sentence, the total must be divisible by 4 (3:1). Thus, the total must be divisible by 6 and 4 or 12. The only number given that is not divisible by 12 is 258.

18. (J) Let us calculate the value of each:

   (F) $(.5)(.3)(280) = 42$
   (G) $(.33)(.7)(160) = 36.96$
   (H) $(2)(.5)(30) = 30$
   (J) $(3)(.4)(40) = 48$
   (K) $(.6)(60) = 36$

19. (D) Simplifying and factoring we get:

$$\frac{12\sqrt{6} - 6\sqrt{50}}{\sqrt{72}} = \frac{12 \cdot \sqrt{2}\sqrt{3} - 6 \cdot 5\sqrt{2}}{6\sqrt{2}}$$

Then cancel:

$$\frac{\cancel{12}^2 \cdot \cancel{\sqrt{2}}\sqrt{3} - \cancel{6}^1 \cdot 5\cancel{\sqrt{2}}}{\cancel{6}\cancel{\sqrt{2}}} = 2\sqrt{3} - 5$$

20. (F) From the given information, it costs $30x$ for the first 30 kilowatt hours. Thus $z - 30$ kilowatt hours remain at y cents per kilowatt hour. Thus $30x + (z - 30)y = (30x) - (30y) + yz = 30(x - y) + yz$.

21. (C) We solve these two equations simultaneously.

$$3y + 2x = 18$$
$$y - 4x = -8$$

Multiply the first equation by 2 and add to the second,

$$6y + 4x = 36$$
$$\underline{y - 4x = -8}$$
$$7y \qquad = 28 \qquad \text{or } y = 4$$

Note that the only point with a y-coordinate of 4 is $(3, 4)$, choice (C).

Substituting back into one of the original equations gives

$$3(4) + 2x = 18$$
$$12 + 2x = 18$$
$$2x = 6$$
$$x = 3$$

Thus $(3, 4)$ is the point.

22. (J) We can set up a proportion, since we have similar triangles.

$$\frac{AB}{AD} = \frac{CE}{DE}$$

Thus, $\qquad \dfrac{AB}{18} = \dfrac{4}{6}$

Therefore, $\qquad AB = 12$

23. (D) There are 216 or $(6 \times 6 \times 6)$ ways of rolling 3 dice. Of these, there are 3 ways of rolling a 4. Thus $3/216 = 1/72$.

24. (G) The point of intersection of these two graphs has an x-coordinate of -1. Substitute -1 into the equation and solve for y.

$$y + 4 = 2x^2$$
$$y + 4 = 2(-1)^2$$
$$y + 4 = 2$$
$$y = -2$$

25. (C) We solve simultaneously

$$6x - 3y = 30$$
$$4x + y = 2$$

Multiply the bottom equation by 3 and add the two equations together.

$$6x - 3y = 30$$
$$\underline{12x + 3y = 6}$$
$$18x = 36 \qquad \text{or } x = 2$$

Thus $x = 2$

Substitute back to one of the original equations and we find that $y = -6$. Thus their sum is -4.

26. (K) From the figure, we use the Pythagorean theorem and find the missing side, x, is 12 inches. Thus, (K) is correct.

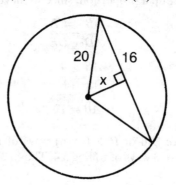

27. (E) To get a ratio of x/y, divide both numbers by 7, leaving

$$x = \frac{3y}{7}$$

and then divide by y, giving $\dfrac{x}{y} = \dfrac{3}{7}$

28. (G) Multiply each term by the lowest common denominator, $4y$. You get

$$12 + 8 = 3y$$

which simplifies to $20 = 3y$

Now divide each side by 3. $y = 6\frac{2}{3}$

29. (C) Since the coordinates of the midpoint are the average of the endpoints, we have the following:

Let (a, b) be the coordinates of the missing endpoint. Since no two points given as choices have the same first (or second) coordinates, it is necessary to find only the first *or* second coordinate.

Thus $\dfrac{(a) + (x)}{2} = 3x$ and $\dfrac{(b) + (y)}{2} = -3y$

Therefore, $a + x = 6x$ and $b + y = -6y$

So, $a = 5x$ and $b = -7y$

Thus $(5x, -7y)$

30. (F) Let x = Jane's weight. Then $2x + 12$ = Tim's weight. Therefore, $x + 2x + 12 = 135$, $3x + 12 = 135$, $3x = 123$, $x = 41$. So Tim's weight is $(2)(41) + 12 = 94$.

31. (A) We have $\left(\dfrac{1}{3 + i}\right)\left(\dfrac{3 - i}{3 - i}\right) = \dfrac{3 - i}{9 + 1} = \dfrac{3 - i}{10}$

32. (H) When you multiply, you add exponents. The product of two negative numbers is a positive number. Rearranging and simplifying gives

$$(5x^2y)(-2xy^2)(-3y^4) = (5 \cdot -2 \cdot -3)(x^2 \cdot x)(y \cdot y^2 \cdot y^4) = 30x^3y^7$$

33. (B) First calculate the discount. Ten percent of $40.00 is $4.00. Subtract this discount from the normal price of $40.00, giving $36.00 after the discount. The 10% tax is calculated on this $36.00 amount, or $3.60. Add this to the $36.00, giving $39.60.

34. (H) The number 8 is the geometric mean between 4 and x, therefore, $\dfrac{4}{8} = \dfrac{8}{x}$ thus $x = 16$. Thus, $AC = 20$.

35. (D) Set up an equation: $6a + 2p = 3a + 6p$. Thus, $3a = 4p$. Multiply both sides by 3, and we have $9a = 12p$. Therefore, the answer must be (D).

36. (F) Since x and z are complementary, $x = 90 - z$. Since x and y are supplementary, $x = 180 - y$. Thus $180 - y = 90 - z$. Solving for z, $z = y - 90$.

37.   Rounding off the numbers gives $\sqrt{2500/100}$, which reduces to $\sqrt{25} = 5$.

38. (G) If there were the term (-100) at the end, the answer would have been -50. (Take the series in pairs, each pair being equal to -1. There are 50 pairs.) Since we are missing the -100 at the end, we must add 100 to -50 and get 50.

39. (D) Count two surfaces for each edge where cubes are connected. Don't forget the six surfaces for the three cubes on the top of the first layer.

40. (K) Divide the first inequality by 2 and we get $6 < x < 9$. Divide the second inequality by 3 and we get $-3 < y < 2$. If we add these two inequalities, we see that statement I is true. If we take these two inequalities and multiply the first by -1, we get $-6 > -x > -9$ or $-9 < -x < -6$. Now adding the two statements together, we get $-12 < y - x < -4$. So II is true.

41. (D) To find the mean, we must average the six scores (add up the scores and divide by the number of scores). The median is the middle score when the scores are in order from lowest to highest or highest to lowest. With an even number of scores, the median is the average of the two middle scores. Now put the scores in order.

$$20, 32, 36, 40, 42, x$$

Since the five answer choices are each greater than the first 5 scores, the median must be the average of 36 and 40, or 38. If we multiply 38 times 6, we get the sum of the six needed numbers.

$$38 \times 6 = 228$$

Since the sum of the first 5 numbers is 170, the sixth number must be 58. You could also have worked this problem by plugging in from the answer choices.

42. (F) If x represents the smallest number, then the 3 numbers can be represented by

$$x + (x + 2) + (x + 4) = 2x + 15$$
$$3x + 6 = 2x + 15$$
$$x = 9$$

Thus, the numbers are 9, 11, and 13, which total 33. Again, you could have used a trial-and-error method of working from the answers. In this particular problem, only 33, choice (F), can be obtained by adding 3 consecutive odd numbers.

43. (B) $\dfrac{(5^2 + 5^1)(5^3 + 5^2)}{5^2} = \dfrac{(25 + 5)(125 + 25)}{25} = \dfrac{(30)(150)}{25} = 180$

44. (H)

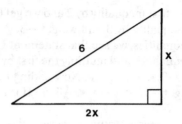

If the shortest side of the triangle is x,

$$x^2 + (2x)^2 = 6^2$$

$$x^2 + 4x^2 = 36$$

$$5x^2 = 36$$

$$x^2 = \frac{36}{5}$$

Now multiplying by $\frac{\sqrt{5}}{\sqrt{5}}$ $x = \frac{\sqrt{36}}{\sqrt{5}} \times \frac{\sqrt{5}}{\sqrt{5}} = \frac{6\sqrt{5}}{\sqrt{5}}$

Since the third side is twice the second, the answer is

$$\frac{12\sqrt{5}}{5}$$

45. (E)

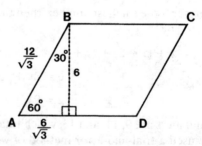

Using the 30-60-90 relationship in a right triangle, we see that the slant height is $12/\sqrt{3}$, which can be changed to $4\sqrt{3}$.

$$\left(\frac{12}{\sqrt{3}} \cdot \frac{\sqrt{3}}{\sqrt{3}} = \frac{12\sqrt{3}}{3} \right)$$

Thus, the perimeter is $4\sqrt{3} + 4\sqrt{3} + 8 + 8 = 8(2 + \sqrt{3})$.

46. (K)

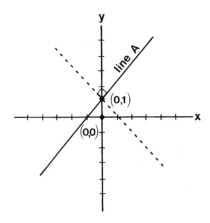

Use the point slope formula.

$$y = mx + b \text{ (where the slope } m = \tfrac{3}{4})$$

A perpendicular line would have a slope that is the negative reciprocal of $\tfrac{3}{4}$, which is $-\tfrac{4}{3}$. This leaves the equation as

$$y = -\frac{4}{3}x + 1$$

We know that the y-intercept is 1, since the line passes through $(0, 1)$. The slope is the negative reciprocal. Now multiply through by 3.

$$3y = -4x + 3$$

Then add $-4x$ to both sides, giving

$$4x + 3y = 3$$

47. (C) If x is the angle, then $(90 - x)$ is its complement and $(180 - x)$ is its supplement. Thus,

$$180 - x = 4(90 - x)$$
$$180 - x = 360 - 4x$$
$$3x = 180$$
$$x = 60$$

48. (K) Multiply by $\dfrac{\sqrt{3}}{\sqrt{3}}$

$$\frac{(\sqrt{5} + 2)}{\sqrt{3}} \times \frac{\sqrt{3}}{\sqrt{3}} = \frac{\sqrt{15} + 2\sqrt{3}}{3}$$

49. (A) Since the slope of the line between (4, 2) and (9, 7) is 1, we can extend the line in both directions giving us the following diagram. We now have several triangles. The large right triangle has an area of 32. The two smallest triangles have areas of 4 and 8. We subtract these from 32, giving 20.

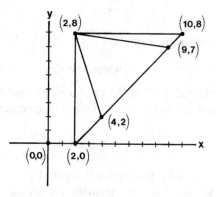

50. (G)

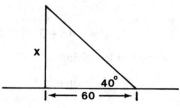

We have $\tan 40° = \dfrac{x}{60}$

So $x = 60 \tan 40°$

51. **(B)** The hexagon is made up of 6 equilateral triangles each having side length of 48/6 = 8.

The height of an equilateral triangle is $\frac{1}{2}$ the base times the height. The triangle is a 30-60-90 right triangle with the sides in the ratio of $1 - \sqrt{3} - 2$. Thus, the area of each equilateral triangle is

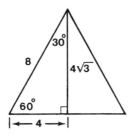

$$A = \frac{1}{2} \times (8) \times 4\sqrt{3}$$

So the area of one of the triangles is $16\sqrt{3}$. Therefore, the whole hexagon is $96\sqrt{3}$.

52. **(H)** Since angles a and b are vertical angles, they are the same size. Thus, angle $b = 50°$. Since angle b and angle c add up to 160°, angle c must be 110°. Therefore, angle d, which is supplementary to angle c, must be 70°.

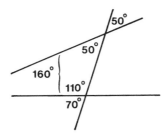

53. **(E)** If Lou averaged 60 on his first four tests, then his total points must have been 240. In order to average 70 on five tests, the total must be 350. Thus, he must score 110 on the fifth test.

54. **(K)** If r is the radius and s is an edge of the square, we could equate the areas.

$$\left(\begin{array}{l} \text{Area circle} = \pi r^2 \\ \text{Area square} = s^2 \end{array} \right) \qquad \pi r^2 = s^2$$

Dividing by r^2 $\qquad\qquad \pi = \dfrac{s^2}{r^2}$

Taking the square root $\qquad \dfrac{s}{r} = \sqrt{\pi}$

Now we have a ratio of side to radius. Then

$$\frac{\text{perimeter of square}}{\text{circumference of circle}} = \frac{4s}{2\pi r} = \frac{4\sqrt{\pi}}{2\pi} = \frac{2\sqrt{\pi}}{\pi}$$

55. **(D)** We proceed as follows:

$$\frac{9 - \dfrac{1}{p^2}}{3 - \dfrac{1}{p}} \quad \frac{\dfrac{9p^2 - 1}{p^2}}{\dfrac{3p - 1}{p}}$$

Invert the denominator and multiply:

$$= \frac{(3p - 1)(3p + 1)}{p^{2^1}} \times \frac{\overset{1}{p}}{(3p - 1)} = \frac{3p + 1}{p}$$

56. (F) The distance around the track is equal to two straight sections plus the circumference of the circle.

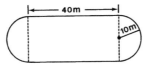

Thus, $40 + 40 + (2)(10)(\pi) = 80 + 20(\pi)$

Factoring out leaves $= 20(4 + \pi)$

57. (A)

$$\frac{(m^6n)^{-2}(mn^{-2})^3}{(m^{-2}n^{-2})^{-2}} = \frac{m^{-12}n^{-2}m^3n^{-6}}{m^4n^4} = \frac{m^{-9}n^{-8}}{m^4n^4} = m^{-13}n^{-12} = \frac{1}{m^{13}n^{12}}$$

58. (H)

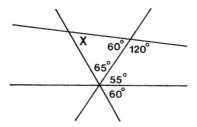

Since angle y is supplementary to 120°, it must be 60°. Angle z plus 55° plus 60° add up to a straight angle of 180°. Thus, angle z is 65°. Since the three angles of a triangle add up to 180°, angle x must be 55°.

59. (D) Use the definition of the tangent.

$$\tan \theta = \frac{\text{opposite side}}{\text{adjacent side}}$$

$$\tan 34° = \frac{50}{x}$$

$$x = \frac{50}{\tan 34°}$$

60. (H) Two equations are represented.

$$\tfrac{1}{2}x = 2y + 6$$

$$y = x + 9$$

Now substituting $x + 9$ in place of y in the first equation gives

$$\tfrac{1}{2}x = 2(x + 9) + 6$$

Simplifying gives $\tfrac{1}{2}x = 2x + 18 + 6$

or $\tfrac{1}{2}x = 2x + 24$

Multiplying through by 2 gives

$$x = 4x + 48$$

Adding $-4x$ to each side gives

$$-3x = 48$$

Dividing by 3 leaves $x = -16$

Plugging back into one of the original equations

$$y = x + 9$$

$$y = (-16) + 9 = -7$$

Thus, the larger value is -7. Using another method, the two equations are represented (could be written) like this:

$$\tfrac{1}{2}x - 2y = 6$$

$$x - y = -9$$

Multiply the first equation by (-2) and add to the second. This gives

$$3y = -21 \quad \text{or} \quad y = -7$$

Thus, $x = -16$. The larger value is -7.

TEST 3: READING

1. (B) Choice (A) is of only minor concern, while (D), according to the passage, is untrue, and (C) cannot be done.

2. (G) The passage calls their *dissimilarity* the *glory* of artists

3. (B) The extended comparison in the first paragraph of the passage likens the unique qualities of certain paintings to qualities of fruits.

4. (F) Though the passage grants education some importance, its chief point is that the artist's talent is inborn.

5. (B) The comparison is used extensively in the first two paragraphs of the passage but not in the third.

6. (H) Though the other elements are important, inborn ability, according to this writer, is the most important factor.

7. (D) The last paragraph suggests a preference for intelligibility, openness, and reality, suggesting the author would not approve of vagueness in art. The first paragraph praises *finish* and *tenderness*.

8. (H) This idea is central to the passage.

9. (B) In the last paragraph, the author specifically objects to dishonesty, affectation, and unreality. The approval of honesty and intelligibility suggests that the author would not object to simplicity.

10. (H) The paragraph suggests teaching artists about the nobility of other artists and virtues including charity, sincerity, and honesty. The implication is that the better person the artist is, the more likely (though *not* certain) it is that the person's art will be good.

11. (C) The two are a father and son. The son narrates the passage after not having seen his father for some time. The last word of the passage makes the relationship clear.

12. (H) There are references to a door and window through which the father has entered his son's room. The mention of the candle in the third paragraph sets the scene at night.

13. **(B)** The speaker corrects his first expression (*I reckoned I was scared . . . but . . . I was mistaken*). Though afraid of his father in the past, he is here only startled.

14. **(G)** The second paragraph, unlike the rest of the passage, uses several similes (*like he was behind vines*) and metaphors (*a tree-toad white, a fish-belly white*). Almost all of the passage uses denotative language and nonstandard grammar.

15. **(C)** The paragraph is at pains to make the visitor appear repulsive. There is no attempt to make him appear sympathetic or pitiable, though he is clothed in rags.

16. **(H)** Throughout the passage, the father is obsessed with the notion that his son is snubbing him and looking down on him as a social inferior. In fact, his son dislikes him for reasons that have no connection with class.

17. **(A)** The passage is a first person (*I*) narration which quotes dialogue (more than one speaker) from a scene that took place in the past.

18. **(G)** The third-to-last paragraph reveals that the mother is dead and, like the father, was illiterate.

19. **(B)** Though choices (C) and (D) are true, his motive is to find out if the report is true. The first words of the last paragraph support this reading.

20. **(H)** He is hostile to all except ignorance. He wishes to stop his son from attending school.

21. **(D)** Though the topics of choices (A), (B), and (C) appear in the passage, the organizing subject matter is Tutankhamen's tomb and its treasures.

22. **(J)** The first paragraph raises the question of why an apparently minor boy king should have been given so rich a tomb. Paragraphs two and three propose an answer to this question.

23. **(C)** The third paragraph says he died at about eighteen, and the first that he died in 1325 B.C. Eighteen years before would be 1343 B.C.

24. (J) These words reflect the attitude of the outraged priests.

25. (B) The third paragraph asserts that the populace *hated to give up all their beloved gods,* so we can assume that the return of the many gods was welcome.

26. (F) Both the first and second statements are plausible inferences. The passage tells us nothing about Akhenaten's tomb; it is Tutankhamen's that is rich.

27. (B) Both the lotus and papyrus are water plants, not surprising when we consider the importance of the Nile to Egyptian life.

28. (J) The passage suggests that the Egyptians believed in all three.

29. (A) Ankh is not a god, but a cross with a loop, symbolic of life.

30. (G) The passage neither proves nor disproves this idea. It asserts only that Tutankhamen's is, so far, *the richest* that has yet been discovered.

31. (B) The states west of the Rockies (Oregon, Washington, California) are likely to have species different from those in states east of the mountains such as New York and Delaware.

32. (F) The second paragraph asserts that fish life in two river systems is not *identical.*

33. (D) The pike is found north of Maryland. The catfish and sunfish are found in both the North and South, but the brook trout occurs only in the South.

34. (H) It is possible that river systems that appear to be separate were connected at times of heavy rain or snow melt.

35. (B) The first and third statements could be used to explain how species got from one system to the other. Because many freshwater species cannot survive in salt water, it is impossible for them to migrate to another water system by way of the ocean.

36. (H) The eel is found as far south as Panama, the only fish in common with freshwater species in the United States.

37. (A) According to the last paragraph, temperature is the chief factor in limiting wider distribution of species. Of the pairs listed here, the temperatures would be most alike in New York and Rhode Island.

38. (H) The last paragraph cites temperature.

39. (B) Since the area most similar in temperature would be most likely to have similar species, Canada is the best answer.

40. (H) Neither choice (F) nor choice (G) refer to fresh water, an important aspect of the subject of this passage. (J) does not have the geographical specificity of (H), and the explanation of cause in the passage is small.

TEST 4: SCIENCE REASONING

1. (B) Find the mark representing 70 miles on the left scale, halfway between 60 and 80. Trace rightward to the temperature line, then downward to the bottom scale. The temperature at that altitude is −15°C.

2. (G) The stratosphere varies in temperature from −60° at its base to −10° at its top, for a total range of only 50°. The range of the troposphere is 80°, the mesosphere 70°, and the thermosphere at least 270°.

3. (A) The mesosphere and troposphere both show lower temperatures as you move upward to higher altitudes. In contrast, the stratosphere and thermosphere both display increasing temperature with increasing altitude.

4. (J) The troposphere has the highest air pressure because it has the most air overlying that level. The variation of air pressure is much simpler than temperature, for the air pressure always decreases with increasing altitude.

5. (A) The rise in temperature upward through the stratosphere is caused by the solar energy absorbed by oxygen molecules at that height.

6. (H) Since those crystals floated in bromoform, they must have a specific gravity less than 2.89. The detection of calcium proves that they must be plagioclase, not quartz or orthoclase.

7. (B) The liquid would have a specific gravity of 3.11, which is the average of the values for bromoform and methylene iodide. In such a liquid, biotite (3.00) would float and hornblende (3.20) would sink. To separate any two crystal varieties, it is necessary to have a liquid of intermediate specific gravity.

8. (H) The crystals must be either augite or biotite and those crystal varieties could be distinguished by detecting aluminum (biotite), calcium (augite), or potassium (biotite). The absence of sodium in Experiment 2 showed that the crystals could not be hornblende.

9. (C) The X-ray fluorescence unit would be much more useful if it could measure the amount of each element detected. For example, a silicon abundance of 20% would indicate hypersthene, augite, hornblende, or plagioclase.

10. (H) The crystals must be either olivine or hypersthene because they have a specific gravity over 3.33 and contain silicon. Unfortunately, olivine and hypersthene have the same elements present and therefore cannot be distinguished with the available apparatus.

11. (A) Possessing a liquid of specific gravity less than 2.89 would permit separating light crystals like plagioclase, quartz, and orthoclase. Choice (C) is not the best because such a liquid could be prepared by mixing bromoform and methylene iodide, without any acetone.

12. (G) Sparrows feed on insects and grasses. Notice the arrows pointing from insects and grasses toward sparrows.

13. (C) The longest food chain on the diagram is: grasses to mice to snakes to weasels to wolves to worms.

14. (G) According to the diagram, the only animals that eat snakes are hawks and weasels. You must look at the arrows in the diagram to answer the questions dealing with the network of feeding relationships.

15. (C) Grasses and trees are the only independent organisms in the diagram. The photosynthesis of green plants derives energy from solar radiation. All the animals in the diagram are dependent on plants or other animals.

16. (J) Since weasels eat rabbits, a reduction in the number of weasels would allow an increase in the number of rabbits. Since bobcats eat rabbits, the larger number of rabbits would allow an increase in the number of bobcats. Probably the chicken farmers do not realize that their weasel campaign could lead to more bobcats.

17. (A) Within the range 0.2 to 0.7 atmosphere, it is true that lower current accompanied the lower pressure. Since the current is proportional to the amount of ionization, the prior hypothesis holds for that pressure range.

18. (J) The battery must be present to produce the current which flows around the circuit. Both meters must be present to measure the current and pressure. However, the vacuum pump could be switched off during one reading; it would have to be switched back on to lower the pressure for the next reading.

19. (B) At lower pressures, there are fewer molecules of nitrogen and oxygen in the flask. Thus the alpha particles encounter fewer molecules to ionize. The lower degree of ionization results in lower currents.

20. (H) The polonium-210 loses half of its radioactivity every 138 days. If the researcher tried to repeat the experiment 90 days later, there would be fewer alpha particles emitted from the source and less ionization of the air. The new current readings would be lower than the original readings.

21. (B) In the pressure range 0.7 to 1.0 atmosphere, the energy of the alpha particles must be completely dissipated in ionization. This would explain why a change of pressure within that range does not affect the degree of ionization: it is as high as it can get.

22. (F) The lining of the flask serves only to conduct current. Substituting aluminum—or any other metal—for the silver should not affect the results. Choice (G) affects the degree of ionization, (H) affects the current directly, and (J) affects the number of alpha particles.

23. (C) The passage mentions Rhesus monkeys as an example of primates. Apes and monkeys are closely related to humans (also classified as primates), so any primate studies would be relevant to human medicine.

24. (J) The statement that few of the animals infected with a supposedly carcinogenic virus actually develop cancers certainly suggests that the case for animal tumor viruses is still uncertain.

25. (D) In the second sentence, Scientist 1 mentions connective-tissue cancer. The following sentence says that cancers of the same kind are called sarcomas.

26. (G) If new cancer-causing agents are discovered frequently, then we do not know all the causes of cancer. Perhaps viruses are a "new" cause yet to be discovered.

27. (A) It is accepted that cancer may be spread by injecting cancerous cells into a healthy animal. To show that some other material in the injected liquid causes the cancer, it is necessary to filter out any cancer cells.

28. (J) Scientist 2 does not accept the evidence that some animal cancers are induced by viruses. If Scientist 1 could prove that point, it would weaken the argument presented by Scientist 2.

29. (D) Scientist 1 implies that only miniscule virus particles are small enough to pass through the filters and remain in the liquid to be injected. If some material besides viruses also passed through the filters, that other material could be the cause of the induced cancers.

30. (J) Iodine forms the weakest bond with hydrogen. The I-H bond has an energy of 71 kcal/mole, less than the value for F-H, Cl-H, or Br-H. It is important for you to realize that a high energy means a strong bond, while a low energy means a weak bond.

31. (B) The Cl-Cl bond has a higher energy, and thus is stronger, than the F-F, Br-Br, or I-I bonds. Notice that the question refers to molecules with two identical halogen atoms.

32. (F) Carbon tetrachloride would be the largest molecule, because the central carbon atom is surrounded by four large chlorine atoms. Look at the first table to see the relative sizes of the atoms. Molecules (G) and (J) are not as large as carbon tetrachloride because they have only one large halogen atom.

33. (B) In the chlorine bonds, Cl-O is 12 kcal/mole less than Cl-F. By analogy, Br-O should be about 12 kcal/mole less than the value for Br-F, which is 57 kcal/mole. 57 minus 12 equals 45 kcal/mole.

34. (J) The best generalization of the bond strengths is that the bond is stronger (energy is higher) between smaller atoms. This explains the very strong bonds with the small hydrogen atom and the very weak bonds with the large iodine atom.

35. (B) The experiments were performed to explore the possibility of gene exchange. The assumption is that the abilities to synthesize leucine and cystine are governed by different genes.

36. (G) Since all organisms need amino acids for metabolism and growth, yet the normal bacteria do not require an external source, they must manufacture the needed amino acids internally.

37. (A) Since the L strain needed a supply of leucine to survive, that strain cannot manufacture its own leucine. However, the strain did not require any cystine nutrient, so it must be able to synthesize its own cystine.

38. (F) The C strain would have been able to grow if supplied with a source of cystine, because it could synthesize all other needed amino acids. The L strain would not have been able to grow under those conditions, for it still had no possible means of obtaining the leucine which it needed but couldn't synthesize.

39. (D) At least one of the two strains must have received the gene permitting it to manufacture the one amino acid that it originally couldn't manufacture. However, the mere growth of colonies does not reveal whether the growing bacteria come from the C strain, the L strain, or both strains.

40. (G) It is possible that the mutant C and L strains lacked more than one gene apiece compared to the normal bacteria. If they each were missing the same gene (plus other missing genes to differentiate the two strains), then even perfect gene exchange in the mixed culture could not have reconstructed the normal gene set. This difficult question is best answered by eliminating the other three choices.

Appendixes

APPENDIX A: ENGLISH REVIEW

The following section contains a brief review of the major concepts, rules, and most common errors usually found in English grammar and usage exams. Many helpful study techniques are also included.

Before reading the review in full, skim through it and read the headings of each section. Then read first those sections that are most important to you, the sections that cover your personal "trouble spots." After you read a section, close the book and try to write a brief summary of what you've read to check your understanding.

PUNCTUATION

Instances of incorrect or omitted punctuation appear on the ACT. The most important marks of punctuation tested are the comma (,) and semicolon (;). Typically, the ACT tests *obvious* and *basic* punctuation skills rather than subjective, stylistic uses of the comma or semicolon.

The Comma

Use a comma

- before words like *and, or, but, so, for,* and *yet* that join two or more complete sentences (each with a subject and verb and able to stand alone and make sense) into a compound sentence:

> The horrifying aftermath of the fire was reported on all the news stations, and the arson squad worked diligently to uncover the cause of the tragedy.
> Linguists expect to find primitive languages simple and uncomplicated, but they find instead that early language systems were strikingly elaborate and complex.

NOTE: To punctuate a compound sentence when the two or more clauses themselves contain commas, a semicolon is sometimes needed. See the review section on the semicolon for further explanation.

- to set off interrupting or introductory words or phrases:

> *Safe in the house,* we watched the rain fall outside.
> *Regrettably,* many of my friends will not attend the party.
> Tom, *after all,* is one of twelve children.
> You home is in Lincoln, Nebraska, *isn't it?*
> One must, *of course,* save a great deal of money before one goes into business for oneself.

- to separate a series of words or word groups:

> The threat of runaway inflation, the heightened tension regarding foreign affairs, and the lack of quality education in many schools are issues that will be addressed in political campaigns for years to come.

- to set off nonessential clauses and phrases that are descriptive but not needed to get across the basic meaning of the sentence:

> Truman, who tried to continue Roosevelt's conciliatory approach to the Soviet Union, adopted a much tougher policy toward the Russians by 1946.

The clause *who tried . . . Union* is not necessary. Truman's name is sufficient and the clause is merely descriptive, not definitional. The clause is then nonessential and therefore set off by commas.

> My wealthy Aunt Em, exceeding the trait of being economical, is so parsimonious she washes paper plates to be used again.

The phrase *exceeding the trait of being economical* is set off by commas because it is extra information and descriptive, not essential and definitional.

Remember, clauses and phrases that *are* essential and definitional are *not* set off by commas.

> Any teacher who ignores the varying and individual skill levels of his or her students is apt to devise lesson plans either too elementary or too advanced for effective sequential learning of new skills.

The clause *who ignores the varying . . . students* is essential; without it the reader might wonder *which* teachers. Because it defines precisely which teachers, it is not set off by commas.

> Nothing was allowed to be published in Iron Curtain countries except material that had secured the approval of the Communist Party.

The clause *that had secured . . . Party* is essential here and is therefore not set off by commas. Without this clause the sentence meaning would be quite ambiguous. Again, the reader would not know *which* material because the definitional clause is necessary here.

- to set off appositives (second nouns or noun equivalents that give additional information about a preceding noun):

> Mr. Johnson, a teacher, ran for Chairman of the School Board.
> Robert's wife, Marsha, played the harp.

When the second noun is needed to identify and to distinguish the first noun from others of its kind, the second noun is not set off with commas:

> The word *tenacious* was misspelled.
> My daughter Wendy loves to swim more than her sister does.

Since there are two daughters, *Wendy* is essential to distinguish which daughter loves to swim, and the word is therefore not set off by commas.

- after introductory clauses or phrases:

> Although the thirteen-year-old boys grew restive under the new discipline policy, the girls seemed unperturbed by it.
> When finishing an essay, do not end with an apology for not having said anything or with an indignant statement about the unfair allotment of time.

The following are some situations in which commas should *not* be used.

Do NOT use a comma

- to separate a subject and its verb or a verb and its complement:

  > Requiring the study of grammar in secondary English classes, is, somewhat controversial.

  The first comma unnecessarily separates *requiring* and *is* (subject and verb); the second separates *is* and *somewhat controversial* (verb and its complement).

- to separate a verb from its object:

  > Dolly Parton combines, a buxom blonde appearance, a homespun country-western sense of humor, and a dynamic vocal range.

  In this sentence the first comma separates *combines* (verb) from *appearance . . . sense . . . range* and splits the verb from the objects.

- to connect independent sentences without also using conjunctions such as *but, and, or, so, for,* and *yet.*

  > At the last board meeting, an irate administrator argued that management should be given the right to fire employees as necessary to enforce board policies, that right was conceded.

  Both a comma and *and* are needed after *policies* to connect the two independent sentences correctly. A semicolon would also be correct here. See the review section dealing with semicolons for more information.

- to set off essential modifying information from the word modified:

  > A steadily increasing incidence of vandalism is an appalling reality, characteristic of the inner-city neighborhoods, in many metropolitan areas.

  The two commas in this sentence are unnecessary and separate modifying phrases from the two words they modify.

NOTE: To avoid some of the punctuation errors involving either misuse of or omission of commas, try reading the sentence out loud (in a whisper) to yourself. Often your ear will catch an error your eye might overlook. Read over the examples in the section headed "Do *not* use a comma," and you will *hear,* in most cases, the correct punctuation.

The Semicolon

Use a semicolon

- to separate two complete sentences when they are not joined by words like *and, but, for, or, nor,* or *yet:*

  The winter was exceptionally cold; once again fuel shortages plagued the northeastern cities.

  Long-awaited relief from the six-month drought was in sight; the barometric pressure readings indicated a rainstorm was on its way.

  A common error in punctuation is to connect sentences such as the two above with a comma only. One way of avoiding this error is to read the sentences out loud. A long pause between the two sentences indicates the need for a semicolon. Also, remember that two independent sentences may be punctuated as separate sentences with periods at the end of each or as two connected sentences punctuated with a semicolon (;) alone or with a comma and a conjunction (, and) (, but) (, or).

- before words like *however, therefore, moreover, then,* and *consequently* when they are used to link two complete sentences:

  It was raining outside; *however* we felt quite warm and dry inside the house.
  I feel happy about my new job; *consequently* I work quickly and efficiently.
  My friend spends afternoon hours watching TV talk shows; *then* he watches situation comedies all evening.

- before words like *and, but, for, or, nor,* and *yet* that join two complete sentences of a compound sentence if either of the two sentences contains a comma:

  Kim, my sister, could not take time off from work in August; but she took her vacation in September to travel to Canada, where she camped for two weeks.

The Colon

Use a colon

- to formally introduce a statement, a quotation, or a series of terms:

    Introducing a statement—The members of the community all hold the following belief: We should all love our neighbors.

    Introducing a quotation—John F. Kennedy is remembered for these words: "Ask not what your country can do for you; ask what you can do for your country."

    Introducing a series—The most familiar punctuation devices are these: the period, the comma, the semicolon, the colon, and the question mark.

Playing the Punctuation Game: Some Extra Practice

In addition to the practice this book provides, you can strengthen your punctuation skill by doing the following. Have a friend recopy for you a long newspaper or magazine article or editorial, leaving out all the punctuation marks. Then your task becomes putting the punctuation marks back in. Use the original article to check your choices. In current magazine and newspaper articles there may be a wide range of uses of some marks of punctuation, especially the comma. Your practice time playing the "Punctuation Game" is well spent, however, because you have practiced looking for the appropriate places for punctuation. Practicing this editing skill will help you on the ACT.

GRAMMAR, USAGE, AND SENTENCE STRUCTURE

Pronouns

- Use *I, he, she, we,* and *they* in place of the *subject* of a sentence. (The subject is the *doer.*):

    Bill wrote a sentence.
    He wrote a sentence.
    I wrote a sentence.

Susan was late for work.
She was late for work.
My family always takes a summer vacation.
We always take a summer vacation.
Jerry's family always takes a summer vacation.
They always take a summer vacation.

- Use *me, him, her, us,* and *them* in place of the *object* of a sentence. (The object is the *receiver.*):

  Bill greeted *Jerry.*
  Bill greeted *him.*
  Bill greeted *me.*
  The boss fired *Susan.*
  The boss fired *her.*
  Camille helped *Christopher and me* pack our suitcases.
  Camille helped *us* pack our suitcasaes.
  The lifeguard saved *three people* from drowning.
  The lifeguard saved *them* from drowning.

- Use *who* as a *subject* (a *doer*):

  Who knocked at the door?
  Do you know *who knocked* at the door?
  No doubt it was a neighbor *who,* a few minutes ago, *knocked* at the door.

- Use *whom* as an *object* (a *receiver*):

  To whom were you *speaking*?
  Your line was busy, and I wondered *to whom* you were *speaking.*
  I'm the person *whom* you *telephoned* yesterday.

PRONOUN REVIEW CHART
PERSONAL PRONOUNS

	Nominative (subject)		Objective (object)		Possessive (ownership)	
	singular	*plural*	*singular*	*plural*	*singular*	*plural*
First Person	I	we	me	us	my mine	our ours
Second Person	you	you	you	you	your yours	your yours
Third Person	he she it	they	him her it	them	his her, hers its	their theirs

RELATIVE PRONOUNS

Nominative (subject)	Objective (object)	Possessive (ownership)
who (persons) which (things) that (things and persons)	whom	whose

Verb Tense

- Most verbs are regular. For these verbs add *-ed* to talk about the past and *will* or *shall* to talk about the future.

    Past: I *walked* yesterday.
    Present: I *walk* today.
    Future: I *will walk* tomorrow.

One way to practice the basic forms of regular verbs is to recite the *past tense* and *past participle* when you are given only the *present tense*. Here are some examples:

Present	*Past* (*-ed*)
I *talk* today.	I *talked* yesterday.
I *help* you today.	I *helped* you yesterday.
I *close* shop early today.	I *closed* shop early yesterday.

Past Participle (-ed)

I have *talked* on many occasions.
I have *helped* you often.
I have *closed* shop early for a week.

- Some verbs are *irregular* and require special constructions to express the past and past participle. Here are some of the most troublesome irregular verbs:

Present	*Past*	*Past Participle*
begin	began	begun
burst	burst	burst
do	did	done
drown	drowned	drowned
go	went	gone
hang (to execute)	hanged	hanged
hang (to suspend)	hung	hung
lay (to put in place)	laid	laid
lie (to rest)	lay	lain
set (to place in position)	set	set
sit (to be seated)	sat	sat
shine (to provide light)	shone	shone
shine (to polish)	shined	shined
raise (to lift up)	raised	raised
rise (to get up)	rose	risen
swim	swam	swum
swing	swung	swung

Subject-Verb Agreement

- If a subject is plural, the verb must be plural; if a subject is singular, the verb must be singular. The following sentence is incorrect:

  Here on the table *is* an *apple and three pears.*

Focus on the verb (*is*) and then locate the subject. In this sentence, the subject (*an apple and three pears*) *follows* the verb.

Since the subject is plural, the verb must be plural, and the sentence should say:

Here on the table *are* an apple and three pears.

Here is another example that is incorrect:

The man, along with his friends and neighbors, support the home-town candidate.

The verb is *support*. Since the subject is singular (*man*), the verb must be singular—*supports* instead of *support*. Notice that in this case many words separate the subject from the verb; subject and verb will not always be close to one another.

Adjectives and Adverbs

- Adjectives describe nouns:

    Holidays are *happy* occasions. (*Happy* describes *occasions*.)
    His was a *narrow* escape. (*Narrow* describes *escape*.)
    Jesse Owens was a *successful* athlete. (*Successful* describes *athlete*.)

- Adverbs describe verbs:

    We all sang *happily*. (*Happily* describes *sang*.)
    He *narrowly* missed an oncoming car. (*Narrowly* describes *missed*.)
    Jesse Owens *successfully* completed the race. (*Successfully* describes *completed*.)

- Making comparisons—Adjectives normally add *-er* or *-est* to make comparisons.

    Use *-er* to compare two items: Cindy was the great*er* of the two athletes.
    Sometimes use *more* to compare two items: Christopher was the *more* handsome of the twins.
    Use *-est* to compare more than two items: Cindy was the great*est* athlete on the team.
    Sometimes use *most* to compare more than two items: Christopher was the *most* handsome member of the family.

Adverbs normally use *more* or *most* to make comparisons:

> Bob ran *more* quickly today than he did yesterday.
> Bob runs *most* quickly in the early morning.

NOTE: The first sentence compares only two items, today and yesterday, and so it requires *more.* The second sentence compares one time (early morning) with many other possible times, and so it requires *most.*

- Use an adjective after a verb that expresses being, feeling, tasting, or smelling.

> Harry seems happy. (not <u>happily</u>)
> Bill feels bad. (not <u>badly</u>)
> The candy tastes sweet. (not <u>sweetly</u>)
> The flowers smell sweet. (not <u>sweetly</u>)

Idiom

To native English speakers, certain expressions "sound right" because they are so commonly used. Such expressions are called "idiomatic" and are correct simply because they are so widely accepted. Here is a list of examples:

Idiomatic	*Unidiomatic*
addicted *to*	addicted *from*
angry *with*	angry *at*
capable *of*	capable *to*
different *from*	different *than*
identical *with*	identical *to*
obedient *to*	obedient *in*
on *the* whole	on *a* whole

Remember that the standard of correctness is standard written English. Be alert to idiomatic expressions not acceptable or characteristic of standard *written* English.

Double Negatives

To use a double negative is incorrect in standard written English. When words like *hardly, scarcely,* and *barely,* considered "negative" words, are used along with other negative words such as *not, no, none, never,* and *nothing* in the same sentence to express the same negative meaning twice, a "double negative" occurs. For example,

> The puppy *didn't* have *no one* to love.

The notion that there is not anyone to love is expressed twice—once by the *didn't* (did + not) and once by *no one.*

> After a hard day's work, Susan *can't hardly* stay awake.

Susan's not being able to stay awake is expressed twice—once with the *can't* (can + not) and again with *hardly.* Here are some other examples of "double negatives":

> You *don't* have *scarcely* anything to worry about.
> The fans *can't hardly* wait for the concert to begin.

NOTE: Merely the occurrence of two negative words in the same sentence does not result in a "double negative" as in the following example:

> I had *no* time available on weekends, so I decided I would *not* take the part-time job offer.

The *no* and the *not* in this sentence express two different negatives and are therefore not considered "double negatives."

Either/Or—Neither/Nor

- Use *either* or *neither* to compare two items (*either* is sometimes used to compare more than two items):

> Uncle Joe will arrive *either* today or tomorrow morning.
> *Neither* of these two shirts fits me very well.

- Use *either* with *or:*

> Uncle Joe will arrive *either* today *or* tomorrow.

- Use *neither* with *nor:*

> *Neither* the white shirt *nor* the blue shirt fits me very well.

NOTE: *Nor* may not be used in a sentence without *neither.* The following sentence is incorrect. *No* rain *nor* snow had fallen for weeks. The sentence should read like this: *Neither* rain *nor* snow had fallen for weeks.

Exact Word Choice

Sometimes words that sound alike are confused with one another. Checking their dictionary meanings will help you to avoid their misuse. Here are some commonly confused words:

1. adapt/adept	9. lay/lie
2. capital/capitol	10. persecute/prosecute
3. compile/comply	11. precede/proceed
4. detain/retain	12. raise/rise
5. elicit/illicit	13. set/sit
6. foreword/forward	14. their/there/they're
7. human/humane	15. weather/whether
8. incite/insight	

Special Problems

Fewer/Less

- *Fewer* is used with *countable* items:

  There are *fewer people* in the room than I had expected.

- *Less* is used with *uncountable* items:

  There has been *less rain* this year than in years past.

Many/Much

- *Many* is used with *countable* items:

  There are *many people* at the meeting tonight.

- *Much* is used with *uncountable* items:

  Frank spends too *much time* worrying about the future.

Sentence Fragments

A sentence fragment is an *incomplete* sentence that is written and punctuated as if it were a *complete* sentence. Here are some examples of sentence fragments.

> *Fragment:* Although Fred must leave for work early each morning.

Problem: Although suggests another action that would make the sentence complete.

Complete Sentence: Although Fred must leave for work early each morning, *he never gets to bed before one A.M.*

Fragment: Hard study, a baseball game with friends, or just some sleep.

Problem: There is no subject (doer) and no verb (action).

Complete Sentence: Tim [subject] could not *decide* [verb] whether to devote his afternoon to hard study, a baseball game with friends, or just some sleep.

Fragment: People who sing loudly and happily in the shower.

Problem: People who signals the need for additional information, what the people who sing do.

Complete Sentence: People who sing loudly and happily in the shower *often start the day feeling optimistic.*

Wordiness

Saying the same thing twice is one common type of wordiness. Here are some examples with the repetitions italicized:

At 8 A.M. *in the morning* it *suddenly* started to rain *without warning.*

In this *modern world* of *today* there are hundreds of *millionaires with a great deal of money.*

Several *separate* and *distinct* programs signaled a new era of economic progress.

Students found the *lectures* Professor Smith gave while he was *speaking* difficult to *understand* and *comprehend.*

Parallelism

Items in a sentence are *parallel* when they have the same *form.* Here are three series of parallel items:

to join the army, to find a job, to enroll in college
joining the army, finding a job, enrolling in college
the army, a job, college

The following sentence *mixes forms,* an example of *faulty parallelism:*

> *Faulty:* Once he turned eighteen, the young man's choices were *joining the army, to find a job, or college.*
> *Correct:* Once he turned eighteen, the young man's choices were *the army, a job, or college.*

Sometimes faulty parallelism occurs in just two items instead of three:

> *Faulty:* The youngster needed to choose between *playing* outdoors with friends and *to study* for a test.
> *Correct:* The youngster needed to choose between *playing* outdoors with friends and *studying* for a test.

Misplaced Modifiers

A misplaced modifier occurs when a *description* does not clearly refer to the *item described:*

> *Faulty: Galloping* across the finish line, *I* realized I had bet on the wrong horse.

The sentence structure indicates that *I* am doing the *galloping.*

> *Correct:* As the winner galloped across the finish line, I realized I had bet on the wrong horse.

Here are some other misplaced modifiers. Notice that in each case the *description* does not clearly refer to the *item described.*

> A *kitten* [item described] was brought out by an *attendant* with a *pitiful meow* [description].
> (The item described is not clearly connected with its description.)
> *To keep cool* [description] during summer weather, my air conditioner ran constantly.
> (The item described—a person—is omitted altogether.)

Corrections:

> A *kitten with a pitiful meow* was brought out by an attendant.
> *To keep cool* during summer weather, *I* run my air conditioner constantly.

Comparisons

- As/than—*As* and *than* are often used to structure comparisons, sometimes incorrectly and incompletely:

  Correct combinations: as . . . as . . . than

      as . . . as

  Incorrect combinations: as . . . than

  Correct sentences:

  She is *as* pretty *as,* if not prettier *than,* any other girl.

  Linda is *as* pretty *as* any of her sisters.

  Incorrect sentences:

  She is *as* pretty, if not prettier *than,* any other girl.

  Linda is *as* pretty *than* any of her sisters.

APPENDIX B: IMPORTANT TERMINOLOGY, FORMULAS, AND GENERAL MATHEMATICAL INFORMATION THAT YOU SHOULD BE FAMILIAR WITH

The following section contains some important terminology, formulas, and general mathematical information that you should be familiar with. Some basic trigonometry terms and functions are shown, even though only a small portion of the test involves trigonometry. Remember, the content area breakdown is basically as follows:

Pre-Algebra and Elementary Algebra   40%
Intermediate Algebra and Coordinate Geometry   30%
Plane Geometry   23%
Trigonometry   7%

Your review of basic skills should be geared in proportion to the areas above.

COMMON MATH TERMS

Natural numbers—the counting numbers: 1, 2, 3, . . .

Whole numbers—the counting numbers beginning with zero: 0, 1, 2, 3, . . .

Integers—positive and negative whole numbers and zero: . . . −3, −2, −1, 0, 1, 2, . . .

Rational numbers—fractions, such as $\frac{3}{2}$ or $\frac{7}{8}$. Since a number such as 5 may be written as $\frac{5}{1}$, all *integers* are *rational numbers.*

Irrational numbers—examples of irrational numbers are $\sqrt{3}$ and π.

Real numbers—real numbers consist of all *rational* and *irrational* numbers.

Imaginary numbers—numbers which involve square roots of negative numbers: $\sqrt{-1} = i, \sqrt{-2} = \sqrt{2}i, \sqrt{-3} = \sqrt{3}i, \sqrt{-4} = 2i, \ldots$

Complex numbers—numbers in the form $a + bi$ where a and b are real numbers: $3 + 2i, 5 + 3i, 7 - 5i, \ldots$

Odd numbers—numbers not divisible by 2: 1, 3, 5, 7, . . .

Even numbers—numbers divisible by 2: 0, 2, 4, 6, . . .

Prime number—number divisible by only 1 and itself: 2, 3, 5, 7, 11, 13, . . .

Composite number—number divisible by more than just 1 and itself: 4, 6, 8, 9, 10, 12, 14, 15, . . .

Squares—the result when numbers are multiplied by themselves, $(2 \cdot 2 = 4)$, $(3 \cdot 3 = 9)$: 1, 4, 9, 16, 25, 36, . . .

Cubes—the result when numbers are multiplied by themselves twice, $(2 \cdot 2 \cdot 2 = 8)$, $(3 \cdot 3 \cdot 3 = 27)$: 1, 8, 27, . . .

MATH FORMULAS

Triangle

Perimeter $= s_1 + s_2 + s_3$

Area $= \frac{1}{2}bh$

Square

Perimeter $= 4s$

Area $= s \cdot s$, or s^2

Rectangle

Perimeter $= 2(b + h)$, or $2b + 2h$

Area $= bh$, or lw

Parallelogram

Perimeter $= 2(l + w)$, or $2l + 2w$

Area $= bh$

Trapezoid

Perimeter $= b_1 + b_2 + s_1 + s_2$

Area $= \frac{1}{2}h(b_1 + b_2)$, or $h\left(\dfrac{b_1 + b_2}{2}\right)$

Circle

Circumference $= 2\pi r$, or πd

Area $= \pi r^2$

Pythagorean theorem (for right triangles) $a^2 + b^2 = c^2$

The sum of the squares of the legs of a right triangle equals the square of the hypotenuse.

Cube

Volume $= s \cdot s \cdot s = s^3$

Surface area $= s \cdot s \cdot 6$

Rectangular Prism

Volume $= l \cdot w \cdot h$

Surface area $= 2(lw) + 2(lh) + 2(wh)$

IMPORTANT EQUIVALENTS

Memorizing the following can eliminate unnecessary computations:

$\frac{1}{100} = .01 = 1\%$

$\frac{1}{10} = .1 = 10\%$

$\frac{1}{5} = \frac{2}{10} = .2 = .20 = 20\%$

$\frac{3}{10} = .3 = .30 = 30\%$

$\frac{2}{5} = \frac{4}{10} = .4 = .40 = 40\%$

$\frac{1}{2} = \frac{5}{10} = .5 = .50 = 50\%$

$\frac{3}{5} = \frac{6}{10} = .6 = .60 = 60\%$

$\frac{7}{10} = .7 = .70 = 70\%$

$\frac{4}{5} = \frac{8}{10} = .8 = .80 = 80\%$

$\frac{9}{10} = .9 = .90 = 90\%$

$\frac{1}{4} = \frac{25}{100} = .25 = 25\%$

$\frac{3}{4} = \frac{75}{100} = .75 = 75\%$

$\frac{1}{3} = .33\frac{1}{3} = 33\frac{1}{3}\%$

$\frac{2}{3} = .66\frac{2}{3} = 66\frac{2}{3}\%$

$\frac{1}{8} = .125 = .12\frac{1}{2} = 12\frac{1}{2}\%$

$\frac{3}{8} = .375 = .37\frac{1}{2} = 37\frac{1}{2}\%$

$\frac{5}{8} = .625 = .62\frac{1}{2} = 62\frac{1}{2}\%$

$\frac{7}{8} = .875 = .87\frac{1}{2} = 87\frac{1}{2}\%$

$\frac{1}{6} = .16\frac{2}{3} = 16\frac{2}{3}\%$

$\frac{5}{6} = .83\frac{1}{3} = 83\frac{1}{3}\%$

$1 = 1.00 = 100\%$

$2 = 2.00 = 200\%$

$3\frac{1}{2} = 3.5 = 3.50 = 350\%$

MEASURES

Customary System, or English System

Length
    12 inches (in) = 1 foot (ft)
    3 feet = 1 yard (yd)
    36 inches = 1 yard

    1760 yards = 1 mile (mi)
    5280 feet = 1 mile
    $5\frac{1}{2}$ yards = 1 rod

Area
    144 square inches (sq in) = 1 square foot (sq ft)
    9 square feet = 1 square yard (sq yd)

Weight
    16 ounces (oz) = 1 pound (lb)
    2000 pounds = 1 ton (T)

Capacity
    8 fluid ounces (fl oz) = 1 cup (c)
    2 cups = 1 pint (pt)
    2 pints = 1 quart (qt)

    4 quarts = 1 gallon (gal)
    8 dry quarts = 1 peck
    4 pecks = 1 bushel

Time

365 days = 1 year   10 years = 1 decade
52 weeks = 1 year   100 years = 1 century

Metric System, or *The International System of Units*
(SI, *Le Système International d'Unités*)

Length—meter
   Kilometer (km) = 1000 meters (m)
   Hectometer (hm) = 100 meters
   Dekameter (dam) = 10 meters

   Meter
   10 decimeters (dm) = 1 meter
   100 centimeters (cm) = 1 meter
   1000 millimeters (mm) = 1 meter

Volume—liter
   Common measures
      1000 milliliters (ml, or mL) = 1 liter (1, or L)
      1000 liters = 1 kiloliter (kl, or kL)

Mass—gram
   Common measures
      1000 milligrams (mg) = 1 gram (g)
      1000 grams = 1 kilogram (kg)
      1000 kilograms = 1 metric ton (t)

MATHEMATICAL WORDS AND PHRASES

Words that signal an operation:

ADDITION   *MULTIPLICATION*
- Sum   - Of
- Total   - Product
- Plus   - Times
- Increase   - At (Sometimes)
- More than   - Total (Sometimes)
- Greater than

SUBTRACTION
- Difference
- Less
- Decreased
- Reduced
- Fewer
- Have left

DIVISION
- Quotient
- Divisor
- Dividend
- Ratio
- Parts

GEOMETRY TERMS AND BASIC INFORMATION

Angles

Vertical angles—Formed by two intersecting lines, across from each other, always equal

Adjacent angles—Next to each other, share a common side and vertex

Right angle—Measures 90 degrees

Obtuse angle—Greater than 90 degrees

Acute angle—Less than 90 degrees

Straight angle, or line—Measures 180 degrees

Angle bisector—Divides an angle into two equal angles

Supplementary angles—Two angles whose total is 180 degrees

Complementary angles—Two angles whose total is 90 degrees

Lines

Two points determine a line

Parallel lines—Never meet; slopes are the same

Perpendicular lines—Meet at right angles; slopes are opposite reciprocals (for example, $\frac{1}{3}$ and -3)

Polygons

Polygon—A many-sided (more than two) closed figure

Regular polygon—A polygon with all sides and all angles equal

Triangle—Three-sided polygon; the interior angles total 180 degrees

    Equilateral triangle—All sides equal

    Isosceles triangle—Two sides equal

    Scalene triangle—All sides of different lengths

    Right triangle—A triangle containing a right angle

In a triangle—Angles opposite equal sides are equal.

In a triangle—The longest side is across from the largest angle, and the shortest side is across from the smallest angle.

In a triangle—The sum of any two sides of a triangle is larger than the third side.

In a triangle—An exterior angle is equal to the sum of the remote two angles.

Median of a triangle—A line segment that connects the vertex and the midpoint of the opposite side.

Quadrilateral—Four-sided polygon; the interior angles total 360 degrees.

    Parallelogram—A quadrilateral with opposite sides parallel

      Rectangle—A parallelogram with all right angles

      Rhombus—A parallelogram with equal sides

      Square—A parallelogram with equal sides and all right angles

      Trapezoid—A quadrilateral with two parallel sides

Pentagon—A five-sided polygon

Hexagon—A six-sided polygon

Octagon—An eight-sided polygon

Circles

Radius of a circle—A line segment from the center of the circle to the circle itself.

Diameter of a circle—A line segment that starts and ends on the circle and goes through the center.

Chord—A line segment that starts and ends on the circle

Arc—A part of the circle

A FEW REMINDERS ABOUT POLYNOMIALS

The Laws of Operation on Polynomials		
Law	Addition	Multiplication
Commutative	$a + (b + c) = (c + b) + a$ $= (b + c) + a$	$a(bc) = (bc)a = (cb)a$
Associative	$(a + b) + c = a + (b + c)$	$(ab)c = a(bc)$
Distributive	$x(a + b - c) = xa + xb - xc$ $(a + b - c)x = ax + bx - cx$	

Laws of Exponents

$$a^m \cdot a^n = a^{m+n}$$

$$(a^m)^n = a^{mn}$$

$$\frac{a^m}{a^n} = a^{m-n}, a \neq 0$$

$$(ab)^n = a^n b^n$$

$$a^0 = 1, a \neq 0$$

$$\left(\frac{a}{b}\right)^n = \frac{a^n}{b^n}, b \neq 0$$

$$a^{-n} = \frac{1}{a^n}, a \neq 0$$

THE QUADRATIC FORMULA

For a quadratic equation in the form $ax^2 + bx + c = 0$, the following quadratic formula is often used:

$$x = \frac{-b \pm \sqrt{b^2 - 4ac}}{2a}$$

By using first the $+$ and then the $-$ sign before the radical we obtain the two roots of the quadratic equation.

SOME BASIC TRIGONOMETRIC RATIOS

$$\sin \theta = \frac{\text{opposite side}}{\text{hypotenuse}} \qquad \cot \theta = \frac{\text{adjacent side}}{\text{opposite side}}$$

$$\cos \theta = \frac{\text{adjacent side}}{\text{hypotenuse}} \qquad \sec \theta = \frac{\text{hypotenuse}}{\text{adjacent side}}$$

$$\tan \theta = \frac{\text{opposite side}}{\text{adjacent side}} \qquad \csc \theta = \frac{\text{hypotenuse}}{\text{opposite side}}$$

The trigonometric functions are related by eight fundamental identities.

The Reciprocal Relations

(1) $\csc \theta = \dfrac{1}{\sin \theta}$

(2) $\sec \theta = \dfrac{1}{\cos \theta}$

(3) $\cot \theta = \dfrac{1}{\tan \theta}$

The Quotient Relations

(4) $\tan \theta = \dfrac{\sin \theta}{\cos \theta}$

(5) $\cot \theta = \dfrac{\cos \theta}{\sin \theta}$

The Pythagorean Relations

(6) $\sin^2 \theta + \cos^2 \theta = 1$

(7) $\tan^2 \theta + 1 = \sec^2 \theta$

(8) $1 + \cot^2 \theta = \csc^2 \theta$

GRAPHS OF THE BASIC TRIGONOMETRIC FUNCTIONS

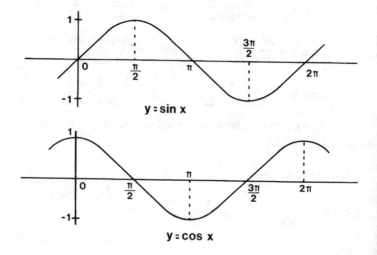

$y = \sin x$

$y = \cos x$

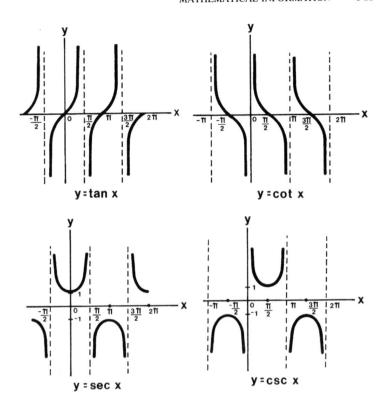

y = tan x

y = cot x

y = sec x

y = csc x

SOME BASIC LOGARITHMS

$Log_{10}1 = 0$, since $10^0 = 1$
$Log_{10}10 = 1$, since $10^1 = 10$
$Log_{10}100 = 2$, since $10^2 = 100$
$Log_{10}1000 = 3$, since $10^3 = 1000$
$Log_2 8 = 3$, since $2^3 = 8$
$Log_3 9 = 2$, since $3^2 = 9$
$Log_2 16 = 4$, since $2^4 = 16$

APPENDIX C: NATURAL SCIENCES TERMINOLOGY

The following section contains *some* of the basic terms often used in Science Reasoning passages. These lists are designed to simply refresh your memory regarding some basic science concepts so that you are more familiar with some of the subject matter in the passages. *Do not memorize* these lists; simply scan the terms to refresh your memory. Your review should be brief. **Remember, the science test is a Science *Reasoning* test.**

BIOLOGY

ADENOSINE TRIPHOSPHATE: A compound with energy-rich phosphate bonds involved in the transfer of energy in cellular metabolism (ATP).

ADRENALIN: A hormone secreted by the adrenal medulla, also called epinephrine.

AGNATHA: A class of vertebrates without jaws. Includes the hagfish and lamprey.

ALGAE: Simple plants containing chlorophyll.

ALLELES: Genes on the same loci of homologous chromosomes but producing contrasting characteristics.

AMINO ACID: An organic compound containing an amino and a carboxyl group; the building blocks of proteins.

AMPHIBIA: A class of vertebrates capable of living both in water and on land; the larval forms have gills and the adults lungs. Includes frogs, toads, and salamanders.

ANGIOPERMAE: The class to which flowering plants belong.

ANNELIDA: A phylum of segmented worms.

ANTIBIOTIC: A substance produced by a microorganism that destroys or inhibits the growth of another microorganism.

ANTIBODY: A substance produced by the body to inactivate a foreign agent (an antigen).

ARACHNIDA: A class of arthropods with no antennae and four pairs of walking legs. Includes spiders, scorpions, ticks, mites, and king crabs.

ARTERY: A blood vessel which carries blood away from the heart.

ARTHROPODS: Segmented invertebrates with jointed appendages and a hard, chitinous exoskeleton.

ASEXUAL REPRODUCTION: Reproduction in one individual, without the union of gametes.

AVES: A class of vertebrates with feathers and wings; the birds.

AXON: The nerve process that conducts the impulse away from the body of a neuron.

BACTERIA: Unicellular organisms without a distinct nucleus and usually without chlorophyll.

BILE: A yellowish-green fluid secreted by the liver which aids in the digestion of fats.

BINOMIAL NOMENCLATURE: The international system of naming organisms using two names, the first generic, the second specific.

BRYOPHYTES: Plants of the phylum Bryophyta; mosses and liverworts.

CALORIE: The amount of heat required to raise the temperature of 1 gram of water 1°C. When capitalized, a unit of heat 1,000 times larger (kilocalorie).

CARBON CYCLE: The exchange of carbon between living things and their environment.

CARTILAGE: The connective tissue composing the bones of vertebrate embryos, largely replaced by bone in adults.

CELL: The basic unit of structure in organisms.

CENTRAL NERVOUS SYSTEM: The brain and spinal cord.

CEREBELLUM: The part of the vertebrate brain which controls muscular coordination.

CEREBRUM: The anterior part of the brain in which conscious mental processes take place.

CHONDRICHTHYES: A class of vertebrates comprising the cartilaginous fishes. Includes sharks, rays, skates, chimeras, and sawfishes.

CHORDATA: The phylum characterized by a notochord, pharyngeal gill clefts, and a dorsal, hollow nerve cord.

CHROMOSOME: A body composed of chromatin granules which appears in the cell nucleus during mitosis; the bearer of hereditary characteristics.

CLASS: The main subdivision of a phylum.

COELENTERATA: A phylum of animals having two layers of cells surrounding a digestive cavity.

CONIFER: A cone-bearing tree.

CORAL: A colonial marine coelenterate of the class Anthozoa.

CRUSTACEA: The class of arthropods characterized by gills and two pairs of antennae. Includes lobsters, crabs, barnacles, water fleas, and sawbugs.

CTENOPHORA: The phylum of marine animals comprising the comb jellies and sea walnuts.

CYTOPLASM: The ground substance of the cell outside the nucleus.

DENDRITE: The branching nerve fiber that conducts impulses toward the neuron.

DEOXYRIBONUCLEIC ACID (DNA): The nucleic acid in the chromosomes that stores genetic information.

DERMIS: The inner layer of the skin; the corium.

DIATOMS: Algae of the phylum Chrysophyta.

DIGESTION: The breakdown of food materials for absorption and assimilation.

DIPLOID: Having homologous pairs of chromosomes; twice the haploid number.

ECHINODERMATA: A phylum of radially symmetrical marine animals with spiny exoskeletons.

ECOLOGY: The study of relations between organisms and their environment.

EMBRYO: An organism in the early stages of development.

ENZYME: An organic catalyst.

EPIDERMIS: The outer layer (cuticle) of the skin.

EVOLUTION: The modification and development of organisms from pre-existing forms.

FAMILY: The main subdivision of an order.

FERTILIZATION: The union of gametes to form a zygote.

FOSSIL: Any naturally preserved remains of an organism.

FRUIT: The mature ovary of a flower.

GAMETE: A germ cell; an egg or sperm cell.

GENE: A unit of heredity located on the chromosome.

GENOTYPE: The genetic constitution of an individual organism.

GENUS: The main division of a family.

GYMNOSPERMAE: A class of vascular plants bearing seeds in cones.

HAPLOID: Having one set of chromosomes as in gametes; half the diploid number.

HEMOGLOBIN: The respiratory pigment of the red blood cells.

HOMOLOGY: The correspondence of body structures of different organisms due to common ancestry. The structures may not have the same function.

HORMONE: A chemical substance produced by an endocrine gland that regulates cell activities.

HYBRID: The offspring of genetically different parents.

INSECTA: A class of arthropods characterized by three distinct body sections, three pairs of legs, and usually two pairs of wings.

INSULIN: A hormone produced by the pancreas which regulates the utilization of sugar.

KREBS CYCLE: The series of enzyme-controlled reactions which convert pyruvic acid to carbon dioxide, water, and energy.

LAMARCK'S THEORY: The belief that acquired characteristics are inherited.

LIGAMENT: A fibrous band which connects bone to bone or supports an organ.

MAMMALIA: A class of warm-blooded vertebrates possessing hair and feeding their young by means of mammary glands.

MEDULLA OBLONGATA: The posterior part of the vertebrate brain.

MEIOSIS: The two successive cell divisions in the formation of gametes which result in four daughter cells, each containing one-half the number of chromosomes of the parent cell. Also called *reduction division.*

METABOLISM: The chemical changes taking place in an organism.

METAMORPHOSIS: The changes in structure that occur in the development of the adult from the larval form.

METAZOA: Multicellular animals.

MITOCHONDRIA: Organelles of the cytoplasm containing enzymes.

MITOSIS: Cell division in which the chromosomes split, forming daughter cells with the same number of chromosomes as the original cell.

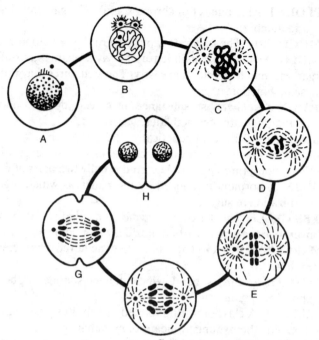

Mitosis. A, resting cell; B, C, and D, prophase; E. metaphase; F, anaphase; G and H, telophase.

MOLLUSKS: Animals of the phylum Mollusca having soft, unsegmented bodies usually protected by a shell.

MUTUALISM: A mutually beneficial relationship between two organisms of different species.

MUTATION: An inheritable change in the structure of a gene.

NATURAL SELECTION: The survival of the best adapted organisms.

NERVOUS SYSTEM: The system composed of the brain, spinal cord, ganglia, and nerves.

NUCLEUS: The spheroid body in the cell containing chromatin and controlling cellular activities.

OOGENESIS: The maturation of egg cells.

ORDER: The main division of a class.

ORGAN: A group of cells or tissues functioning as a whole.

OSMOSIS: The diffusion of fluid through a semipermeable membrane separating two solutions, from the less dense to the more dense.

OSTEICHTHYES: The class of vertebrates comprising the bony fishes.

OXYGEN DEBT: The amount of oxygen needed to oxidize the lactic acid built up in the muscle cells during heavy exercise.

PARASITE: An organism that lives on or in another organism, deriving food at the expense of its host.

PERICARDIUM: The outside membrane of the heart.

PHALANGES: The bones of the toes and fingers.

PHENOTYPE: Appearance of an organism, as opposed to its genetic constitution.

PHOTOSYNTHESIS: The synthesis of carbohydrates by green plants in the presence of sunlight.

PHYLUM: A main division of the plant or animal kingdom.

PISTIL: The central portion of a flower, consisting of the ovary, style, and stigma.

PITUITARY: The endocrine gland located at the base of the brain whose hormones regulate other glands.

PLASMA: The liquid part of the blood.

PLASMOLYSIS: The shrinking of cells as a result of loss of water by osmosis.

PLASMOPTYSIS: The bursting of cells due to an excessive intake of water by osmosis.

PLASTIDS: Organelles of the cytoplasm involved in food synthesis and storage.

PLATYHELMINTHES: An animal phylum comprised of flatworms.

POLLEN: The mature microspores of seed plants.

POLLINATION: Fertilization by the transfer of pollen from an anther to a stigma.

PORIFERA: The animal phylum constituted by the sponges.

PROTEIN: A complex organic compound made up of amino acids.

PROTOPLASM: The living material of the cell.

PROTOZOA: A phylum of one-celled animals.

REFLEX: A response to a stimulus.

REPTILIA: A class of scaly vertebrates which includes the turtles, lizards, snakes, alligators, and crocodiles.

RESPIRATION: Biological oxidation.

RIBOSOMES: Organelles of the cytoplasm concerned with protein synthesis.

SEPTUM: A wall separating two cavities.

SEXUAL REPRODUCTION: Reproduction involving the union of an egg and sperm cell.

SPECIES: The main division of a genus.

SPERM CELL: A male gamete.

SPORE: An asexual reproductive cell or structure.

SYMBIOSIS: The close living association of organisms of different species in which both benefit.

TAXONOMY: The science of the classification of organisms.

TISSUE: A group of specialized cells having the same function and structure.

TOXIN: A substance produced by an organism that is poisonous to another organism.

TRAIT: An inherited characteristic.

TRANSPIRATION: Evaporation of water from plants.

TROPISM: A growth movement of an organism in response to a continuous stimulus.

VACUOLE: A fluid-filled space in the cytoplasm that contains food material or wastes.

VEIN: A vessel which conveys blood to or toward the heart.

VERTEBRATA: A subphylum of chordates characterized by a well-developed brain, a backbone, and, usually, two pairs of limbs.

VIRUS: A simple, self-reproducing form of matter, often an infectious agent.

VITAMIN: An organic compound needed in small quantities for normal metabolism.

ZYGOTE: The cell resulting from the fusion of two gametes; the fertilized ovum.

To illustrate the mode of classifying living things, let us consider the dandelion from the plant kingdom and man from the animal kingdom.

DANDELION

Kingdom
Plantae
  Phylum
  Tracheophyta
    Class
    Angiospermae
      Order
      Campanulales
        Family
        Compositae
          Genus
          Taraxacum
            Species
            Taraxacum officinale

MAN

Kingdom
Animalia
  Phylum
  Chordata
    Class
    Mammalia
      Order
      Primates
        Family
        Hominidae
          Genus
          Homo
            Species
            Homo sapiens

KINGDOM PLANTAE

Subkingdom Thallophyta
(primitive plants)
Phylum Cyanophyta
(blue-green algae)
Phylum Euglenophyta
(euglena-like organisms)
Phylum Chlorophyta
(green algae)
Phylum Chrysophyta
(diatoms)
Phylum Pyrrophyta
(dinoflagellates)
Phylum Phaeophyta
(brown algae)
Phylum Rhodophyta
(red algae)
Phylum Schizomycophyta
(bacteria)
Phylum Myxomycophyta
(slime molds)
Phylum Eumycophyta
(molds and yeasts)
Subkingdom Embryophyta
(higher plants)
Phylum Bryophyta
(mosses and liverworts)
Phylum Tracheophyta
(vascular plants)

KINGDOM ANIMALIA

Subkingdom Protozoa
(unicellular animals)
Phylum Protozoa
(protozoa)
Subkingdom Metazoa
(multicellular animals)
Phylum Porifera
(sponges)
Phylum Coelenterata
(coelenterates)
Phylum Platyhelminthes
(flatworms)
Phylum Aschelminthes
(roundworms)
Phylum Echinodermata
(echinoderms)
Phylum Mollusca
(mollusks)
Phylum Annelida
(segmented worms)
Phylum Arthropoda
(arthropods)
Phylum Chordata
(chordates)

CHEMISTRY

ABSOLUTE TEMPERATURE: Temperature in degrees absolute (Kelvin) equals temperature in degrees centigrade plus 273. Zero degrees absolute is considered absolute zero.

ACID: A hydrogen-containing compound which yields hydrogen ions in water and turns blue litmus red.

ALKALI METALS: Group IA in the periodic table: Li, Na, K, and Kb.

ALKALINE EARTH METALS: Group IIA in the periodic table: Be, Mg, Ca, and Sr.

ALLOY: A metallic solution of a solid element in a solid element; the two or more elements of an alloy are miscible when melted, and do not separate out when the alloy solidifies.

ALPHA PARTICLE: An atomic structural unit, identical with a helium atom minus its two electrons; a product of radioactive disintegration.

ANION: A negatively charged ion; an anion in electrolysis moves toward the anode, or positive pole.

ANODE: The positive electrode.

ATOMIC NUMBER: The number of protons in an atomic nucleus, equal to the nuclear charge; the number of electrons in a neutral atom.

ATOMIC WEIGHT: The weight of an atom of an element relative to the weight of an atom of C^{12}; each possible isotope of an element will have a different weight, and the usual atomic weight of an element is an average of these.

AVOGADRO'S NUMBER: 6.02×10^{23} (the number of molecules in a gram molecular weight or one mole of a substance).

BASE: A metallic hydroxide which, when water soluble, yields hydroxide ions in solution and turns red litmus blue.

BETA PARTICLE: An electron emitted from the nucleus of an atom during radioactive disintegration.

BOYLE'S LAW: The volume of a gas varies inversely with pressure at constant temperature.

CATALYST: A nonreacting component in a chemical reaction which alters the speed of the reaction.

CATHODE: The negative electrode.

CATION: A positively charged ion; a cation in electrolysis moves toward the cathode, or negative pole.

CHARLES'S LAW: The volume of a gas varies directly with absolute temperature at constant pressure.

COMPOUND: A homogeneous substance formed by chemical union of two or more elements in constant proportions by weight.

CONDENSATION: The liquefaction of a vapor.

CONSERVATION OF ENERGY, LAW OF: Energy may be changed from one kind to another, but never lost or gained. Types of energy include mechanical (potential, kinetic), electrical, electromagnetic (radiant), and thermal (heat).

CONSERVATION OF MASS, LAW OF: There is no detectable gain or loss of total mass in chemical change.

CRYSTAL: A solid in which the atoms are arranged in a symmetrical regular pattern so that the form of the solid is that of a geometrical figure, with crystal faces along axes and at definite angles.

DENSITY: Mass per unit volume of a substance.

DISSOCIATION: Separation of a compound in solution to positive and negative ions.

ELECTRON: The smallest known particle with a negative unit charge and a mass which is 1/1837 that of the hydrogen atom: in atomic theory, electrons form a negatively charged cloud about the nucleus of an atom; electron movement constitutes electricity.

ELEMENTS: Substances which cannot be broken down into simpler substances without a change in their characteristic properties.

EQUILIBRIUM: The point at which two opposing chemical reactions balance.

EVAPORATION: A change of a substance from a liquid to a gas.

FISSION: The splitting of an atom nucleus into parts, with the release of energy, by particle bombardment.

FUSION: The melting of a solid to form a liquid; nuclear fusion is the union of isotopes of lighter elements at high temperature to form heavier nuclei, with release of energy.

HALF-LIFE: The time required for the radioactivity of a substance to drop by half.

HALOGENS: Nonmetallic salt- (and acid-) forming members of Group VIIA of the periodic table: F, Cl, Br, and I.

HYDROLYSIS: Chemical decomposition of a compound by reaction with water.

ION: A charged atom or group of atoms formed by the loss or gain of one or more electrons.

ISOTOPES: Isotopes of an element have the same number of protons and electrons and show the same chemical behavior, but they have differing numbers of nuclear neutrons and thus a different weight; isotopes may be stable or radioactive.

METALS: Elements that tend to lose electrons and form cations.

MIXTURE: Substances mixed, in any proportion, without reaction.

MOLE: Abbreviation for molecular weight.

MOLECULAR WEIGHT: The sum of the weights of the atoms in a unit of a compound.

MOLECULE: The smallest unit of a compound which can have a free existence as a chemical entity.

NEUTRALIZATION: The chemical reaction of an acid with a base in such proportion (as in titration to an end point) that a salt and water are formed.

NEUTRON: A fundamental (subatomic) particle of zero charge; in atomic theory, neutrons, along with protons, are nucleons which make up the nuclei of atoms.

NOBLE GASES: Also called inert gases, the relatively nonreactive elements, He, Ne, Ar, Kr, and Xe.

NONMETALS: Elements that tend to gain electrons and form anions.

NUCLEUS: The atomic center of an element made up of neutrons and protons (nucleons), the center of mass.

OCTET RULE: A metallic element tends to give, or a nonmetallic element tends to gain, electrons to achieve an outer electron configuration of eight electrons.

OXIDATION: An increase in valence by the loss of electrons.

pH: Logarithm of the reciprocal of hydrogen ion concentration.

PROTON: A subatomic particle, carrying a unit positive charge; hydrogen ions are sometimes considered protons; in atomic theory, protons, along with neutrons, make up the nuclei of atoms, with the number of protons equal to the atomic number of the atom.

RADIATION: Generally, radiation includes not only radiant energy, but radioactive emanations, disintegration products, and subatomic particles.

RADIOACTIVE DISINTEGRATION: Spontaneous decay of a radioactive element by ejection of particles from nuclei, with subsequent transmutation to another element.

REACTION: Any change, usually chemical, that results in the formation of one kind of molecule from another.

REDUCTION: A decrease in valence by gain of electrons.

SALT: A cation-anion compound where the cation is a metal or a positive radical and the anion, a nonmetal or a negative radical.

SOLUTE: The substance which dissolves in a solvent to form a solution.

SOLVENT: Usually, the liquid in which a solute is dissolved.

SUBLIMATION: The process in which a substance changes directly from a solid to a gas, without an intermediate liquid stage.

VALENCE: A numerical representation of the bonding (combining) capacity of an atom or a radical; the number of electrons to be donated or accepted.

LIST OF FIRST 20 ELEMENTS

1. Hydrogen	6. Carbon	11. Sodium	16. Sulfur
2. Helium	7. Nitrogen	12. Magnesium	17. Chlorine
3. Lithium	8. Oxygen	13. Aluminum	18. Argon
4. Beryllium	9. Fluorine	14. Silicon	19. Potassium
5. Boron	10. Neon	15. Phosphorous	20. Calcium

Periodic Table of the Elements

Metals   Non-metals   Rare Gas Elements

IA	IIA	IIIB	IVB	VB	VIB	VIIB	VIII	VIII	VIII	IB	IIB	IIIA	IVA	VA	VIA	VIIA	0
1 H 1.00797																	2 He 4.0026
3 Li 6.939	4 Be 9.0122											5 B 10.811	6 C 12.01115	7 N 14.0067	8 O 15.9994	9 F 18.9984	10 Ne 20.183
11 Na 22.9898	12 Mg 24.312											13 Al 26.9815	14 Si 28.086	15 P 30.9738	16 S 32.064	17 Cl 35.453	18 Ar 39.948
19 K 39.102	20 Ca 40.08	21 Sc 44.956	22 Ti 47.90	23 V 50.942	24 Cr 51.996	25 Mn 54.9380	26 Fe 55.847	27 Co 58.9332	28 Ni 58.71	29 Cu 63.546	30 Zn 65.37	31 Ga 69.72	32 Ge 72.59	33 As 74.9216	34 Se 78.96	35 Br 79.904	36 Kr 83.80
37 Rb 85.47	38 Sr 87.62	39 Y 88.905	40 Zr 91.22	41 Nb 92.906	42 Mo 95.94	43 Tc (99)	44 Ru 101.07	45 Rh 102.905	46 Pd 106.4	47 Ag 107.868	48 Cd 112.40	49 In 114.82	50 Sn 118.69	51 Sb 121.75	52 Te 127.60	53 I 126.9044	54 Xe 131.30
55 Cs 132.905	56 Ba 137.34	57 La* 138.91	72 Hf 178.49	73 Ta 180.948	74 W 183.85	75 Re 186.2	76 Os 190.2	77 Ir 192.2	78 Pt 195.09	79 Au 196.967	80 Hg 200.59	81 Tl 204.37	82 Pb 207.19	83 Bi 208.980	84 Po (210)	85 At (210)	86 Rn (222)
87 Fr (223)	88 Ra (226)	89 Act† (227)															

*Lanthanide Series

58 Ce 140.12	59 Pr 140.907	60 Nd 144.24	61 Pm (145)	62 Sm 150.35	63 Eu 151.96	64 Gd 157.25	65 Tb 158.924	66 Dy 162.50	67 Ho 164.930	68 Er 167.26	69 Tm 168.934	70 Yb 173.04	71 Lu 174.97

†Actinide Series

90 Th 232.038	91 Pa (211)	92 U 238.03	93 Np (237)	94 Pu (242)	95 Am (243)	96 Cm (247)	97 Bk (247)	98 Cf (249)	99 Es (254)	100 Fm (253)	101 Md (256)	102 No (254)	103 Lw (257)

PERIODS 1 2 3 4 5 6 7

Atomic weights shown below the symbols are based on Carbon-12.

PHYSICS AND ASTRONOMY

ACCELERATION: The time-rate change of velocity.

ARCHIMEDE'S PRINCIPLE: A body immersed in a fluid is lifted by a force equal to the weight of the fluid displaced by the body.

ASTEROID: A planetary fragment or minor planet. Most of the thousands of known asteroids are between the orbits of Mars and Jupiter. Ceres is the largest asteroid.

CHARGE: An elementary property of matter. There are two kinds of electrical charges, positive and negative. Charges of like sign repel each other, and charges of unlike sign attract each other.

COMET: A diffuse body which glows with a prominent tail when its orbit brings it near the Sun.

ECLIPSE: A solar eclipse occurs when the moon passes between the earth and the sun; a lunar eclipse occurs when the earth passes between the sun and the moon, so that the earth's shadow darkens the moon.

ENERGY, KINETIC: Energy resulting from a body's motion.

ENERGY, POTENTIAL: The energy of a body due only to its position.

FORCE: A force causes a body to accelerate.

FREQUENCY: The number of vibrations of a wave per unit time.

JUPITER: The fifth planet from the sun is the largest in the solar system, with a diameter 11 times that of the earth. Of Jupiter's many moons, the largest is Ganymede.

LENS: A transparent material shaped to *refract* light in certain ways. The faces of a lens are usually sections of spheres, either concave or convex.

MAGNETIC POLES: The magnetic effects which appear to be concentrated at the ends of a bar magnet are referred to as the "north" and "south" poles.

MARS: The fourth planet from the sun, with a diameter 53% that of the earth. Mars has two small satellites, Phobos and Deimos.

MASS: The measure of inertia.

MERCURY: The small planet closest to the Sun, with a diameter 39% that of the Earth.

MIRROR: A surface that *reflects* light and thereby forms reflected images.

MOMENTUM: The product of mass and velocity.

NEPTUNE: The eighth planet from the sun, with a diameter nearly four times that of the earth. Neptune has two satellites, the largest being Triton.

PENDULUM: A mass hanging on the end of a string or other support so that it is free to move.

PLUTO: The ninth planet from the sun was discovered in 1930. Its only known moon is Charon.

REFRACTION: The bending of a wavefront, or a ray at the interface between two media.

SATURN: The sixth planet from the sun has very prominent rings composed of many fragments of ice. Of Saturn's numerous moons, the largest is Titan.

SPECTRUM, ELECTROMAGNETIC: The total range of frequencies or wavelengths of electric and magnetic waves, including radio and light waves and gamma rays.

URANUS: The seventh planet from the sun has a diameter almost four times that of the earth. Uranus has five moons and a faint set of rings.

VELOCITY: The time-rate change of position of an object.

VENUS: The second planet from the sun is very nearly the same size as the earth. Venus is cloaked by dense, hot clouds.

WAVE (MECHANICAL): A disturbance that moves through a deformable medium.

WORK: The product of force and distance.

THE SOLAR SYSTEM
(Elements Relative to Earth = 1)

Planet	Distance from Sun	Sidereal Period	Radius	Mass	Moons
Mercury	0.39	0.24	0.38	0.05	0
Venus	0.72	0.62	0.96	0.82	0
Earth	1.00	1.00	1.00	1.00	1
Mars	1.52	1.88	0.53	0.11	2
Asteroids	2.8	(thousands of small bodies)			
Jupiter	5.2	11.9	11.0	317.8	16
Saturn	9.5	29.5	9.2	95.1	17
Uranus	19.2	84.0	3.7	14.5	5
Neptune	30.1	164.8	3.5	17.2	2
Pluto	39.5	248.4	0.5	0.002	0

The sidereal period is the time for a planet to make one revolution around the sun. Earth is 93 million miles from the sun, has a sidereal period, or year, of 365 days and has a radius of 4000 miles. From the table one may calculate that Jupiter, for example, is about 500 million miles from the sun, takes almost 12 Earth years to travel around the sun, and has a radius of about 44,000 miles; the mass of this giant planet is nearly three times that of all other planets combined.

TEMPERATURE CONVERSION SCALES

The three most common scales for measuring temperature are: **Fahrenheit** (°F), **Celsius,** or *centigrade,* (°C), and **Absolute,** or *Kelvin,* (°K). The temperature scale conversion formulas are

$$°F = (9/5 \times °C) + 32$$
$$°C = (°F - 32) \times 5/9$$
$$°K = 273 + °C$$

Boiling point of water: 212°F, 100°C, 373°K
Freezing point of water: 32°F, 0°C, 273°K
Lowest possible temperature (absolute Zero): −459°F, −273°C, 0°K

SYSTEMS OF UNITS

System	Length	Mass	Time	Force
mks (meter-kilogram-second)	meter	kilogram	second	newton
cgs (centimeter-gram-second)	centimeter	gram	second	dyne
fps (foot-pound-second)	foot	slug	second	pound

COMMON UNITS OF MEASUREMENT

Units of length

1 meter (m) = 39.37 in.
1 centimeter (cm) = 10^{-2} meter = 3.9×10^{-1} in.
1 kilometer (km) = 10^3 meters = 6.2×10^{-1} mile
1 millimeter (mm) = 10^{-3} meter = 4×10^{-2} in.
1 mile (mi) = 5280 ft = 1760 yd = 320 rd
1 rod (rd) = 5.50 yd = 16.5 ft
1 yard (yd) = 3 ft
1 foot (ft) = 12 inches (in.)
1 Angstrom (Å) = 10^{-8} cm
1 micron (μ) = 10^{-4} cm

Units of mass

1 slug = 1 pound/g, where g = 980 cm/sec^2 = 9.8 m/sec^2 or 32 ft/sec^2
1 kilogram = 10^3 grams

Units of force

1 dyne (dy) = 1 gm cm/sec^2
1 newton (nt) = 1 kg m/sec^2
1 pound (lb) = slug ft/sec^2

Units of work and energy

1 electron volt (eV) = electron change × 1 volt = 1.6×10^{-19} joule
1 joule = 1 nt m = 10^7 erg
1 erg = 1 dy cm

Units of power
1 watt = 1 joule/sec = 10^7 erg/sec
1 ft lb/sec = 1/550 horsepower (hp)

Units of heat
1 calorie = 4.19 joule
1 kilocalorie (kcal) = 1000 calories (cal)
1 British thermal unit (BTU) = 252 cal = 0.252 kcal

Units of circular measure
1 degree = 1.745×10^{-2} radian
1 radian = 57.30 degrees

PHYSICAL CONSTANTS
Speed of light c = 3.00×10^8 m/sec
Equatorial radius of the earth = 6.378×10^6 m = 3963 mi
Polar radius of the earth = 6.357×10^6 m = 3950 mi
Mass of the earth = 5.983×10^{24} kg

GEOLOGY

ALLUVIUM: Sediment deposited by a stream, within or along it.
AQUIFER: A bed of rock that carries water, being both porous and permeable.
ARTESIAN WELL: A water well drilled into a confined aquifer.
ATOLL: A coral reef enclosing a lagoon, left by the disappearance of the island in the center.
BASALT: An igneous rock formed from lava.
BATHOLITH: The largest size pluton, more than 40 square miles in exposed area.
CALDERA: A volcanic cone enlarged by explosion or collapse of the summit.
CIRQUE: A spoon-shaped hollow eroded by a glacier at the head of a mountain valley.
COAL: A sedimentary rock composed of partly decayed and buried plant material.

CONGLOMERATE: A sedimentary rock consisting of gravel or material of mixed sizes.

CONTINENTAL DRIFT: The hypothesis of moving continents.

CONTINENTAL SHELF: The zone lying between the shore and the continental slope.

CONTINENTAL SLOPE: The zone lying between the continental shelf and the ocean basin.

CORE: The center of the earth, including the outer core and the inner core.

CRUST: The outer zone of the earth, above the Mohorovičić discontinuity.

DELTA: A triangular deposit of stream sediment in a body of water.

DIASTROPHISM: Movements within the solid earth, including folding and faulting.

DIKE: A tabular body of igneous rock that intruded older rock.

EPICENTER: The place on the earth's surface nearest to the origin of an earthquake.

EROSION: The removal of rock by water, ice, and wind.

EXTRUSIVE ROCK: Igneous rock cooled from lava or explosive material at the surface of the earth.

FAULT: A crack in rock along which displacement has occurred.

FOLD: Bent or warped rock.

FORMATION: The unit of geologic mapping.

GLACIER: A moving body of ice and snow.

GNEISS: A coarse metamorphic rock.

GRANITE: An igneous rock consisting of feldspar and quartz.

IGNEOUS ROCK: Rock formed by the solidification of molten rock.

INTRUSIVE ROCK: Igneous rock cooled from magma within the crust of the earth.

LAVA: Molten rock at the surface of the earth.

LIMESTONE: Sedimentary rock composed of calcium carbonate as the mineral calcite.

MAGMA: Molten rock within the earth.

MANTLE: The zone of the earth between the crust and the core.

MARBLE: A metamorphic rock derived from limestone.

MEANDER: A curve in a stream.

METAMORPHIC ROCK: One formed by the transformation of an igneous or sedimentary rock.

METAMORPHISM: Transformation of igneous or sedimentary rock into metamorphic rock.

MINERAL: A natural, inorganic chemical element or compound.

MOHO: The boundary between the crust of the earth and the mantle.

ORE: A natural source of metal.

OROGENY: Mountain building.

PALEONTOLOGY: The study of ancient life through fossils.

PERMAFROST: Permanently frozen ground.

PETROLEUM: A liquid fuel from the transformation of plant and animal remains.

PLUTON: A body of intrusive igneous rock.

QUARTZITE: A metamorphic rock derived from sandstone.

RADIOMETRIC DATING: Determining geologic age of a rock by measuring its concentration of radioactive elements.

RELIEF: The variation in elevation in an area.

RICHTER SCALE: A scale measuring earthquake magnitude.

SANDSTONE: A sedimentary rock composed of sand-sized particles.

SCHIST: A medium-grained metamorphic rock.

SEDIMENTARY ROCK: One formed by accumulation of particles at the earth's surface, especially by settling in a body of water.

SEISMIC: Pertains to an earthquake.

SHALE: A sedimentary rock composed of very small particles.

SILL: A tabular body of igneous rock intruded parallel to older strata.

SLATE: A fine-grained metamorphic rock that splits into smooth sheets.

SOIL: Decomposed rock and humus.

STRATA: Layers of sedimentary rock; singular is *stratum.*

SUPERPOSITION, LAW OF: In an undisturbed sequence of strata, the younger bed is deposited atop the older bed.

TECTONIC: Pertains to deformation of the earth.

TILL: Rocks and mud deposited by a glacier.

TOPOGRAPHY: The shape of the earth's surface.

TSUNAMI: A giant wave caused by an earthquake, miscalled a *tidal wave.*

UNCONFORMITY: A buried surface of ancient erosion; a time lapse in the geologic record.

UNIFORMITARIANISM: The principle that the present is the key to understanding the past.

VOLCANIC: Pertains to igneous rock extruded at the earth's surface.

WATER TABLE: The upper limit of ground saturated with water.

WEATHERING: The physical and chemical breakdown of rock.

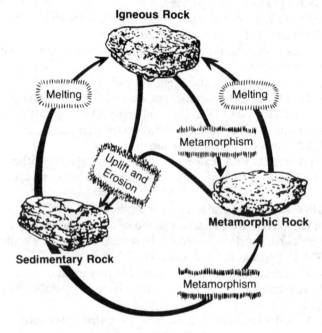

ROCK CYCLE

This diagram outlines the basic rock cycle in which one rock may be derived from or changed into another. (From: *View of the Earth, An Introduction to Geology* by John J. Fagan. Copyright © 1965 by Holt, Rinehart and Winston, Inc. Reprinted by permission of Holt, Rinehart and Winston, Inc.)

GEOLOGIC TIME SCALE

Era	Period	Epoch	Began Millions of Years Ago	Duration in Millions of Years	Dominant Life Forms
Cenozoic	Quaternary	Recent		(Late archeologic and historic time)	
		Pleistocene	1	1	
	Tertiary	Pliocene	13	12	Mammals
		Miocene	25	12	
		Oligocene	36	11	
		Eocene	58	22	
		Paleocene	63	5	
Mesozoic	Cretaceous		135	72	
	Jurassic		181	46	
	Triassic		230	49	Reptiles
Paleozoic	Permian		280	50	
	Pennsylvanian		330	50	
	Mississippian		355	25	Amphibians
	Devonian		405	50	Fishes
	Silurian		425	20	
	Ordovician		500	75	
	Cambrian		600	100	Invertebrates
Precambrian:					
Proterozoic and			1,600	1,000	Algae
Archeozoic			5,600	4,000	No life

FINAL PREPARATION: "The Final Touches"

1. Make sure that you are familiar with the testing center location and nearby parking facilities.
2. The last week of preparation should be spent primarily on reviewing strategies, techniques, and directions for each area.
3. Don't *cram* the night before the exam. It's a waste of time!
4. Remember to bring the proper materials to the test—identification, admission ticket, three or four sharpened Number 2 pencils, a watch, and a good eraser.
5. Start off crisply, concentrating first on the items that you can do most easily, and then coming back and trying the others.
6. If necessary, try to eliminate one or more of the choices, and then guess. There is no penalty for guessing, so answer every question.
7. Mark in reading passages, underline key words, write out information, make notations on diagrams, take advantage of being permitted to write in the test booklet.
8. Make sure that you are answering "what is being asked" and that your answer is reasonable.
9. Using the TWO SUCCESSFUL OVERALL APPROACHES (p. 7) is the key to getting the ones right that you should get right—resulting in a good score on the ACT.